*From Educational Experiment
to Standard Bearer*

# From Educational Experiment to Standard Bearer
## University 101 at the University of South Carolina

Daniel B. Friedman, Tracy L. Skipper, and Catherine S. Greene

THE UNIVERSITY OF
SOUTH CAROLINA PRESS

© 2022 University of South Carolina

Published by the University of South Carolina Press
Columbia, South Carolina 29208

www.uscpress.com

Manufactured in the United States of America

31 30 29 28 27 26 25 24 23 22
10 9 8 7 6 5 4 3 2 1

Library of Congress Cataloging-in-Publication Data
can be found at http://catalog.loc.gov/.

ISBN: 978-1-64336-365-3 (hardcover)
ISBN: 978-1-64336-366-0 (paperback)
ISBN: 978-1-64336-367-7 (ebook)

# CONTENTS

# TABLES AND FIGURES

## Tables

## Figures

# FOREWORD

## Fifty Years Later: Looking Back, Looking Ahead, Giving Credit, Sustaining, and Adapting the Vision

*John N. Gardner*

Here we are, after 50 years, ready and able to tell a story that has been waiting patiently to be told. This is a story about us, the University of South Carolina and our people, and about the needs of first-year higher education students the world over. This foreword comprises a set of reflections on the now-globally replicated University 101 course and first-year experience concepts.

Of course, we all have our own stories. Our university has its own story and is still writing that story well into its third century. This story is about helping students write their own narratives more successfully than might have been possible were it not for what is reported here. This story is about many things that mattered in 1970 when our tale begins and continue to matter 52 years later as we celebrate the 50th anniversary of University 101 and its global offshoot, the First-Year Experience movement in higher education.

But it is also a much bigger story. For this reason, I begin by saying what it is not:

- This is not the story of a single leader, innovator, or sustainer.
- Nor is this the story of an initiative du jour that passed into the dustbins of university history.
- This is not the tale of an educational fad.
- Finally, this is not the description of a silver bullet for solving issues related to academic performance, retention, or graduation.

Rather, the University 101 story engages four interconnected themes: (a) leadership, (b) a response to demands for justice and equity in the academy and the larger society, (c) educational innovation, and (d) a different approach to college students and their success.

## ■ Leadership

One of the unique aspects of the University 101 story is that it was an initiative conceived by a university president, Thomas F. Jones, who led the University of South Carolina from 1962 to 1974. It flourished not just due to Jones's successors' patronage and support, but also because of the value placed on mentoring future leaders—leaders of the course—and the students the course served and the members of the larger higher education community. This story demonstrates what a university can accomplish if it stays focused for half a century on its highest aspirations and continually builds on, sustains, and learns from its successes.

From the origins of the course, a movement was born. In 1982, we launched an annual series of national conferences known as The First-Year Experience. The first meeting hosted 173 participants; annual attendance at these meetings now averages two thousand educators from across the United States and the world. What started as a US domestic movement was exported beyond these borders in a series of International Conferences on The First-Year Experience from 1986 to 2013. A university-based national research and resource center emerged in 1987 and continues to this day as the National Resource Center for The First-Year Experience and Students in Transition. In addition to convening the Annual Conference on The First-Year Experience and other professional development events, the National Resource Center produces scholarly research and publications on this area of higher education.

## ■ Justice and Equity

Related to the theme of leadership is the story of how great universities pursue social justice and stimulate and share innovation around the world. In 1970, four distinct historical movements collided on the Columbia campus of the University of South Carolina (UofSC): (a) the antiwar movement, (b) the women's rights movement, (c) the students' rights movement, and (d) the civil rights movement. In the second week of May 1970, coterminous with the expansion of the Vietnam war by the US incursion into Cambodia, student protests erupted at Kent State, Jackson State, and UofSC, among others. A student protest held on the historic Horseshoe became a riot when the South Carolina National Guard teargassed hundreds of students that had assembled there. This represented an improvement in response to student protests in the state. Just 27 months earlier, in February 1968, a crowd of several hundred Black college students gathered to demand the end of segregation of a bowling alley in Orangeburg, South Carolina. They were confronted by South

Carolina Highway Patrol officers who opened fire, injuring approximately 30 protesters and killing three—most shot in the back or side as they tried to escape. Unlike the Orangeburg Massacre, as the event became known, no lives were lost in the Columbia protest.

The students fleeing the Horseshoe moved up a few hundred feet and barricaded President Jones in his office. When he eventually emerged from the sit-in, he announced: "[T]he students have given me an extended opportunity to reflect on the meaning of student behavior!" Doing what university presidents often do when faced with a crisis, he formed a committee to study the causes of the student riot and what could be done to prevent such behavior in the future.

By explicitly addressing students' rights, responsibilities, and opportunities through the University 101 course, the university hoped to ensure enduring societal improvement and greater equity in the treatment of first-year students, regardless of background.

## ■ Educational Innovation

What emerged slightly more than two years later in July 1972 was the UofSC Faculty Senate's approval to launch an educational experiment: a three-credit, pass/fail course, University 101, the Student in the University. The UofSC model for the so-called *first-year seminar,* a course type dating back to 1882, contained something truly original: mandatory faculty development prior to teaching the course. The specific intent was to use the course as a vehicle to promote a more humanizing, student-focused beginning collegiate experience, in what had become by 1972 a large, urban, racially integrated (accomplished peacefully[1]) research university, and to teach students "to love the University." In short, Jones saw in University 101 the potential to solve two problems: (a) preventing student riots by bonding them to the university and (b) helping faculty and staff significantly improve their teaching and their relationships with students.

The course launched in the fall of 1972 with fewer than 20 sections, and I was one of those inaugural faculty. Two years later, outgoing President Jones appointed me to be the first faculty leader for the course, a position I held from 1974 to 1999.

The result was the birth of a unique course genre: the contemporary first-year seminar. A large part of our story is how this educational innovation was sustained. The course quickly became a model in US higher education for the work of *assessment,* a term that did not emerge until 1985. UofSC began doing assessment in the 1974–75 academic year to measure whether and how the course was achieving its objectives, leading to the surprise finding of increased student retention rates, especially for less well-prepared and minority students.

In part because of these assessment findings, as early as five years after its founding, University 101 began to be replicated on other campuses in the United States and Canada (dating from 1977). Soon the University 101 concept was enjoying very rapid replication on hundreds of other campuses.

We also integrated the different talents and knowledge of faculty, student affairs/student success personnel, and student leaders in powerful partnerships that wove the course into the larger fabric of the institution. For example, one of these partnerships involved the embedding of University 101 and a companion bookend course University 401, a senior seminar, in the University's Quality Enhancement Plan through the creation of USC Connect (now the Center for Integrative and Experiential Learning), a vehicle for helping students identify and engage in beyond-the-classroom learning experiences that complement their academic program and help them reach their educational and professional goals.

The founding years between 1972 and 1999 were succeeded by many necessary steps to institutionalize, refine, improve, redesign as appropriate, and expand a wide range of activities and components of both University 101 Programs and the National Resource Center. During this time, we have seen extraordinary refinements in the assessment practices applied to the courses, the development of new instructional resources, and the creation of an extraordinary cadre of undergraduate and graduate peer leaders who co-teach every section of University 101.

### ■ Student Learning and Success

Perhaps the most important thread in this decades-long story is the focus on student learning and success. We began by focusing on a humanistic educational experiment designed to improve the beginning college experience. We learned that focusing on and assisting college students improved their retention and graduation rates. We also inspired many students to engage in learning for its own sake, laying the foundation for lifelong learning and success.

What began as an improvement initiative focused on the first year of college grew to include other college student transitions, for example, the sophomore year, the transfer experience, and the senior-year experience, with conferences and scholarly publications to support both UofSC's and the larger higher education community's related educational endeavors.

This broadened focus became further institutionalized with the University's adoption in 1998 of the University 401 course, The Senior Experience, now a popular elective for the University's departing students helping them to make a successful transition to life after UofSC.

In the second half of our history, we have weathered the Great Recession of 2008 and, most recently, the COVID-19 pandemic and related economic depression, all spurs to further innovation for students needing more support than ever before. We have been blessed especially by having a succession of new leaders for these programs and university-wide stakeholders and participants who have moved the original course and the National Resource Center to hitherto unimaginable levels of educational impact on the Columbia campus, throughout the University of South Carolina system, and around the globe.

And thus, the stage was set, the foundation laid, during the first 50 years. This book, in its rich detail, is a tribute to the University 101 story as written by thousands of participants. It is also an opportunity for us to consider and envision how these themes—leadership, social justice and equity, educational innovation, and student learning and success—will play out over the next half-century.

# PREFACE

*Daniel B. Friedman*

In 1992, I enrolled as a first-year student at Appalachian State University in Boone, North Carolina. I entered college without knowing a single person, without a fully developed skill set to succeed academically, and with very little understanding of what college was all about. Fortunately, I enrolled in a freshman seminar course that put me on a trajectory for success. The class helped me develop meaningful friendships with classmates, several of whom I keep in touch with 30 years later. It also supported my transition and academic success, making me feel that I mattered and that I belonged. The course was a highlight of my college experience.

My instructor, Dr. Rennie Brantz, became my mentor and advisor, and ultimately, my supervisor when we worked together years later. Clearly, this was a transformative experience that contributed significantly to my college transition and degree completion. It also became a significant part of my professional life as I moved from peer leader for Freshman Seminar and student assistant in the office to the assistant director and, finally, the program director.

Dan Friedman's first-year seminar class at Appalachian State University, 1992

But my experience, and the experiences of countless students who have benefited from their first-year seminars, would most likely never had happened if not for a series of protests that occurred on the campus of the University of South Carolina (UofSC) in May 1970, leading to the creation of University 101. Paul Fidler, an assistant vice president of student affairs, conducted early, robust assessment of the course, and Provost Keith Davis instructed John Gardner, the course's director, to "go out and sell" the idea. Word quickly caught on that this course succeeded in getting students to stay, do better in school, maximize their college experience, and ultimately graduate at higher rates.

In 1986, a team from Appalachian State hopped in a 15-passenger van and drove down the mountain to Columbia, South Carolina, to attend the Annual Conference on The Freshman Year Experience—a meeting hosted by Gardner and the University 101 staff. During the van ride back, the Appalachian State team sketched out the idea for developing a freshman seminar class based on the "South Carolina model," which began in 1987.

The work of John Gardner and his colleagues at UofSC generated a ripple effect that I benefited from as a first-year student. I imagine hundreds of institutions repeated Appalachian State's course development process throughout the 1980s and 1990s. And now, according to the 2017 National Survey on the First-Year Experience, 74% of colleges and universities in the United States offer some form of a first-year seminar (Young, 2019). If John and his colleagues had not shared these approaches, my freshman seminar experience would not have happened. Nor would it have been a reality for the millions of students who have taken a course like this across the world, and the first-year experience movement may not have taken root.

Yet, it did take root. The creation of what is now the National Resource Center for The First-Year Experience and Students in Transition at the University of South Carolina provided forums for disseminating research findings and best practices and opportunities for people to learn from one another about issues pertaining to the first college year. Not only did the course and the National Resource Center launch a subfield of higher education research and practice, but they also spurred a larger movement focused on improving the early college experience of entering students. So, in addition to being a student beneficiary, I am also a professional beneficiary of that educational experiment, having dedicated my career to a field that would not have existed if not for the work of faculty and staff at the University of South Carolina.

University 101 at the University of South Carolina marks its 50th anniversary in 2022. The program has continually been recognized as the international leader in first-year seminars. This book celebrates this milestone while examining the impact of the course on the university and the global higher education landscape. It tells the story of how the course came to be, its impact on first-year students, upper-level students serving as peer leaders, faculty and staff instructors, and the university community and culture. The book also explains how this "educational experiment" launched a movement known as the First-Year Experience. Finally, the book analyzes the factors contributing to the course's success and sustainability, inspiring and allowing other institutions to replicate this approach.

This book project began as an effort to commemorate the course as it approached this milestone anniversary. Still, we also know that at the University of South Carolina and elsewhere, first-year seminars have supported student learning, retention, and graduation for countless students—in many cases, for students who are at higher risk of not succeeding in college. In addition to celebrating the success of an individual program, this book also provides us with an opportunity to reflect on the conditions that contributed to University 101's longevity and its impact on students, faculty, staff, and the larger university community. What worked here may not fit every campus, but we hope that administrators, faculty, and staff find inspiration here for shaping institutional cultures to support student learning and success through well-designed first-year seminar programs.

## ■ Volume Overview

The book's contributors include authors selected for their expertise and ability to consider the first-year seminar's significance historically and as an educational innovation. Current program staff also contributed to the book, documenting where the program is now. All contributors consulted archival documents, interviewed former staff and friends of the program to ensure an accurate representation of its evolution, and contemplated the best way to celebrate the program's accomplishments and its constituents while honoring the efforts of those who have contributed to its development over time. We owe a special debt to Elsie Watts Froment. Her doctoral research on educational innovations emerging from the social protest movements in the United States in the late 1960s and early 1970s served as a primary resource for tracing the early development of the course and understanding the roles and motivations of those involved in its creation. On behalf of the book's editors, I would like to thank everyone who contributed their time and energy to crafting this volume. An overview of the contents follows.

In the foreword, John N. Gardner, founding director and architect of University 101, a world-renowned scholar and leading figure in higher education, offers a brief reflection on 50 years of the first-year experience movement and the impact University 101's creation has had on setting an international agenda for student success.

Chapter 1 traces the origins of University 101 by situating the development of the course at the intersection of two strands of the student protest movements of the 1960s and 1970s: (a) student rebellion against paternalistic and increasingly bureaucratic postsecondary education institutions and (b) student activism related to the war in Vietnam. The course emerges as a solution to the problems raised by these two themes, seeking to make the research university more humanistic in its outlook and fostering a sense of belonging for students and connection to the institution.

Picking up from the course's origins, Chapter 2 explores the conditions that contributed to the adoption of this educational initiative at colleges and universities in the United States and worldwide. The chapter situates University 101 in the larger context of extended orientation courses as the original prime mover for this course genre and as reflecting larger national trends. It concludes with a reflection on the impact of this model on higher education, including how it provided a common language and purpose for first-year seminars, launched a broader commitment to student success, and reshaped the landscape of faculty development.

Chapter 3 provides an overview of the University 101 course, including the philosophy, goals, outcomes, and course requirements. It explains the process that is implemented to ensure the continued relevance and excellence of the course by regularly and intentionally revisiting the course requirements and outcomes. This framework would be helpful for institutions seeking to build or revise a first-year seminar.

Chapter 4 analyzes and explains the factors that lead to a successful program and course, including sense of belonging, early alert, and engaging pedagogies. This chapter explains these and other institutional and programmatic aspects that lead to a successful program. Readers who wish to build a similar program will understand the primary elements on which to focus.

Chapter 5 is devoted to highlighting the impact of University 101 on student success through institutional retention and graduation rate comparisons for participants and nonparticipants and students' perceptions of their learning and the value of the course. This chapter demonstrates University 101's impact on first-year students as they seek opportunities to learn, grow, get involved, connect with others, and become part of the university community. Several student stories about the personal impact of the course on adjustment and success conclude the chapter.

Chapter 6 provides an overview of who teaches the course and the process for preparing, developing, and supporting instructors to ensure a high-quality experience. Ongoing instructor development is critical to the success of a first-year seminar as the course is only as good as the person teaching it. Thus, institutions must invest heavily in faculty development. The authors share the University 101 faculty development model along with advice for other institutions. Last, the chapter explores the myriad positive benefits teaching has on instructors, such as greater satisfaction with the institution, increased understanding of students, and adoption of new teaching strategies in other courses they may teach. The investment in faculty development pays dividends far beyond the benefits to the students in the first-year seminar.

Chapter 7 explores the use of peer leaders to support new students and co-teach the U101 class. It explains who these leaders are and how they are selected, trained, and supported. Moreover, it offers an analysis of the impact peer leaders have on first-year students and the success of the course, as well as how peer leaders benefit themselves from this experience.

Chapter 8 explains the importance of integrating the seminar into the fabric of the institution. University 101 is successful, in large part, because it unites offices across the institution in one shared commitment: to support students through the transition to college and beyond. Over the past 50 years, University 101 Programs has become central to a network of connections across the institution by engaging a diverse faculty and including numerous campus offices in the design and implementation of the course itself. Through collaboration on committees, the development of the *Transitions* textbook, and the delivery of Campus Partner Presentations, University 101 Programs has institutionalized the work of the first-year seminar across the University of South Carolina's campus. This chapter also explores how campus partnerships enable University 101 to support students through their first year and beyond.

Finally, Chapter 9 provides a conclusion that highlights the most significant takeaways, lessons learned, and insights to practitioners on other campuses.

To showcase the broad reach of University 101, we have included four case studies of four first-year seminars inspired by the South Carolina model, representing various institutional types in the United States and abroad.

Finally, readers will find brief sketches of University 101 leadership and supporters throughout the volume—both as a testament to their contributions to the program's successes and as an exemplar of the wide-ranging institutional buy-in needed to sustain educational innovation across five decades.

I hope this book will serve as an inspiration and road map for other institutions to invest in this proven concept and to focus on the ingredients that lead to a successful program. Future students, much like my younger self, are relying on it.

## *Reference*

Young, D. G. (Ed.). (2019). *2017 National Survey on the First-Year Experience: Creating and coordinating structures to support student success.* University of South Carolina, National Resource Center for The First-Year Experience & Students in Transition.

Chapter 1

# Origins of University 101 at the University of South Carolina

*Christian K. Anderson*

In the fall of 1972, 239 first-year students, called "freshmen" at the time, stepped into classrooms around the University of South Carolina campus to take a newly created class: "University 101. The Student in the University." The idea came from a retreat the previous year during which administrators (including the university's president), faculty, and students considered the future of the institution. They proposed 10 project areas that the university community should undertake, one of which was an "experimental freshman program." However, the true origins of University 101 trace to student dissatisfaction with an increasingly impersonal university that did not seem to cater to their needs or interests and the unrest on campus in the spring of 1970.

## ■ The University of South Carolina in the 1960s

The 1960s were a time of change for the University of South Carolina (UofSC), just as it was for institutions of higher education around the country. Campuses grew at unprecedented rates, which included new groups of students at recently desegregated institutions. The size of faculties and research dollars received from the federal government and foundations, especially at research-focused universities, increased dramatically. Students pushed back against restrictions of all kinds: against the idea of *in loco parentis*, against being drafted into a war that many considered to be unjustified, and against racist ideologies that pervaded not just government and institutional policies but also cultural norms. Student life was an unequal experience for both men and women. Though some strictures had started to dissipate by the end of the 1960s, women's lives in dormitories and around campus were more regulated in terms of dress codes and curfews, resulting in a time of great change and turmoil on American college campuses, manifested by the number of protests organized by students.

Students around the country advocated for self-determination—especially about political activity—and for a voice in university decisions regarding class sizes, the quality of teaching, and curricular changes (Altbach, 1974/1997; Lipset, 1971/1993; Thelin, 2018). Students expressed dissatisfaction with feeling like they were merely cogs in a university machine and commonly expressed that they did not want to be known merely "as a number." The student protest movements of the 1960s grew in response not just due to the McCarthyism of the 1950s (Cohen, 2009), but also due to the explosive growth of universities during this period and the antiwar sentiment among students (Thelin, 2019). For some campuses, student protests of the 1960s are defining symbols of their history. At the University of California–Berkeley, for example, the Free Speech Movement drew national and international attention, prompting students to travel to the Bay Area to be a part of it.

Such changes were more gradual on some campuses than others. Dan Carter recalls his time as a UofSC student in the 1960s as one where fellow students were generally conservative or, perhaps more accurately, politically apathetic. It was a place ruled by tradition. He drew the ire of fellow students when he refused to stand for the band's rendition of "Dixie" at a football game in 1961, and three members of Kappa Alpha dragged him down the stairs of the stadium. Instead of punishing his abusers, the dean informed him that his civil rights activities might "embarrass" the university (Carter, 2013). Through the student newspaper, *The Gamecock*, however, he found others who shared his liberal views, and together they formed the South Carolina Council on Human Relations (SCCHR). He admits it was a small group.

Even though UofSC students were, by and large, not active in the protests of the early 1960s, Columbia and the state of South Carolina were witness to several protests. In January 1961, Black students from Friendship Junior College launched what became known as the "Jail, No Bail" strategy with their sit-in at a lunch counter in Rock Hill (Donaldson, 2021). And on March 3, 1961, about 200 students—mostly from Allen University and Benedict College (two Historically Black Colleges and Universities [HBCUs] in Columbia) and local high schools—marched from Zion Baptist Church to the State House to protest racism. The students were arrested for disturbing the peace. Their lawyers argued for their right to peaceably assemble, and the resulting Supreme Court decision, *Edwards vs. South Carolina* (1963), became a landmark free-speech case. Only one UofSC student was involved: Frederick Hart, a first-year student who was watching the procession (Lesesne, 2001). When asked if he agreed with the Black students, Hart was arrested along with 188 others. He received harassing phone calls and even death threats from white supremacists. The dean of students, George Tomlin, suggested that he leave campus, prompting him to drop out.

The fight for equality came to campus in 1963 when Henrie Montieth, represented by Matthew J. Perry, sued for admission. Perry had successfully desegregated Clemson in January of that year. In May, about 200 students protested the possible desegregation of the campus, burning a cross in front of the president's house (Lesesne, 2001, p. 143). The court ruled in Montieth's favor in July, and on September 11, 1963, she registered for classes alongside Robert Anderson and James Solomon. South Carolina became the last Southern flagship university to desegregate. Dean of Students Charles Witten and other administrators worried about the violence that had plagued the desegregation of the University of Mississippi and other campuses and created an "I-Day" (integration day) plan to avoid the same from happening in Columbia. The continuing process of integration would come slowly. No Black faculty members were hired until 1968, the first Black athletes joined university sports teams in 1969, and the Afro-American Studies Program was not approved until 1970 (Lesesne, 2001).

The campus could be described as "cozy" and "collegial," which was hardly unique to South Carolina at the time (Thelin, 2018). Interest in protesting racism and in the antiwar movement developed slowly and sporadically in the 1960s. In 1967, General William C. Westmoreland, a Spartanburg native, was awarded an honorary degree in Rutledge Chapel, and a group of 29 students (no match for the 150 police on guard or the hundreds of pro-Westmoreland students) showed up to protest. Inside the chapel, professor of chemistry Thomas Tidwell stood after the conferral of the honorary degree and held up a sign proclaiming, "I Protest: Doctor of War" (Matalene & Reynolds, 2001, p. 187). Tidwell's protest may have signaled a departure for faculty who were "largely provincial and professionally comfortable" (Watts, 1999, p. 27).

Student Vickie Eslinger expressed her concerns about the lack of support from the administration for student concerns and initiatives regarding social and racial issues. In a letter to President Jones, she mentions the "obvious absence" of administrators at a lecture on campus by Dick Gregory, a Black comedian and civil rights activist. She challenged Jones's and the faculty's true commitment to education: If they could not listen to a controversial voice such as Gregory's, "then I question the right of those particular people to try to *educate* anyone" (emphasis original, quoted in Matalene & Reynolds, 2001, p. 186).

While these conflicts were brewing, the university experienced unprecedented growth. In the 1950s, the enrollment averaged about 4,300 students, growing to 5,661 by 1960, 9,150 by 1965, and 14,484 by 1970. There were only 318 graduate students in 1960 but 2,006 a decade later, an increase of 531% (Lesesne, 2001, pp. 137, 166). During the 1960s, the campus was abuzz with activity to build new facilities, develop and expand academic programs, improve the faculty, pursue more grant money from the federal government and other sources, revise the curriculum, and modernize the organizational structure. The university added new research centers to support faculty; Jones brought new programs, such as Upward Bound, to increase access to disadvantaged students; and added a new honors program to attract high-achieving students.

This transformation of "Carolina from a small, intimate college into a research university" did not come without growing pains for faculty, students, and the community (Lesesne, 2001, p. 185). One history professor lamented in *The Gamecock* in 1969 that students merely had to sit "through the required courses" and endure "$x$ hours of tedium." This, he argued, led to the mistaken belief "that the student has been educated. In reality, he has only been processed" (quoted in Lesesne, 2001, p. 196). Some students argued that faculty were disengaged from teaching because of their focus on research. They further complained that they were just a number, or even less, "a hole in an IBM card" (p. 197).

The pushback against the new impersonal university was on display in *The Gamecock*. Student body vice president Thorne Compton and treasurer Jim Mulligan wrote in 1966: "The student at Carolina often wonders where his place is in this computerized institution." They commented that despite organizing as students,

> We learned rapidly, however, that concern for student opinion was either totally absent, or based on an intricate system of administrative politics. . . . The heart of the problem seems to be that while the University spends great sums of money and staffs itself well, solely for the benefit of students and the solution of their problems, the individual student and his problems are neglected in the machinery of administration. We have repeatedly found frustration, closed doors, and interested but helpless people in our pursuit of student concerns. We have gone to the bottom and worked up, and to the top and worked down, with the same result. (quoted in Matalene & Reynolds, 2001, pp. 185–186)

Compton and Mulligan's concerns presage the very issues that the University 101 program would address just a few years later.

## ■ The UFO Coffeehouse: A Place of Organizing and Protest for Students and GIs

UofSC student activism throughout the 1960s was limited. However, students became increasingly frustrated by what they saw as an impersonal institution. Their frustrations predisposed some to become more politically active when the conditions were right. Here, the story of the UFO Coffeehouse becomes important in understanding the events at UofSC in May 1970, both because of the antecedents that ultimately led to campus protests and the creation of University 101 and because of the parallels between the coffeehouse and student movements.

Historian David Parsons points out in his book *Dangerous Grounds: Antiwar Coffeehouses and Military Dissent in the Vietnam Era* (2017) that the relationship between college students and GIs is more complicated than is generally understood. The popular image of the antiwar protester, commonly assumed to be a college student, is of someone spitting on the GI headed to war or the veteran returning home. Instead, Parsons highlights the strong antiwar sentiment existing among both soldiers and veterans who were often allies of student protesters.

GIs and college students during this period shared several characteristics. Soldiers on base and students on campus were both transitory, although the former was much more so than the latter. Also, both were subject to control by authority figures: the GIs to military authority and students to the philosophy that the institution stood in place for parents (i.e., *in loco parentis*) and thus should control their lives. Students around the country were increasingly pushing against this idea. While both soldiers and students were subject to formal rules and regulations, they also had to answer to peers. Peer pressure took the form of social expectations or, in some cases, hazing or harassment to force compliance with group norms. Antiwar coffeehouses and student protesters demanded more respect for the voices of young people and for some degree of self-governance. This was true in Columbia, where some students from UofSC and other area colleges identified with soldiers' inability to speak out against the war and felt similarly discounted by campus administrators. Increased policing of students also raised tensions and made restrictions (perceived and real) feel intolerable.

The first of the several antiwar coffeehouses to spring up near military bases around the country and globe was the UFO, founded in Columbia, South Carolina, in January 1968 by Fred Gardner and Donna Mickleson (Parsons, 2017). The UFO name was a play on "USO," the social and entertainment organization that served members of the military and their families, which had a club just a few blocks away in downtown Columbia. Located at 1732 Main Street, the UFO Coffeehouse was directly across from city hall and next door to an upscale restaurant, the Elite Epicurean. As one of the Epicurean's owners explained, "we catered to the establishment and they to the anti-establishment" (quoted in McAninch, 1995, p. 364).

At the time, Fort Jackson was one of the largest and most important training bases for the US Army, with a population of about 20,000 soldiers. It was important to the city of Columbia and the state of South Carolina, and both local and national politicians were invested in its success (Parsons, 2017). Camp Jackson had been founded in 1917 to train WWI soldiers and became increasingly important during WWII and subsequent war efforts. The political and business communities embraced the transformation of Columbia into a military town. The USO located in downtown Columbia was one of the busiest in the country (Moore, 1993, p. 413). While Fort Jackson was one of the first military bases to integrate in the South, Black soldiers did not enjoy the same privileges off base. Military officials carefully navigated directives to desegregate the base while respecting local Jim Crow restrictions (Myers, 2006), leading to a separate USO for Black soldiers.

Fort Jackson was also a site of the growing GI movement, as the coalition of antiwar military personnel came to be known. Howard Levy, an army doctor stationed at Fort Jackson, refused to train medics headed to Vietnam. In 1967, Levy was dishonorably discharged and sentenced to three years in a military prison. He was not alone. As the war became more unpopular, the number of insubordination cases increased. Columbia, as both a military and college town in the South, was primed for the kinds of activity Gardner's UFO would bring.

Fred Gardner, a 1963 graduate of Harvard, was a journalist and former editor for the *Harvard Crimson* (Parsons, 2017). He worked as an editor for *Scientific American* after college graduation and then enlisted in the Army Reserves. After completing his training at Fort Polk in Louisiana, he moved to San Francisco, the epicenter of the Free Speech and counterculture movements. He realized the Left was missing an opportunity to involve active-duty soldiers in the antiwar movement, especially those drafted into the US Army, where there was growing disaffection within the ranks. Gardner saw the potential in "an alliance of soldiers and civilians" (Parsons, 2017, p. 17). The "hip antiwar coffeehouses" of the Bay area were, Gardner believed, a good model for a place to foster a dialogue between antiwar soldiers and civilians. Levy's story caught Gardner's attention, and he decided to start his coffeehouse in Columbia (Parsons, 2017).

Gardner's vision for the coffeehouse was that civilians would take the lead from GIs and then serve as a support for "empowering disaffected soldiers to channel their energy into political action" (Parsons, 2017, p. 19). Of course, some of the civilians attracted to the UFO would be local college students, including those from UofSC.

The UFO was immediately popular. While generally sedate during the day, with people sipping coffee and having conversations, it became louder in the evenings as patrons listened to music, turned up on the hi-fi stereo, or enjoyed live performances by touring musicians (Parsons, 2017). A *New*

*York Times* reporter compared it to hipster establishments one might find in Greenwich Village. This atmosphere did not jive well with the local conservative culture. The Columbia chief of detectives declared: "We just feel like we don't want it in town" (quoted in Parsons, 2017, p. 21), and federal, state, local, and military police combined forces to close the UFO. State police and the FBI sent undercover agents to spend time at the UFO. Fort Jackson even stationed MPs outside the coffeehouse to report on and intimidate soldiers who visited. Staff and visitors were often arrested on minor charges.

Within a month of its opening, GIs were meeting at the UFO to share ideas and plans (Parsons, 2017). They organized a February "pray-in" to be held at a chapel on base where soldiers could express their doubts about the war and pray for peace. In the summer of 1968, Norman Mailer visited the UFO and spoke to a crowd of about 200, some of whom were undoubtedly SLED (South Carolina Law Enforcement Division) officers and informants (Moore, 1993). In fact, Mailer asked undercover agents in the audience to please stand and introduce themselves (Parsons, 2017). National activists took note of the UFO, and toward the end of 1968, Fred Gardner collaborated with Howard Levy, the Army doctor serving time for insubordination; Dr. Benjamin Spock, the famous pediatrician; Noam Chomsky, famed MIT linguistics professor and activist; and others to create the US Servicemen's Fund (USSF) to support antiwar efforts, including the coffeehouse network.

In the early months of 1969, a Black draftee, Joe Miles, reluctantly arrived at Fort Jackson and immediately started enlisting other Black soldiers in his antiwar cause (Parsons, 2017). The UFO served as an organizational hub for his group, called GIs United Against the War in Vietnam. On March 20, 1969—just over a year after the pray-in protest—about 200 soldiers assembled outside their barracks to protest the war. Others shouted support from the windows of their rooms. The next day, Fort Jackson authorities arrested nine soldiers on charges that they had incited a riot. One of the nine was an informant, so those charged became known as the "Fort Jackson Eight." The story soon made national headlines, becoming a public relations nightmare for the Army and a victory for the GI Movement. A central question in their case was whether those in uniform enjoyed the same First Amendment protections as other citizens.

Students at UofSC took note. More than 40 showed up in support of the Fort Jackson Eight at their hearing at the US District Court in Columbia, holding signs, including one that read, "Free the Ft. Jackson Eight" (Ball, 1969, p. 3). The *Gamecock* regularly reported on the case throughout the spring. Student leaders of AWARE (created in 1966 and later aligned with Students for a Democratic Society or SDS) invited the lawyer for the Eight to campus to speak ("AWARE Speaker Fails to Appear," 1969; "Soldiers' Defender

Kraus leading the march down Main Street, stopping in front of the shuttered UFO

Comments on Case," 1969). His speech was the subject of letters to the editor from students. Concerned students saw the cause of the Fort Jackson Eight as their own.

Once the Jackson Eight were released, FBI agents and local police continued harassing the UFO, ultimately resulting in its closure by the city and the arrest of the owner on January 13, 1970 (Parsons, 2017). The following day Jon Kraus, an untenured instructor of political science who also served as president of the ACLU of South Carolina, paraded in front of the UFO and City Hall, promoting a rally to be held on campus (McAninch, 1995; Parsons, 2017). He was forced to move it to Valley Park (later renamed Martin Luther King, Jr. Park), however, because UofSC would not allow nonstudents to attend the rally. About 300 gathered at the park to hear speakers, including Dr. Howard Levy, who had been released from military prison by this point, and Lee Weiner, one of the Chicago Seven. At the end of the rally, Kraus led a march down Main Street, stopping in front of the shuttered UFO (Parsons, 2017).

On February 8, 1970—the second anniversary of the Orangeburg Massacre—student supporters filled Drayton Hall, a large auditorium on campus, to rally for the UFO (Hope & Wannamaker, 1970). President Jones made clear in a statement that the university was not obligated to allow rallies and required the organizers to retract an invitation to the general public, limiting the number of non-student attendees to no more than 50 of about 500 total seats (McAninch, 1995). Speakers came from the Black Liberation Movement, the Women's Liberation Movement, the UFO Offense Coalition, the Puerto Rican Independence Movement, and writers for the Fort Jackson independent newspaper, *Short Times*. Zack Dais, a representative from the

Black Awareness Coordinating Committee at South Carolina State, gave a commemorative address and talked about how to organize for the future.

The Columbia city prosecutor, solicitor John Foard, paid no heed to the protests. A WWII veteran and experienced litigator, he was determined to close the UFO and oust its owners from the city. Tom Broadwater, an African American lawyer for the fledgling South Carolina chapter of the ACLU and a relatively recent law school graduate, was the attorney for the UFO. He was no match for Foard. Columbia historian John Hammond Moore (1993) called Foard's prosecution and attempt to oust professors from Columbia College and UofSC a "witch hunt" (p. 409), and Parsons (2017) referred to the trial as "bizarre" (p. 83). Foard was known to sometimes break into religious song and even drop to his knees to supplicate to the jury (McAninch, 1995). During the trial, Foard read from the *Berkeley Barb*, an underground newspaper available at the coffeehouse, as evidence that the UFO was a "cesspool of evil" (Parsons, 2017, p. 83). Foard's witch hunt extended to President Jones, calling his efforts to control the campus "weak," and he appeared personally before the Trustees in July 1970 asking them to fire Jones, but to no avail.

William Shepard McAninch (1995), a former UofSC law professor, provided a legal analysis of the UFO case. He put the situation in context, explaining that this was the era of the Chicago Seven and the 1968 Democratic Convention, the Black Panthers, a growing distaste for the war in Vietnam, and closer to home, the killing of three South Carolina State College student in the "Orangeburg Massacre." The era was imbued with a "we/they" mentality. As he explains, "While most of us were in fact somewhere in between, it often appeared that our world was split into two camps, and nowhere was this division more apparent than in the 1700 block of Main Street in Columbia, South Carolina" (p. 365).

Students sought to create a permanent space for a "UFO in Exile" in the Russell House (Lesesne, 2001; McAninch, 1995; Parsons, 2017). They held regular meetings to continue the kinds of discussions that took place at the UFO and to support the owners during the trial. Foard soon came after them, as well. He instigated drug raids on campus, investigated *The Gamecock* for obscenity, and tried to restrict gatherings in the Russell House (Parsons, 2017). Obtaining both a guilty verdict and sentence for the UFO owners was not enough for Foard. He went after any professor who had testified for the defense, claiming that they "don't belong at the university" (McAninch, 1995, p. 378). The UofSC chapter of the American Association of University Professors (AAUP) made a strong statement supporting academic freedom and urged the university to resist Foard's pressure. Nonetheless, Kraus was fired (as was a professor at Columbia College). On April 13, 1970, the day before the UFO trial began, FREAK (Freedom of Research in Every Aspect of Knowledge, a student organization) staged a sit-in of the administration building to protest the arrest of two students on drug charges and the way the police had dealt with students (Lesesne, 2001). The event was disruptive but peaceful. Jones expressed sympathy for the students' position but said the rule of law had to be respected. The speaker of the South Carolina House of Representatives, Solomon Blatt, declared that the student protesters "should be run off campus by sundown" (quoted in McAninch, 1995, p. 370).

On April 14, the university barred the UFO owners from campus, and plainclothes police officers patrolled the Russell House. The AAUP chapter criticized Foard's heavy hand in interfering with the campus. Student body president Mike Spears presented a resolution from a hastily formed "Student Emergency Coalition for Academic Freedom at USC" to the Board of Trustees. The resolution stated, "The University community is disturbed, dismayed and distressed by the brazen attempts by a few ill-informed local politicians to exercise unjust and dictatorial control over the University of South Carolina" (Lesesne, 2001, p. 214). The board referred their request for support for the "students' academic freedom, freedom of association and freedom from police or political restrictions" to a committee without further action. This only served to further alienate the students. Ultimately, the UFO was a "physical symbol for the students' struggle against authority" (Parsons, 2017, p. 85).

■ **"The Months of May"**

On May 4, 1970, Ohio National Guard troops killed four students at Kent State University, enraging students around the country and sparking protests from coast to coast. UofSC was no exception. Historian Henry Lesesne explains how this all came to a head in Columbia:

> The University was awash in grievances, among them the drug arrests . . . Foard's attack on the University's faculty and administration, police patrols in their student union, the board's refusal to support rights to academic freedom, the U.S. invasion of Cambodia, the senseless killings at Kent State, the University's heavy-handed clearing of minority neighborhoods near campus, and a general sense on the part of students that the administration and board of trustees did not recognize or defend their constitutional rights as students. (Lesesne, 2001, p. 214)

The events of the preceding months brought together a coalition of students and faculty, including AAUP members, AWARE students, FREAK, the Emergency Coalition that had presented the resolution to the trustees, the Inter-Fraternity Council, the still-nascent Association of Afro-American Students, and the Student Senate. Brett Bursey, a UofSC student and former

AWARE leader who had been barred from campus for burning a Confederate flag in protest and vandalizing a draft board office, chaired the coalition. They called for a strike to be held on Thursday, May 7, 1970 (Broadhurst, 2020; Lesesne, 2001; Watts, 1999).

At UofSC, the day began as any other normal class day. By midday, about 500 protesters had assembled at the flagpole on the Horseshoe (Lesesne, 2001; "The Months of May," 1970). They demanded that the flag be lowered to honor those killed at Kent State. Another (much smaller) group of students yelled in support of keeping the flag up. Around 2:00 p.m., the protest moved to the Russell House, where the student leaders seized the building keys, expelled university officials, and locked the doors. Some student leaders

Students gathered for a protest in front of the flagpole on the Horseshoe

Students protesting in front of the Russell House

Students crowding in protest on the Horseshoe

Students storming Osborne Administration Building

who had initially supported the strike now disavowed it, including the student body president. The South Carolina Highway Patrol and SLED officers arrived at 5:15 p.m., and an hour later, National Guard troops arrived. The possibility of violence was very real as some students threw rocks and other objects at law enforcement. This incident resulted in 42 student arrests, all of whom were suspended from the university.

On Friday, May 8, about 1,000 students gathered at the flagpole on the Horseshoe and marched to the State House, a block away (Lesesne, 2001; "The Months of May," 1970). They demanded amnesty for the arrested students. A petition was circulated and signed by 723 students and faculty lamenting the "lack of a responsive channel of communications" that had led to the Russell House takeover (Lesesne, 2001, p. 216). After a quiet weekend, tensions flared the following week. Monday, May 11, was Confederate Memorial Day, a state holiday. The trustees met that day at 2:30 p.m. in the administration building to discuss the disciplinary cases of the students. By 3:15 p.m., about 300 students had come to the building to protest the treatment of their classmates and to demand amnesty. Tensions escalated, and students stormed the building, ransacking offices on the first floor. Trustees were barricaded on the second floor, protected by police, even as students attempted to negotiate their way up the stairs. The crowd eventually grew to more than 2,000 protestors.

Protesters crowding the halls of Osborne Administration Building

Police officer speaking to crowd of protesters

Once again, SLED officers and National Guard troops were called in to quell the situation. They dispersed the crowd with tear gas as the students yelled, "Power to the People!" (Lesesne, 2001, pp. 216–217). Ironically, the governor was in Washington, D.C., attending a conference at the White House on student unrest. Upon his return, he declared a state of emergency and issued a curfew. The faculty held an emergency meeting on May 12 in the Town Theatre to affirm the students' rights to academic freedom and assembly while also condemning any violence. Meanwhile, students were holding a rally in nearby Maxcy–Gregg Park, one of many to be held that week. That evening, 15 faculty members came to various dormitories to hold "rap sessions" with students, which some credited with helping quell further violence. Nonetheless, rumors swirled, including that the Weathermen Underground were coming to burn the campus. Jones met with leaders of student groups to address their concerns. During that week, faculty continued to hold rap sessions, and about 100 spent the night on campus.

Actress and antiwar activist Jane Fonda was in town to drum up antiwar support among soldiers (Moore, 1993). She spoke on May 14 to about 2,000 in Maxcy–Gregg Park, delivering a "sermon on non-violence" (Moore, 1993, p. 410). Tensions grew at the park as word spread of the arrest of two more student leaders. Fonda urged the students to "get political," not violent, but she did not understand that the Columbia protests were about more than just the war (Lesesne, 2001).

Novelist Pat Conroy (1995) captures the mood of the May 1970 protests in his novel *Beach Music*. The narrator, a student at the University of South Carolina, talks of hearing about the killings at Kent State:

> A fearful discharge of energy was set off in the hearts of those us who had long ago grown accustomed to our roles as wards of the state. We poured out of dormitories and fraternity and sorority houses and left our books untended in library carrels . . . Disoriented and without any sense of purpose, we registered incomprehension, grief, and betrayal over the senseless murder of four of our own. (p. 547)

Conroy's narrator emphasizes that these killings by the National Guard did not take place at "the already-radicalized Harvard or Columbia" but in the heartland of America, where students were like those at South Carolina: acquiescent to authority. This fictionalized story of the "months of May" provides insight into the psychology of students—the anger and confusion and the awakening of many who were previously apathetic or even sympathetic to US involvement in Vietnam.

I had never been a part of something so much larger than myself. My hands trembled with fury and my mouth was dry; I felt irrational and murderous, yet curiously not angry as I walked with the students, many crying around me. (p. 547)

It was a turning point for students on campus: "You could feel the thrill of lethargy set afire" (p. 548).

## ■ Born of Protest: The Creation of University 101

President Jones knew that he had serious challenges ahead after the May 1970 events. And he knew that students would need a significant voice in finding the answers to those challenges. As early as the summer of 1970, a committee was assembled to write a summary and report about the events of that spring. The report, titled "The Months of May" (1970), was mailed as part of the university's alumni magazine with a preface from Jones. The title is not explained but likely acknowledges that while May was a crucial turning point, the crisis on campus had been building for several months before that.

Jones assembled groups of administrators, faculty, staff, and students for a series of meetings of the President's Committee on Academic Atmosphere to discuss the university's future (Lesesne, 2001). These meetings, some held as off-campus retreats, allowed students to air grievances—about the lack of communication, alienation among Black students, class sizes, and lack of meaningful interaction with faculty, to name a few—but also to channel them into solutions. The culminating "think tank" retreat was held at Camp Gravatt near Aiken in October 1971.

The think tanks produced many ideas, which *The Gamecock* announced on the front page on October 4, 1971 (Fellenbaum). The story describes 10 areas: (a) improving academic advisement, (b) improving peripheral services such as the bookstore, (c) developing intensive experiences such as the honors programs, (d) creating an experimental freshman program, (e) introducing new living–learning experiences including ones that involve faculty, (f) dealing with outside political pressures on the institution, (g) personalizing instruction and improving student motivation, (h) recruiting academically motivated students, (i) responding more effectively to the educational needs of the state, and (j) making UofSC the nucleus for cultural and scientific excellence.

The Camp Gravatt report outlined the particular challenges faced by first-year students and how the university might address them in an "Experimental Freshman Program" (Heckel et al., 1973). The following proposed course description was submitted for approval to the Faculty Senate (which had been created just two years previous) on July 12, 1972:

University 101. The Student in the University (No credit). The purposes
of higher education, and potential roles of an individual student within
a university and within other learning environments. Open to freshmen
only. Approval for one year.

The committee also provided a detailed outline of the course design, the
associated faculty training, and information about the curriculum (Heckel et
al., 1973). They argued that if it proved valuable, it should be made a permanent part of the curriculum and, if not, it should be abandoned, and better
alternatives pursued.

College administrators had long been trying to figure out how to "turn the
bewildered freshman as speedily as possible into a college man" (Finnegan
& Alleman, 2013, p. 97). Orientation courses were introduced as early as 1888
(Fitts & Swift, 1928), with the first in a seminar format at Reed College in 1911
(Koch & Gardner, 2006). Such courses served both administrative (orienting
the student to their new environment) and curricular (introducing them to
their field of study and to ways of studying) goals.

YMCA organizations led orientation efforts on many campuses. As
campuses grew more secularized and new student personnel departments
emerged, the role of the campus YMCA slowly faded (Setran, 2007; Finnegan
& Cullaty, 2001). At South Carolina, the YMCA initially handled student
orientation, but this function was slowly taken over by the university as it
introduced more student services and counseling. By 1965, the YMCA no
longer held its own orientation (Watts, 1999). Without the YMCA, a different
approach for integrating first-year students into university life was needed.

Yet, the organizers of this new experimental course at South Carolina
were attempting to go beyond a mere orientation course. They recognized
that the first-year experience is unique: a time of adjustment, learning, and
trying to set a course of study. Possible hazing or harassment made these
adjustments all the harder. New students arrived on campus with the expectation to succeed but without the "skills of studenthood" (quoted in Dwyer,
1989, p. 38). Educators responded with institutional initiatives to help novice
students develop these skills. They needed to address these practical matters
as well as tackle the more fundamental issue of making the university a more
humane place for intellectual self-discovery.

In April 1972, a faculty committee issued a report, "Proposal for An Experimental Freshman Program" (Atkinson et al.). They had studied existing
orientation programs and corresponded with other universities. Their proposal outlined the aims of the initiative and the plan for its implementation
while also recognizing some of the impending problems. The aim was both
philosophical and practical: to help the student understand the meaning and

purpose of higher education and become a more self-aware person while also learning about facilities and resources available on campus. They proposed that 150 students would take the course the first term with 10 faculty members, representing various disciplines with large enrollments in first-year courses, who were dedicated to an increased level of interaction with the students. As such, they recognized that the selection of faculty was crucial. The proposed course would have a mix of academic and practical content and be graded on a pass/fail basis. They also suggested that the program needed an administrator as soon as feasible and that it should coordinate with other experimental programs already in place. (Atkinson et al., 1972). J. Manning Hiers was charged with the initial coordination of the program.

Former dean of students Charles Witten reflected on the creation of University 101:

> During the years of the student revolt and the cultural revolution, we had several big retreats attended by student leaders and some key faculty members and administrators. . . . The idea of this new course was to introduce students to the world of learning. Learning is a terrific thing. If college can do nothing else for students, it must teach them how to learn. It is our duty. When people go out for jobs, the outfit they work for is going to train them for 6 months to a year. So, to teach them how to learn is the key. (Lowery, 2002)

Jones personally invited the first group of instructors to teach the course. Witten recalled, "I remember the head of the philosophy department taught the course, and his faculty members said how wonderful the change in his attitude was after learning what students were about" (Lowery, 2002). The course's impact on faculty was also evident in a letter that Jim Comer, associate professor of art, wrote to Jones in December 1972. Comer energetically embraced the new program, writing that teaching the course was "extremely rewarding," educationally beneficial to both him and students, and served as a "flywheel" for starting other programs (personal communication, December 12, 1972).

In 1973, the university offered 44 sections serving 751 students (Watts, 1999, p. 269), and by the 1975–1976 academic year, the program had grown to 1,258 students. John N. Gardner, director of the program, wrote in a memorandum on November 15, 1976, that 180 faculty (one third of them tenured professors) had been trained as University 101 instructors. Special sections of the course were in place for Upward Bound students, "mature" students (what we now refer to as nontraditional), commuter students, students in particular majors (e.g., journalism, nursing), those participating in a living–learning program, and even one for students in prison. Gardner explained that Paul Fidler, the university's academic planning officer and assistant vice president for student affairs, evaluated the effectiveness of the program and that other colleges and universities had already inquired about the course. At least two (University of Cincinnati and University of Texas at Austin) were basing new initiatives on it. Although still young, University 101 had clearly arrived.

### ■ The Humanistic Experiment

Jones introduced a number of innovative ideas while president, such as the Contemporary University and University Without Walls. While the Contemporary University provided students a one-semester hiatus from the traditional university curriculum, the University Without Walls was a complete break from it, allowing students to design their own educational experience (Lesesne, 2001). Both programs were short-lived but represented Jones's commitment to finding ways to better serve student needs. This approach also underscored his desire to humanize the research university. Paul Gray, former MIT president (1980–1990) and one of Jones's students, said of his former professor: "It was education over the whole spectrum, for it was Tom who first urged me to read Herodotus, Whitehead, and Tocqueville; it was he who told me where to look, just north of Scollay Square, for a used set of Harvard Classics. It was he who insisted that all relationships and all actions respect the humanity of those who were involved" (quoted in Dresselhaus et al., 1984, p. 144).

Jones, who had worked at the Naval Research Laboratory as a civilian during WWII (1941–1947) and later served in leadership roles in several scientific organizations (Dresselhaus et al., 1984), had come to embrace the human relations perspective. Black activists and white allies saw human relations as race relations and used the theory in the freedom struggle and to prepare for the sit-ins that created the necessary publicity for their movement (Whittington, 2013). Jones's perspective on the connection between human relations and civil rights is unclear, but the shared language may help explain why activist students found common ground with him. Both Jones (see Watts, 1999) and the activists (Whittington, 2013) saw human relations as a means of increasing empathy and decreasing reliance on authoritarian models of leadership.

President Jones's various reform efforts, and especially the introduction of University 101, can be described best as an attempt to combine and reconcile two aspects of the university experience: the research focus and the student experience. The American university is a conglomeration of various influences from England, Scotland, and Germany (Geiger, 2015). The British collegiate ideal called for faculty and students to live in close proximity and study, eat, and pray together but with external governing boards instead of full faculty self-governance. Americans studying for advanced degrees in Germany in the 19th century returned with a commitment to key values about the purpose of higher education: *Wissenschaft*, the pursuit of pure science or knowledge for knowledge's sake; *Lehrfreiheit*, academic freedom; and *Lernfreiheit*, the freedom of students to choose their own course of studies.

American universities put great value in providing both high-impact research and first-rate student experiences. Reconciling the values of *Wissenschaft* and the collegiate experience was clearly at the heart of the experimental freshman program proposed at Camp Gravatt. Jones realized this is what he needed to do at UofSC to fulfill his mission of a research-focused yet humanistic university. The student riots had exposed that the time for it was overdue.

As Elsie Watts (1999) explained, "The transformation of higher education in accordance with the research ideal carried with it tensions concerning education for life" (p. 1). What Jones and others were after was a *holistic* development of the student, a way to reconcile these two tensions. Aligning these perspectives is no small task because the pull of the research ideal is what defines faculty life, and faculty productivity ultimately defines a university's success. Yet, the collegiate experience defines a student's success. For Jones, the ideal university was one that "fit the student instead of the student having to fit the university" (Lesesne, 2001, p. 221). That these considerations arose from student protests provides new meaning and historical context for student activism.

In his introduction to a monograph about University 101, Jones (1973) explains that

> University 101 is an experimental program that attempts to modify both the professor and the student to survive in a new educational dimension. By its very nature, University 101 attempts to communicate with all students, not just the very bright, or conversely, not just the disadvantaged. (p. 2)

The course eventually engaged both experiential and cognitive factors to enhance learning and would mutually benefit both the professor and the student.

## ■ Conclusion

Critics of student activism often argue that this work does not always provide lasting results, that it has "minimal impact on either society or the university"

(Altbach, 1974/1997, p. 209), and that students "seldom have been interested in participating in academic governance" (p. 211). Lipset (1971/1993) argued that students are interested in attacking but not substantively changing the university in ways that are meaningful. Clark Kerr famously quipped,

> One of the most distressing tasks of a university president is to pretend that the protest and outrage of each new generation of undergraduates is really fresh and meaningful. In fact, it is one of the most predictable controversies that we know. The participants go through a ritual of hackneyed complaints, almost as ancient as academe, while believing that what is said is radical and new. (quoted in Thelin, 2018, pp. 98–99)

Kerr's glib response to student concerns showed a lack of understanding of how meaningful many student complaints were. However, the birth of University 101 reveals that student activism was an important catalyst for educational reform and an example of how students can have "profound impacts" on political and social structures (Boren, 2001, p. 3). In such moments of crisis, students can find themselves "at the center of extremely powerful sociological, political, and physical forces" (Boren, 2001, p. 4). In the case of University 101, the combination of students demanding change and an insightful president understanding how to react brought about this and other reforms.

While students on Southern campuses were slower to use the tactics of protest and civil disobedience, their stories are no less significant. During the 1960s student movement, "one dependable way for journalists to demonstrate just how far the wave of activism had spread was to describe its effects on the campuses of the Southeast" (Turner, 2001, p. 103). President Jones used a similar metric when he commented about the protests on campus: "This is Carolina. For this to happen here, something must be wrong" (Lesesne, 2001, p. 221). What was wrong, he realized, was that the university had grown too impersonal and was not *humane* enough (Watts, 1999). The university's motto, "Emollit Mores Nec Sinit Esse Feros" means, after all, "Learning humanizes character and does not permit it to be cruel." Jones's solution was to listen to and collaborate with students in an effort to humanize the university.

Fred Gardner's UFO Coffeehouse was short-lived, but its effects are long-lasting. It created an environment for people to come together and reason about the state of the world. Ultimately, it could not survive the collective attacks by those threatened by ideas that ran counter to the predominant culture. But it provided a place to dream of a different, more humane world, including for UofSC faculty and students.

The University 101 program, under the direction of John Gardner shortly after its creation until 1999 and others since, has spawned a national research center and an international movement on the first-year experience. The program that grew directly from the student activism of the late 1960s at UofSC—especially the protests during the "Months of May" in 1970—has not only survived but thrived and grown. The next chapter explores the early development and national prominence of University 101, reflecting on its role as a launching point for a global movement focused on the first-year experience in higher education.

## References

Altbach, P. G. (1997). *Student politics in America: A historical analysis.* Transaction Publishers. (Original work published in 1974).

Atkinson, F. D., Caldwell, W. H., Heckel, R. V., Hiers, J. M., Mulvaney, R. J. & Rempel, R. A. (1972). *Proposal for an experimental freshman program.* University of South Carolina.

AWARE speaker fails to appear. (1969, April 22). *The Gamecock,* 3.

Ball, M. (1969, April 29). 40 students attend soldiers' hearing. *The Gamecock,* 3.

Boren, M. E. (2001). *Student resistance: A history of the unruly subject.* Routledge.

Broadhorst, C. (2020, Spring). 50 years of May. *Carolinian: University of South Carolina Alumni Magazine,* 13–20.

Carter, D. T. (2013). Foreword: Deep South campus memories and the world the sixties made. In R. Cohen & D. J. Snyder (Eds.), *Rebellion in black & white: Southern student activism in the 1960s* (pp. vii–xviii). Johns Hopkins University Press.

Cohen, R. (2009). *Freedom's orator: Mario Savio and the radical legacy of the 1960s.* Oxford University Press.

Conroy, P. (1995). *Beach music.* Doubleday.

Donaldson, B. (2021, April 9). "Our ultimate choice is desegregation or disintegration" – Recovering the lost words of a jailed civil rights strategist. *The Conversation.* https://theconversation.com/our-ultimate-choice-is-desegregation-or-disintegration-recovering-the-lost-words-of-a-jailed-civil-rights-strategist-155675.

Dresselhaus, M. S., Rosenblith, W. A., Tribus, M., & Zimmerman, H. (1984). Thomas Franklin Jones: 1916–1981. In *Memorial Tributes: National Academy of Engineering, Volume 2* (pp. 141–146). The National Academies Press. https://doi.org/10.17226/565.

Dwyer, J. O. (1989). A historical look at the freshman year experience. In M. L. Upcraft, J. N. Gardner, & Associates, *The freshman year experience: Helping students survive and succeed in college* (pp. 25–39). Jossey-Bass.

Fellenbaum, C. (1971, October 4). Group proposes new ideas. *The Gamecock,* 1.

Finnegan, D. E., & Alleman, N. F. (2013). The YMCA and the origins of American freshman orientation programs. *Historical Studies in Education, 25,* 95–114.

Finnegan, D. E., & Cullaty, B. (2001). Origins of the YMCA universities: Organizational adaptations in urban education. *History of Higher Education Annual, 21,* 47–77.

Fitts, C. T., & Swift, F. H. (1928). *The construction of orientation courses for college freshmen.* University of California Press.

Geiger, R. L. (2015). *The history of American higher education: Learning and culture from the founding to World War II.* Princeton University Press.

Heckel, R. V., Hiers, J. M., Finegold, B. & Zuidema, J. (1973). *University 101: An educational experiment.* University of South Carolina, Social Problems Research Institute.

Hope, H., & Wannamaker, J. (1970, February 9). UFO backers gather at USC. *The Gamecock,* 1.

Jones, T. (1973). Introduction. In R. V. Heckel, J. M. Hiers, B. Finegold, & J. Zuidema, *University 101: An educational experiment* (pp. 1–5). University of South Carolina, Social Problems Research Institute.

Koch, A. K., & Gardner, J. N. (2006). The history of the first-year experience in the United States: Lessons from the past, practices in the present, and implications for the future. In A. Hamana & K. Tatsuo (Eds.), *The first-year experience and transition from high school: An international study of content and pedagogy.* Maruzen Publishing.

Lesesne, H. H. (2001). *A history of the University of South Carolina: 1940–2000.* University of South Carolina Press.

Lipset, S. M. (1993). *Rebellion in the university.* Transaction Publishers. (Original work published in 1971).

Lowery, J. W. (2002, Spring/Fall). Dr. Charles Witten: A conversation about a remarkable life and career. *Palmetto Practitioner: Issues in Student Affairs.* https://web.archive.org/web/20080220204609/http://www.sccpaweb.org/palmettopractitioner/2002/index.html.

Matalene, C. B., & Reynolds. K. C. (2001). *Carolina voices: Two hundred years of student experiences.* University of South Carolina Press.

McAninch, W. S. (1995). The UFO. *South Carolina Law Review, 46*(2), 363–379.

The months of May. (1970). *University of South Carolina Magazine.*

Moore, J. H. (1993). *Columbia and Richland County: A South Carolina community, 1740–1990.* University of South Carolina Press.

Myers, A. H. (2006). *Black, white, & olive drab: Racial Integration at Fort Jackson, South Carolina, and the Civil Rights Movement.* University of Virginia Press.

Parsons, D. L. (2017). *Dangerous grounds: Antiwar coffeehouses and military dissent in the Vietnam era.* University of North Carolina Press.

Setran, D. P. (2007). *The college "Y": Student religion in the era of secularization.* New York: Palgrave Macmillan.

Soldiers' defender comments on case. (1969, May 2). *The Gamecock,* 3.

Thelin, J. R. (2018). *Going to college in the sixties.* Johns Hopkins University Press.

Thelin, J. R. (2019). *A history of American higher education* (3rd ed.). Johns Hopkins University Press.

Turner, J. (2001). From the sit-ins to Vietnam: The evolution of the student activism on southern college campuses, 1960–1970. *History of Higher Education Annual, 21,* 103–135.

Watts, E. (1999). *The freshman year experience, 1962–1990: An experiment in humanistic higher education* [Unpublished doctoral dissertation]. Queen's University.

Whittington, E. L. (2013). Interracial dialogue and the southern student human relations project. In R. Cohen & D. J. Snyder (Eds.), *Rebellion in black & white: Southern student activism in the 1960s* (pp. 83–105). Johns Hopkins University Press.

# Chapter 2

# The University 101 Model

**Transforming Higher Education in
the United States and Abroad**

*Tracy L. Skipper*

The University of South Carolina (UofSC) May 1970 protests gave birth to University 101, but the course also owes a debt to President Thomas Jones's desire to educate more South Carolinians, especially those from disadvantaged backgrounds, while still advancing the university as a major research institution. As Elsie Watts (1999) noted in her history of the first-year experience movement, University 101 (UNIV 101) was one of several educational experiments Jones promoted in the late 1960s and early 1970s, including Upward Bound and University Without Walls. At the heart of all these experiments was a student-centered philosophy that Jones believed would make the research university a more humane place.

The key to Jones's vision for institutional transformation was changing the way faculty taught so that students would become engaged in the academic enterprise and learn to love the university. University 101 was designed to acquaint students with the central purposes of higher education; help them understand their role as a person and student within the university; and guide them to its resources by changing the way faculty saw their students, themselves, and their relationships to others at the institution. The emphasis on changing the institution to better serve students is perhaps the defining characteristic of Jones's model. Yet, initiatives for first-year students were often designed to remediate their personal and academic inadequacies so that they would be better suited to the college culture—what scholars of educational equity might call a deficit model (see, e.g., Harris & Bensimon, 2007; Witham & Bensimon, 2012). By grounding his initial approach in the human potential movement, Jones rejected the deficit model in favor of a talent development approach to addressing the struggles he observed in his university and among his students. Further evidence of this talent development approach is his desire to create a course to serve all students in the university—"not just the very bright, or conversely, not just the disadvantaged" (Jones, 1973, p. 2).

A first-year seminar was not a new concept when it was introduced at UofSC in 1972. However, South Carolina is credited with the birth of the seminar—or at least the seminar in its current form. Why did an educational initiative that had waxed and waned in American higher education since the late 19th century (Gordon, 1989) suddenly find its footing in Columbia, South Carolina in the mid-1970s? In short, Jones's course tapped into larger shifts in American higher education, and the structure that grew up around UNIV 101 contributed to its longevity, driving institutional transformation at the University of South Carolina and reshaping how educators across the world would see the first college year for the next five decades.

## ■ The Right Solution at the Right Time

The South Carolina model spoke to two crises in American higher education in the latter half of the 20th century: (a) a looming student retention crisis and (b) a growing dissatisfaction with higher education. In scanning the educational landscape, Jones recognized that declining student enrollment in colleges and universities would be compounded by decreased funding for higher education at the federal level. To survive, institutions would need to do more to retain the students they did enroll and the tuition dollars they brought with them. In many cases, institutions would seek to "fix" their entering students, remediating possible deficits to increase their chances of survival. However, Jones (1973) saw his course as more than "survival training" (p. 3); instead, he suggested the course would help students develop a bond with their professors—one that opened them to additional learning experiences at the university and helped them find meaning in those experiences. Thus, the emphasis was less on fixing entering students and more on transforming the environment they entered.

Still, while "retention in the interests of the student"—educating a wider and more diverse population of South Carolinians—was the primary rationale for Jones's first-year seminar, "he used retention in the interests of the financial health of the institution as a selling point to ensure its survival" (Watts, p. 265). The initial course pilot was managed by the Social Problems Research Institute (SPRI); their report on UNIV 101 demonstrated modest but encouraging results, especially for less academically prepared entering students (Heckel et al., 1973). Course participants had lower predicted GPAs but earned slightly higher grades and completed more credit hours during their first two semesters than students who did not take the course.

Yet, these initial findings were not enough to ensure the course's survival. When William H. Patterson succeeded Jones as president of South Carolina in 1974, Jones's educational experiments, including UNIV 101, came under scrutiny. Patterson conditioned the future of the course on John Gardner's (director from 1974 to 1999) ability to prove that students and the university benefitted from UNIV 101 through "credible research data" (Watts, 1999, p. 278). Paul Fidler, a staff member in the emerging area of student affairs, was brought in to do the assessment. Fidler (1991) studied sophomore return rates for course participants from 1973 to 1988 and confirmed the compensatory impact of participation in UNIV 101 observed by SPRI. Students enrolling in the seminar during this period continued to have lower predicted GPAs than nonparticipants, with provisionally admitted students and undeclared majors (two groups of students at high risk for attrition) overrepresented in the course sample. Nevertheless, students who enrolled in the course were more likely to return for their second year of college than those who elected not to take the course. Other research on the course demonstrated its positive impact on sophomore return rates for African American students (Fidler & Godwin, 1994) and on graduation rates (Shanley & Witten, 1990). Once South Carolina demonstrated the retention benefits of its model, other institutions looked to it as a potential solution to their own enrollment woes.

Connected to the enrollment and retention crisis were growing calls for the reform of undergraduate education in the early to mid-1980s. President Ronald Reagan's Commission on Education produced several reports detailing the problems of secondary and postsecondary education and offering recommendations for their reform (e.g., *A Nation at Risk, Involvement in Learning, To Reclaim a Legacy*). The Study Group on the Conditions of Excellence in American Higher Education's (1984) *Involvement in Learning* highlighted the transformations that had taken place in higher education in the preceding three decades, including rapid increases in enrollment; changes in enrollment patterns (i.e., later entry into college, part-time attendance, and longer times to degree); the shifting nature of relationships between institutions and both students and faculty; and greater control of higher education institutions at the state level. Because the number of colleges and universities did not keep pace with the growth of student enrollment in higher educations, institutions became larger and more complex, often to the detriment of students:

> The greater the size of the institutions, the more complex and bureaucratic they tend to become, the fewer the opportunities for each student to become intensely involved with intellectual life, and the less the personal contact between faculty and students. (Study Group, 1984, pp. 11–12)

First-year students, in particular, received short shrift: "closed out of course selections, treated impersonally, and given lower priority in academic advising than sophomores, juniors, and seniors" (Study Group, 1984, p. 26). The curriculum was also becoming increasingly specialized and fragmented. Now more than ever, students needed help navigating the academic landscape if they were to not only survive but also succeed in college. The Study Group affirmed the critical importance of transforming the way institutions designed the first year of college to shore up undergraduate education.

The South Carolina model, conceived as a vehicle for institutional transformation, anticipated and responded to many of the issues raised by these reports. Reflecting on the course after its initial pilot, President Jones (1973) described it as "an experimental program that attempts to modify both the professor and the student to survive in the new educational dimension" (p. 2). Indeed, the course helped acclimate students to the postsecondary environment and the complex educational bureaucracy that is the research university. More important, it sought to transform the way students were taught and how they learned by focusing on intellectual engagement and personal development as opposed to remediation or mere skills acquisition. In a 1980 presentation, Gardner highlighted the course's role in providing faculty with new and effective ways to communicate subject matter to students. By helping faculty develop new teaching skills, UNIV 101 addressed another concern raised by the Study Group (1984)—that is, increasing students' active involvement in the learning enterprise by offering first-year students classes that "provide adequate opportunities for intense intellectual interaction between students and instructors" (p. 25). The following section takes a closer look at how the course structure responded to these larger concerns about US undergraduate education.

## ■ The South Carolina Model in Context

In 2008, George Kuh identified the first-year seminar as one of 10 high-impact practices (HIPs) that contributed to increased rates of student retention and engagement. Learning communities, service-learning, and common intellectual experiences (e.g., reading experiences, convocations, etc.) were also highlighted as HIPs. By the time Kuh codified these experiences, many of them had been operating on campuses for 20 years or longer in response to those twin concerns of retaining students and providing engaging educational experiences. Like first-year seminars, learning communities were an earlier educational innovation that reemerged and gained traction during the 1980s (Goodsell Love, 1999).

By focusing on the conditions of students' educational experiences rather than on the characteristics of entering students, HIPs serve as potential vehicles of talent development and institutional transformation. Scholars and practitioners have studied HIPs to determine the factors that contribute to their effectiveness. In 2013, Kuh and O'Donnell articulated several key characteristics that define HIPs, such as

- performance expectations set at appropriately high levels;
- significant investment of time and effort by students over an extended period of time;
- interactions with faculty and peers about substantive matters;
- experiences with diversity (i.e., exposure to and interaction with people and circumstances different from those with which students are familiar);
- frequent, timely, and constructive feedback;
- periodic, structured opportunities to reflect and integrate learning;
- opportunities to discover relevance of learning through real-world applications; and
- public demonstration of competence (p. 10).

These characteristics have largely been present in UNIV 101's overall structure since its inception. The following section examines evidence of these characteristics within the larger context of extended orientation seminars and UNIV 101, in particular, drawing on more than a quarter century of national survey research.[1]

### An Extended Orientation Seminar

In a 1980 presentation to a faculty development conference, Gardner described the goals of UNIV 101 as

- providing orientation to the purposes of higher education in general and to the University of South Carolina in particular,
- helping students adjust to the university and develop a positive attitude about the university and college-level learning processes,
- improving retention rates, and
- providing faculty with new and effective ways to communicate subject matter to students and with greater knowledge about the university and the services available to assist students.

Later, this type of course would be defined by Barefoot (1992)[2] as an extended orientation seminar in the following manner:

> Sometimes called freshman orientation, college survival, or student success courses. May be taught by faculty, administrators, and/or student affairs professionals. Content will likely include introduction to campus resources, time management, study skills, career planning, cultural diversity, and student development issues.

Since 1991, landscape analyses of the first-year seminars have explored course objectives.[3] The two primary objectives most consistently reported from 1991 to 2017 were (a) orientation to campus resources (an average response frequency of 56.1%) and (b) develop academic skills or academic success strategies (an average response frequency of 53.7%). In the early years of the survey administration, *easing the transition or adjustment to college* rounded out the three most important course objectives.[4] Since the 2012 administration, *develop a connection with the institution* has been among the top-three objectives identified as most important.[5] These goals largely mirror those of the course at its inception, suggesting its influence on the development of these courses nationally. The remainder of this section explores structural elements of the extended orientation course that mark it as a high-impact educational practice.

### Time on Task and High Expectations

### Credit Hours and Course Grading

Since its inception, UNIV 101 has been offered as a three-credit-hour course, which sets it apart from other extended orientation seminars. Responses to national surveys on first-year seminars indicate that 50% to 60% of extended orientation courses are offered for a single credit hour (see Figure 2.1). These courses are much less likely to be offered for three credit hours, with only about one quarter of respondents reporting this pattern in recent years. As Friedman notes in Chapter 4, the amount of credit earned offers the course

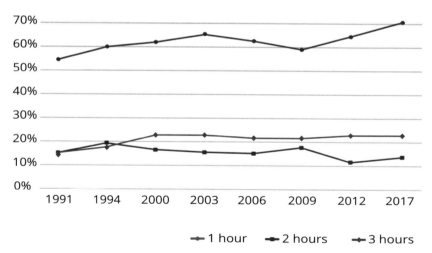

**FIGURE 2.1.** Number of credit hours assigned to extended orientation seminars, 1991–2017.

legitimacy and contributes to its overall effectiveness. In part, course effectiveness can be tied to more opportunities for time on task afforded more by contact hours, of which credit hours are a proxy.

Closely related to credit hours earned are considerations of course grading. Barefoot and Fidler (1992) reported that 36% of extended orientation seminars were graded on a pass/fail basis on the 1991 survey administration; that number, however, declined steadily to just over 10% in 2017 (Young, 2019). Like many extended orientation courses, UNIV 101 was initially graded on a pass/fail basis. In the early 1990s, Gardner successfully lobbied the Faculty Senate's curriculum committee to change the grading policy. According to Gardner (personal communication, February 26, 2021), students were the impetus for the change:

> we'd been hearing from students that they wanted it to be a letter grade because a number of them were complaining that they were having to do too much work for a pass. And it was, you know, hey, this is a real course. Make it a real course like my other courses. Or we had students tell us, "If I could get an A in here, I'd really do a lot more work." Or say, "If this were letter graded, I would take it more seriously."

Students clearly communicated that they wanted greater alignment between institutional expectations and the effort required to pass the course. More important, students wanted the institution to hold them to higher expectations and indicated their willingness to meet those expectations.

## Course Assignments

Assigning a letter grade to the course communicates a certain level of expectation about UNIV 101 as an academic experience. More important, instructors are required to include writing assignments (both formal and informal); oral presentations; and projects, papers, or exams that "challenge students to reflect upon and synthesize the major course goals" (Friedman & Sokol, 2021, Chapter 1, p. 9). National data also point to the role of writing in first-year seminars. For example, 42.5% of respondents to the 2012–2013 National Survey on First-Year Seminars indicated that they included opportunities to produce and revise writing in the first-year seminar; more than one quarter of extended orientation seminars included this writing focus (see Skipper, 2014). These requirements signal both high expectations for student performance in the course and for their investment of time and effort.

### *Constructive Feedback*

Setting high expectations for student performance is meaningful only to the extent that students receive timely, constructive feedback on how they are performing. To support instructors in providing meaningful feedback to students, University 101 Programs provide sample writing and presentation assignments and accompanying rubrics through the *University 101 Faculty Resource Manual* and in an online resource repository.

### Instructor Presence

The extended orientation seminar has involved a range of campus professionals in instruction throughout its history, with faculty (average response of 85%) followed by student affairs administrators (average response rate of 63.2%) being most commonly reported as seminar instructors. As greater attention has been paid to educational and career planning in the first college year, more institutions have reported involving academic advisors in seminar instruction (ranging from about one third in 2003 to more than half in 2017). In many cases, the seminar instructor serves as the first-year academic advisor for students in their section. Chapter 6 offers additional insight on who teaches the course at UofSC.

The importance of instructor presence in achieving the aims of UNIV 101 is evidenced by the prominent role that instructor training has played in the course since its inception. The original training model—45 hours spread over three weeks—was soon shortened to 1 week. Initial training for UNIV 101 instructors now takes place in a three-day workshop, and it is supplemented by a robust calendar of faculty development initiatives, including

UNIV 101 instructors after Teaching Experience Workshop

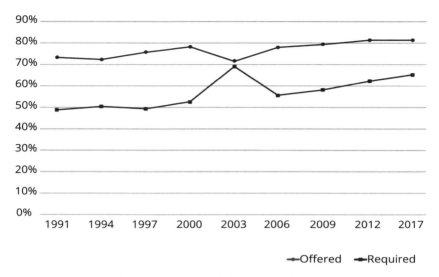

FIGURE 2.2. Connection of instructor training to extended orientation seminars, 1991–2017. *Note.* Data by seminar type not available for 1997 and 2003 survey administration. Percentage reflects responses across all seminar types.

online resources, brown-bag lunches, and an annual one-day conference (see Chapter 7). Instructor training is a ubiquitous feature of extended orientation courses nationally, and increasingly it is required (Figure 2.2). Yet, the South Carolina model is unique in its intentional, year-round approach to faculty development. Of the institutions offering instructor training between 2000 and 2017, slightly more than one third reported that training was a half day or less; about one quarter of respondents offered a daylong training event. The attention to faculty development ensures that instructors are ready to engage students in educationally meaningful ways within and beyond the classroom, as described in the next section.

### Interactions With Peers and Instructors

As an extended orientation seminar, UNIV 101 emphasizes building community and provides opportunities for students to engage with their peers about a range of issues important to their success in college, their personal health and well-being, their relationships with others, and their future employment opportunities. The discussion-based format of the course, emphasis on active learning, and small-group processing creates a strong framework for peer interaction. University 101 Programs and its campus partners provide funding for dinner dialogues, meals hosted by instructors in their homes, and beyond-the-classroom experiences to encourage instructors to explore opportunities for interaction outside the formal classroom setting.

An initiative frequently connected to first-year seminars is the common reading experience (increasing from 27.4% on the 2009 administration to 38.5% in 2017)—an experience designed to introduce students to the intellectual life of college before classes begin. The First-Year Reading Experience was launched at the University of South Carolina in 1994. While initially serving a small number of entering students, it expanded to include the entire first-year class in 2005. After hearing a speaker associated with the common reading (often the author), new students may meet with their UNIV 101 class to get to know one another prior to the first official class meeting, visit exhibits connected to the reading, and/or engage in a discussion of the text. By asking students to engage their UNIV 101 classmates in conversation about a challenging text early in their college experience, the course directors establish a baseline for the kinds of intellectual exchanges they hope to see in UNIV 101 and elsewhere in the undergraduate experience. See Chapter 8 for additional discussion of this initiative.

### Opportunities for Reflective and Integrative Learning

The course's student-centered nature is evident in its emphasis on reflective writing assignments. Students are also encouraged to explore and plan for experiential learning opportunities beyond the first year through University 101's partnership with the Center for Integrative and Experiential Learning. Service-learning is one such experience. Like learning communities and common reading initiatives, service-learning is often connected to the first-year seminar. About one quarter to one third of respondents across survey administrations report embedding service-learning in the first-year seminar. Service experiences are an important opportunity for engaging first-year students beyond the classroom and are incorporated in many sections of UNIV 101 at South Carolina.

Colleges and universities frequently link the seminar to other educational initiatives supporting persistence and important social and academic outcomes. On the 1994 survey administration, respondents were asked whether the seminar was linked to one or more other first-year courses—that is, whether the seminar was part of a learning community. The practice of embedding a seminar in a learning community grew steadily through the 1990s and early 2000s, reaching a peak of 39.5% in 2009. The most recent survey administration suggests that about one third of respondents linked a seminar to other first-year courses (see Young, 2019). Henscheid and colleagues (2016) explored the role of first-year seminars in learning communities, identifying several possible functions for the course. These include such things as

- building community;
- serving as a space to explore concepts across courses, sometimes accomplished through shared assignments or visits from the faculty teaching the other course(s) in the learning community;
- enhancing academic skills, behaviors, and dispositions important to academic achievement;
- focusing on career exploration;
- linking the social with the academic; and
- providing opportunities to process concepts related to the learning community theme or to learning in general (see pp. 26–31).

The Common Courses program, a partnership between University Housing, University 101 Programs, and the College of Arts and Sciences (A&S), created living–learning communities at UofSC (Lichterman et al., 2016) and "allow[ed] first-year students to take both a U101 course and core introductory course . . . in A&S with peers who live in their residence hall" (p. 140). The UNIV 101 course served as a site for curricular integration, drawing on content from the core course as a source of reflection or for teaching study skills or notetaking. The seminar also promoted social and academic connections by intentionally integrating beyond-the-classroom activities connected to themes and concepts in the core course.

The extended orientation model that emerged in South Carolina tapped into larger concerns about higher education in the 1970s and 1980s. Structural conditions at UofSC supported the course's longevity, encouraged its adoption (and adaptation) by other campuses, and set the stage for wider educational transformation. The final sections of this chapter describe the conditions that contributed to UNIV 101's role in launching a larger movement and highlight three enduring outcomes of that movement.

### ■ Starting a Conversation About Student Success

Almost from the beginning, other colleges and universities sought to replicate the South Carolina model, specifically its emphasis on faculty development. Awareness of the course was no accident, however. John Gardner had been "ordered to 'go out and sell 101' to the US higher education community" by then provost Keith Davis (J. N. Gardner, personal communication, February 18, 2021). In his November 1976 annual report, Gardner noted that he had corresponded with individuals from more than 60 institutions seeking information about the course. Interest in the seminar was spurred by a write up in the June issue of *Nexus*, the newsletter of the American Association of Higher Education, and presentations at the American College Personnel Association and the National Orientation Directors Association annual meetings. The following year, University 101 received the outstanding innovative program award from the National Association of Student Personnel Administrators (Watts, 1999). See also "National Recognition for University 101."

Colleges and universities began to replicate the course on their own campuses during the mid-to-late 1970s and beyond (see Appendix A for examples). Gardner noted in the 1976 annual report that both the University of Cincinnati and the University of Texas at Austin were actively developing pilots "based directly on our model" and that two other institutions were working on proposals to share with University 101. Interest among Canadian institutions (e.g., University of Guelph, University of British Columbia, University of Toronto, and McGill University) also emerged during this period (Watts, 1999, p. 321).

## National Recognition for University 101

**1977 NASPA Outstanding Innovative Program.** University 101 was recognized as an outstanding innovative program.

**2002 Institution of Excellence in the First College Year.** One of 13 US colleges and universities recognized for an intentional, comprehensive approach to first-year student education; continuous improvement driven by meaningful assessments; broad impact on significant numbers of students; enduring institutional support and leadership for first-year initiatives; and involvement of a broad range of stakeholders in first-year programs.

**2011 NASPA Gold Award—Faculty Development.** The University 101 Instructor Development Process received the Gold Award in Excellence for Administrative, Assessment, Information Technology, Fundraising and Professional Development. UofSC received the Grand Silver overall.

**2018 NASPA Gold Award—Peer Leader Program.** University 101 Programs was recognized for its efforts to develop and support peer leaders in the Student Union, Student Activities, Greek Life, and Leadership category.

**U.S. News & World Report—No. 1 Public University for The First-Year Experience/University 101 Course.** The University of South Carolina has long been recognized as an exemplar for the first-year experience and first-year seminar and has been ranked as the number 1 Public University for the First-Year Experience several times.

An initial step for many campuses in replicating the program was sending delegates to the University 101 Teaching Experience Workshop (TEW). Designed to prepare faculty, staff, and administrators to lead the course at South Carolina, the workshop was also made available to visitors from outside the university. An early workshop advertisement described several aims with broad appeal, including

- modeling a broad range of teaching tactics for the classroom,
- exploring the purpose of higher education for today's students,
- challenging those who teach to challenge those who learn,
- modeling group dynamics for the classroom and beyond, and
- presenting interactive techniques for teaching first-year students.

In addition to opening the TEW to visitors, Gardner and the staff of SPRI, who designed the initial training, took the faculty development workshop to individual colleges, visiting Georgia College in fall 1977 and Clarion College in Pennsylvania in 1978 (Watts, 1999).

The wide dissemination of the model by Gardner and his colleagues through conference presentations, publications, and on-campus consultations and trainings was no doubt partially responsible for its replication on other campuses. To be sure, that they had evidence to demonstrate the educational effectiveness of their program—something of a rarity at that time—also played a large role. Moreover, the course's national prominence in those early years was almost as important as its demonstrated effectiveness in its remaining viable at the University of South Carolina (see, e.g., Watts, 1999, p. 315).

### The Beginning of a National Movement

By 1978, the number of external requests for information about UNIV 101 had grown to 260, reaching 340 by the spring of 1980 (Watts, 1999). To manage some of these information requests and "provide a network for course advocates and give their efforts greater legitimacy," Gardner hosted the National Conference on the Freshman Orientation Course/Freshman Seminar Concept in Columbia, South Carolina, in 1982. The meeting was attended by approximately 175 higher education faculty, staff, and administrators from the United States and Canada (Watts, 1999). In 1983, the meeting, rebranded as the Annual Conference on The Freshman Year Experience, drew more than 400 educators to South Carolina. The national conferences gave the course greater attention and increased the workload of its small staff.

Gardner sought and received approval from the South Carolina Commission on Higher Education in 1986 to establish the National Center for the Study of the Freshman Year Experience, now the National Resource Center for The First-Year Experience and Students in Transition (Watts, 1999). The National Resource Center assumed management of the conference series and launched a study focused on "enumerat[ing] the first-year seminars operating in America" in 1988 (Watts, 1999, p. 364; see Fidler & Fidler, 1991).

When the National Resource Center was launched in July 1987, one of the primary purposes was to establish a literature base on the first-year experience. A practitioner-focused newsletter was launched in May 1988, followed by the first issue of the *Journal of The Freshman Year Experience* that fall. The National Resource Center also published the first installment of *The Freshman Year Experience* monograph series in 1988, John Whitely and Norma Yokota's study of character development in the first college year and beyond.

The National Resource Center provided a platform for promoting the South Carolina model, amplifying the message shared in the decade or so after the course's founding. Staff from University 101 Programs were frequently tapped to present extended sessions on faculty development, peer leadership, and course assessment at national and international conferences and other professional development events hosted by the National Resource Center. The *Journal of The First-Year Experience in Students in Transition* published four studies on the impact of UNIV 101 on students and faculty or on specific practices that contributed to course effectiveness (see Fidler, 1991; Fidler & Moore, 1996; Fidler et al., 1999; Reynolds & Nunn, 1998). Four additional studies were published on programs explicitly modeled on South Carolina's UNIV 101 (see Davis, 1992; Hoff et al., 1996; Koutsoubakis, 1999; Zimmerman, 2000). A Google Scholar search completed in March 2021 (see "University 101 in the Literature") highlights the far-reaching impact of the UNIV 101 model on the research and practice literature.

The National Resource Center also prompted ongoing course innovation. Reflecting on the symbiotic relationship between University 101 and the National Resource Center, Gardner (personal communication, February 26, 2021) noted, "we were learning through our publications great stuff that others were doing that we could be doing . . . , too." The involvement of peer leaders in course instruction is a good example of this. Gardner learned about the practice at a conference and wondered why they were not doing it at South Carolina. He tapped a student worker to serve as his peer leader for a section of UNIV 101 and was so pleased with the result that he asked Dan Berman, then codirector for the course, to implement a peer leader component for the program. Peer leader involvement is now a key feature of University 101, with every section having a peer or graduate leader assigned to assist with the course (see Chapter 7 for more on the peer leader program).

## University 101 in the Literature

University 101's presence in the research and practice literature suggests its wide influence on the development of first-year seminars nationally and on the first-year experience movement. In March 2021, a Google Scholar search for "first-year seminar" AND "South Carolina" yielded 1,650 hits for sources published between 1993 and 2020. Of these, 150 referenced the University 101 course in some substantive way.

In the literature reviewed, University 101 was acknowledged as the originator or source of first-year seminars in the late 20th century or as being responsible for the form's revival (n = 76). Early research on retention and graduation rates for course participants (i.e., Fidler, 1991; Fidler & Godwin, 1994; Fidler & Moore, 1996; Shanley & Witten, 1990) was also cited frequently (n = 53). Individual searches for each of these published studies may suggest an even more wide-ranging impact of the course on student success practice. Sources also mentioned the history or origins of University 101, its connection to the first-year experience movement (n = 33), or descriptions of the course (n = 19). Discussion of the course figures in a range of publication types including doctoral dissertations and master's theses (n = 77), journal articles (n = 40), and book chapters (n = 10).

University 101 maintains an annotated bibliography of publications that have referenced the course in a significant way (e.g., as a site or subject of research, as a program model) on its website.

### International Interest

Throughout the early 1980s, Gardner entertained inquiries about the course model from educators in the United Kingdom, Germany, and Australia (Watts, 1999). In July 1986, the first International Conference on The First-Year Experience was hosted at Newcastle-Upon-Tyne; the series would last for 27 years. International collaborations have continued and resulted in the creation of national or regional networks in Australia, New Zealand, Canada, and Europe. To facilitate the global conversation about the first college year and student success, the National Resource Center hosts an international advisory board with representation from Australia, the Bahamas, Canada, Belgium, Japan, Kuwait, Mexico, New Zealand, Saudi Arabia, South Africa,

Turkey, and the United Kingdom. In 2015, the University of South Carolina and the University of Johannesburg entered into an agreement to form a sister center, the South African Centre for The First-Year Experience. These national and regional networks allow for continued collaboration with South Carolina's National Resource Center alongside more focused attention on the unique higher education context within a country or region.

### Beyond the First College Year

As the National Resource Center assumed responsibility for a growing portfolio of conferences and professional development events, the conversation broadened beyond first-year seminars to educational strategies and initiatives to improve student learning, development, and success in the first college year and beyond. Explorations of the transition out of college, that is the senior year experience, the sophomore year, and the transfer experience, made their way onto the conference agenda—often in specialized meetings—and into the publications of the National Resource Center. To reflect this broadened focus, the Center changed its name to its current title in 1998. The research agenda of the Center showed similar expansion. While the study of first-year seminars has remained a core of the research efforts, national studies have also explored initiatives in the sophomore and senior years and the experiences of peer leaders in higher education settings in the United States, the United Kingdom, South Africa, Australia, and New Zealand.

### ■ The Broader Impact of the South Carolina Model on Higher Education

As suggested earlier, the research and practice emerging from University 101 Programs and the National Resource Center laid the groundwork for broader conversations about effective educational practices that both support student learning, success, and development and have the potential to transform our institutions. This closing section highlights three ways UNIV 101 has impacted higher education in the United States: (a) providing a common purpose and language about the beginning college experience, (b) focusing on student success instead of student survival, and (c) understanding the transformative power of faculty development.

### Common Purpose and Language

The synergy between University 101 Programs and the National Resource Center helped craft a common language and purpose for first-year seminars, and later student success writ large, for the higher education community.

Staff at the National Resource Center first began the effort to count and categorize first-year seminars in the late 1980s. A closer look at how institutions describe their first-year seminars—regardless of type—suggests the broad impact of the extended orientation model on undergraduate education in the first year. This is perhaps most evident among colleges and universities describing a hybrid model, which is defined as having elements of two or more types of seminars.[6] Descriptions of hybrid seminars from the 2009 NSFYS ($n = 194$) and from the 2012 NSFYS ($n = 185$) were analyzed to explore whether and how elements of extended orientation were present in this course type.

Several prominent themes emerged, the most common of which was combining elements typically found in the extended orientation seminar with an academic seminar of some type. For example, an academic seminar with uniform content might also incorporate topics related to college transition or personal development as this description suggests:

> Students are prepared for a successful academic career through the cultivation of valued skills in the liberal arts such as critical reading and analysis, writing and discussion, argument and debate. Students are exposed to a series of primary texts, compiled by the course faculty, dealing with a range of diverse creative, intellectual and ethical ideas. Students are introduced to many helpful campus resources as well as university transition strategies such as time-management, study skills, information literacy, note-taking, utilizing technology, and coping with test anxiety.

Topic-driven academic seminars might also embed content more typical to the extended orientation model:

> All of our courses share course goals related to academic success strategies, life management skills, and familiarity with campus resources— fitting the extended orientation definition. However, each section must also have a subject of inquiry; typically, this is linked to an academic discipline.

Respondents were equally likely, albeit less common, to describe combinations of extended orientation with basic study skills or with major- or discipline-specific courses. In the latter case, the discipline-specific course tends to function as an introduction to the major. One major-specific hybrid was defined in the following way:

> It is primarily an extended orientation session, with a component that is specific to each discipline. Students have a program-based activity/ field trip that is specific to their own major. Additionally, the paper that

each student must write is the same basic assignment, but is meant to be written about their own hopes/aspirations within a particular major.

Two additional patterns that emerged from the analysis included (a) embedding extended orientation content into a general education course (e.g., first-year writing) or another required course unique to the institution (e.g., financial literacy) and (b) employing an adjunct model, either by adding a lab hour for extended orientation content to another course or requiring a series of supplementary activities. Institutions might take this route out of concern about adding an additional course into already-crowded major maps, especially if there are policies in place that penalize students or institutions when students graduate with excess credit hours.

The variety of ways institutions approach structuring the first-year seminar, and the particular emphasis on themes from the extended orientation model, suggests an inherent value in the approach launched at South Carolina. It also speaks to the ingenuity of institutions in finding ways to meet the academic and personal transition needs of entering students within the realities of different institutional contexts and values systems.

### A Focus on Undergraduate Student Success

Perhaps more important than the revival of a particular course type, the work at the University of South Carolina helped launch a broader commitment to student success—not just in the first year but also throughout the college experience. While University 101 Programs was incorporating service initiatives and a common reading into its course and experimenting with learning communities, their colleagues in the National Resource Center were promoting these initiatives through publications and professional development events. Just as the early research on UNIV 101 suggested a compensatory effect for underprepared and underrepresented students, the conversations around student success have evolved beyond simply promoting individual practices to considering the extent to which those practices support the success of historically marginalized populations.

Paul Fidler and others' pioneering efforts to assess the effectiveness of UNIV 101 remain a model for other institutions of higher education. Yet, there has also been an emphasis on moving beyond simply documenting the impact of educational initiatives on academic performance and persistence to understanding how (or which elements of) those initiatives shape student outcomes and for whom.

Early definitions of student success were grounded in easy-to-observe metrics, such as persistence, academic performance, progression toward degree, and graduation. Conversations about student success now focus more broadly on student learning outcomes (see Gahagan et al., 2010; Friedman, 2012) and noncognitive factors, such as strengths, mindset, resilience, and sense of belonging (see Baldwin et al., 2020; Schreiner et al., 2020). The work of University 101 Programs and the National Resource Center have continued to push this conversation forward.

*Faculty Development*

When President Jones launched UNIV 101, he sought to humanize the university by transforming the faculty. Evidence suggests that the emphasis on faculty development may be one of the most important and far-reaching impacts of the course. Campus-based research studies on the impact of first-year seminars suggest that the course has a powerful impact on those who teach it. In one particular set of studies (see Barefoot, 1993), the University of Wyoming found that faculty became more centered on students after teaching the course, and Central Missouri State University reported that faculty learned more about first-year students and the university, used new teaching techniques in the seminar, and tried them in other courses. Similarly, Appalachian State University found that faculty improved their teaching and developed new pedagogical approaches, which were then applied in discipline-based courses (Friedman, 2005). Faculty at Appalachian State also reported increased knowledge about the university and its resources and an increased sense of vitality and collegiality. Studies published in the *Journal of The First-Year Experience and Students in Transition* (e.g., Fidler et al., 1999; Wanca-Thibault et al., 2002) echo these findings.

## ■ Conclusion

In concluding her study of the first-year experience movement, Watts (1999) suggested that the movement ultimately fell short of President Jones's desire to humanize the research university. To be sure, many of the tensions that animated student unrest and discontent in the late 1960s and early 1970s— inequities in access and opportunity across gender, race, and class lines; a demand for relevance in the curriculum; a desire to be treated as an individual—persist in higher education in 2022. The pandemic and accompanying economic crisis, nationwide protests for racial justice in 2020, and the political turmoil of the 2020 presidential election have laid bare the ongoing challenges and possibilities for higher education. Yet, Jones's vision remains as relevant today as it was in 1972. Moreover, 50 years of evidence speaks to the potential transformative power of the first-year seminar and other high-impact practices. Unfortunately, few institutions have been able to implement these initiatives at scale in the way that UofSC has or to sustain them across generations of students, faculty, and administrative leaders. The rest of this volume tells the story of sustaining this educational innovation at scale in the hopes that sharing that story will bring us closer to realizing Thomas Jones's vision for undergraduate education.

## References

Atkinson, F. D., Caldwell, W. H., Heckel, R. V., Hiers, J. M., Mulvaney, R. J., & Rempel, R. A. (1972, April 10). *Proposal for an experimental freshman program.* University of South Carolina, University 101 Programs.

Baldwin, A., Bunting, B., Daugherty, D., Lewis, L., & Steenbergh, T. (2020). *Promoting belonging, growth mindset, and resilience to foster student success.* University of South Carolina, National Resource Center for The First-Year Experience and Students in Transition.

Barefoot, B. O. (1992). *Helping first-year college students climb the academic ladder: Report of a national survey of freshman seminar programming in American higher education.* [Doctoral dissertation, College of William & Mary – School of Education]. W&M Scholar Works. https://dx.doi.org/doi:10.25774/w4-4p9k-8r77.

Barefoot, B. O. (1993). *Exploring the evidence: Reporting outcomes of freshman seminars* (Monograph No. 11). University of South Carolina, National Resource Center for The Freshman Year Experience.

Barefoot, B. O., & Fidler, P. P. (1992). *1991 National Survey of Freshman Seminar Programming: Helping first-year college students climb the academic ladder.* University of South Carolina, National Resource Center for The Freshman Year Experience.

Barefoot, B. O., & Fidler, P. P. (1996). *The 1994 National Survey of Freshman Seminar Programs: Continuing innovations in the collegiate curriculum* (Monograph No. 20). University of South Carolina, National Resource Center for The Freshman Year Experience and Students in Transition.

Davis, B. O. (1992). Freshman seminar: A broad spectrum of effectiveness. *Journal of The Freshman Year Experience, 4,* 79–94.

Fidler, P. P. (1991). Relationship to freshman orientation seminars to sophomore return rates. *Journal of The Freshman Year Experience, 3,* 7–38.

Fidler, P. P., & Fidler, D. S. (1991). *First National Survey on Freshman Seminar Programs: Findings, conclusions, and recommendations* (Monograph No. 6). University of South Carolina, National Resource Center for The Freshman Year Experience.

Fidler, P. P., & Godwin, M. A. (1994). Retaining African-American students through the freshman seminar. *Journal of Developmental Education, 17* (3), 34–40.

Fidler, P. P., & Moore, P. S. (1996). A comparison of effects of campus residence and freshman seminar attendance on freshman dropout rates. *Journal of The Freshman Year Experience, 8*(2), 7–16.

Fidler, P. P., Neururer-Rotholz, J., & Richardson, S. (1999). Teaching the freshman seminar: Its effectiveness in promoting faculty development. *Journal of The First-Year Experience, 11*(2), 59–74.

Friedman, D. (2005). Appalachian State University. In B. F. Tobolowsky, B. E. Cox, & M. T. Wagner (Eds.), *Exploring the evidence: Reporting research on first-year seminar, Volume III* (Monograph No. 42, pp. 13–17). University of South Carolina, National Resource Center for The First-Year Experience and Students in Transition.

Friedman, D., & Sokol, K. (Eds.). (2021). *University 101 faculty resource manual.* University of South Carolina, University 101 Programs.

Friedman, D. B. (2012). *The first-year seminar: Designing, implementing, and assessing courses to support student learning and success. Vol. 5: Assessing the first-year seminar.* University of South Carolina, National Resource Center for The First-Year Experience and Students in Transition.

Gahagan, J., Dingfelder, J., & Pei, K. (2010). *A faculty and staff guide to creating learning outcomes.* University of South Carolina, National Resource Center for The First-Year Experience and Students in Transition.

Gardner, D. P. (1983, April). *A nation at risk: The imperative for educational reform.* National Commission on Excellence in Education, U. S. Department of Education. (ERIC Document No. ED 266006).

Gardner, J. N. (1976, November 15). *Annual report on the health of our program.* Available University 101 Programs, University of South Carolina.

Gardner, J. N. (1980, February 29). *University 101: A concept for improving university teaching and learning.* Paper presented at the Fourth Annual Conference on Faculty Development and Evaluation, Orlando, Florida. (ERIC Resource No. ED192706).

Goodsell Love, A. (1999). What are learning communities? In J. H. Levine (Ed.), *Learning communities: New structures, new partnerships for learning* (Monograph No. 26, pp. 1–8). University of South Carolina, National Resource Center for The First-Year Experience and Students in Transition.

Gordon, V. P. (1989). Origins and purposes of the freshman seminar. In M. L. Upcraft, John N. Gardner, & Associates, *The freshman year experience: Helping students survive and succeed in college* (pp. 183–197). Jossey-Bass.

Harris, F., III, & Bensimon, E. M. (2007). The equity scorecard: A collaborative approach to assess and respond to racial/ethnic disparities in student outcomes. *New Directions for Student Service, 120,* 77–84. https://doi.org/10.1002/ss.259.

Heckel, R. V., Hiers, J. M., Finegold, B., & Zuidema, J. (1973). *University 101: An educational experiment.* University of South Carolina, Social Problems Research Institute.

Henscheid, J. M, Skipper, T. L., & Young, D. G. (2016). National practices for combining first-year seminars and learning communities. In L. Chism Schmidt & J. Graziano (Eds.), *Building synergy for high-impact educational initiatives: First-year seminars and learning communities* (pp. 19–40). University of South Carolina, National Resource Center for The First-Year Experience and Students in Transition.

Hoff, M. P., Cook, D., & Price, C. (1996). The first five years of freshman seminars at Dalton College: Student success and retention. *Journal of The Freshman Year Experience, 8*(2), 33–42.

Jones, T. (1973). Introduction. In R. V. Heckel, J. M. Hiers, B. Finegold, & J. Zuidema, *University 101: An educational experiment* (pp. 1–5). University of South Carolina, Social Problems Research Institute.

Koutsoubakis, D. (1999). A test of effectiveness of a one-term freshman orientation program at the foreign campus of an accredited private American university. *Journal of The First-Year Experience, 11*(2), 33–58.

Kuh. G. D. (2008). *High-impact educational practices: What they are, who has access to them, and why they matter.* Association of American Colleges and Universities.

Kuh, G. D., & O'Donnell, K. (2013). *Ensuring quality and taking high-impact practices to scale.* Association of American Colleges and Universities.

Lichterman, H. L., Friedman, D. B., Falluca, A., & Steinas, J. E. (2016). Common courses: A developing linked coursework perspective. In L. Chism Schmidt & J. Graziano (Eds.), *Building synergy for high-impact educational initiatives: First-year seminars and learning communities* (pp. 139–149). University of South Carolina, National Resource Center for The First-Year Experience and Students in Transition.

National Resource Center for The First-Year Experience and Students in Transition. (2002). *The 2000 National Survey of First-Year Seminar Programs: Continuing innovations in the collegiate curriculum* (Monograph No. 35). University of South Carolina.

Padgett, R. D., & Keup, J. R. (2011). *2009 National Survey of First-Year Seminars: Ongoing efforts to support students in transition* (Research Reports on College Transitions No. 2). University of South Carolina, National Resource Center for The First-Year Experience and Students in Transition.

Reynolds, K. C., & Nunn, C. E. (1998). Engaging freshmen in classroom discussion: Interaction and the instructor techniques that encourage it. *Journal of The First-Year Experience, 10*, 7–24.

Schreiner, L. A., Louis, M. C., & Nelson, D. D. (2020). (Eds.). *Thriving in transitions: A research-based approach to college student success* (2nd edition). University of South Carolina, National Resource Center for The First-Year Experience and Students in Transition.

Shanley, M. G., & Witten, C. H. (1990). University 101 freshman seminar course: A longitudinal study of persistence, retention, and graduation rates. *NASPA Journal, 27*(4), 344–352.

Skipper, T. L. (2014, February 16). Writing in the first-year seminar: A national snapshot [Concurrent session]. Annual Conference on The First-Year Experience, San Diego, CA. http://sc.edu/nrc/system/pub_files/1549472505_0.pdf.

Study Group on the Conditions of Excellence in American Higher Education. (1984, October). *Involvement in learning: Realizing the potential of American higher education.* National Institute of Education.

Tobolowsky, B. F., Mamrick, M., & Cox, B. E. (2005). *The 2003 National Survey on First-Year Seminars: Continuing innovations in the collegiate curriculum* (Monograph No. 41). University of South Carolina, National Resource Center for The First-Year Experience and Students in Transition.

Tobolowsky, B. F., & Associates. (2008). *2006 National Survey of First-Year Seminars: Continuing innovations in the collegiate curriculum* (Monograph No. 51). University of South Carolina, National Resource Center for The First-Year Experience and Students in Transition.

Wanca-Thibault, M., Shepherd, M., & Staley, C. (2002). Personal, professional, and political effects of teaching a first-year seminar: A faculty census. *Journal of The First-Year Experience & Students in Transition, 14*, 23–40.

Watts, E. (1999). *The freshman year experience, 1962–1990: An experiment in humanistic higher education* [Unpublished doctoral dissertation]. Queen's University.

Whiteley, J. M., & Yokota, N. (1988). *Character development in the freshman year and over four years of undergraduate study* (Monograph No. 1). University of South Carolina, National Resource Center for The Freshman Year Experience.

Witham, K. A., & Bensimon, E. M. (2012). Creating a culture of inquiry around equity and student success. In S. D. Museus & U. M. Jayakumar (Eds.), *Creating campus cultures: Fostering success among racially diverse student populations* (pp. 46–67). Routledge.

Young, D. G. (Ed.). (2019). *2017 National Survey on the First-Year Experience: Creating and coordinating structures to support student success.* University of South Carolina, National Resource Center for The First- Year Experience & Students in Transition.

Young, D. G., & Hopp, J. M. (2014). *2012–2013 National Survey of First-Year Seminars: Exploring high- impact practices in the first college year* (Research Report No. 4). University of South Carolina, National Resource Center for The First-Year Experience & Students in Transition.

Zimmerman, A. (2000). A journal-based orientation course as a predictor of student success at a public two-year technical college. *Journal of The First-Year Experience, 12*, 29–43.

# Chapter 3

# The South Carolina Model Today
## Philosophy, Goals, and Course Delivery

*Daniel B. Friedman*

University 101 (UNIV 101) remains true to its historical roots. The course's original intent was to create a dialogue between students and the instructor about important aspects of the college experience and to improve the academic orientation of entering students (Heckel et al., 1973). At its core, the course is still focused on these aims 50 years later. UNIV 101 is designed to help new students make a successful transition to the University of South Carolina, both academically and personally, by fostering a sense of belonging; connecting students to the life, culture, and people of the university; helping students discover the resources and opportunities available to them; articulating to students the expectations of the university and its faculty; and helping them refine their purpose, meaning, and direction. This chapter explores the course's current philosophy, goals, outcomes, and content.

### ■ University 101 as an Extended Orientation

As noted in the original aims of the course, UNIV 101 serves as an extended orientation to the university. Any learning environment, such as summer orientation, welcome week, or the first-year seminar, is limited in what it can accomplish in the time allotted. Thus, careful consideration should be given to not only what students need most but when they are most ready to fully understand and benefit from a topic or learning experience. Giving students what they need, when they need it, and when they are ready for it is an important framework that guides the design of this course, as well as conversations about how it fits within the larger strategy for an integrated first-year experience. This philosophy was present in the original course proposal, which noted that "the coordination of this experiment with other similar programs is important. Many orientation efforts already exist in individual departments, colleges, and the university in general. This experiment should not operate in isolation from them" (Heckel et al., 1973, p. 12). As such,

University 101 Programs staff intentionally coordinate with the various induction programs across campus to ensure the best possible coverage and timing of educational opportunities.

Orientation programs are typically designed to provide information about academic programs, administrative processes, resources, and cocurricular life. They also exist to establish a sense of community for students and clarify the campus culture (Greenfield et al., 2013; Mullendore & Banahan, 2005). Furthermore, Young (2019) found that the top activities for orientation programs included introducing campus resources, services, and facilities; academic advising; and course registration. Given the amount of information packed into a short time, there is a limit to how much a student can absorb. Moreover, the context for learning may not be present for many of these front-loaded initiatives. When students attend orientation, they have a few basic needs on their minds, such as where they will live and with whom, what classes they will take, whether they will like the people they attend the classes with, and whether they can see themselves in this place.

Given the limitations of students' capacity and readiness to absorb new information, threading the induction period throughout the first semester is a more respectful and impactful way to support someone's transition to a new environment. As Mullendore and Banahan (2005) noted, "All of this is not accomplished in a one- or two-day orientation event, but it can and should be done through a comprehensive, multifaceted orientation process at the time of admission and continuing through the entire first year" (p. 391).

Similarly, program designers and instructors should be wary of front-loading a first-year seminar, since much of what students need and when they are ready for it may not become apparent until later in their first semester and may actually be at two very different times. For example, some would argue that academic strategies, as a topic, should be addressed early in the semester, particularly in the first two weeks, so that students can begin preparing appropriately for their coursework. However, the University of South Carolina is a selective institution, and many students enter believing they will not need academic support. Thus, receptivity to learning about this topic early in the term is muted. Moreover, students do not fully comprehend the level of rigor, workload, and expectations of college work until they have taken their first tests or received feedback on their first papers or projects. Students typically get their first grades on major assignments in mid-September, at which point they begin to assess whether their current approach is working. This is an ideal time to discuss academic strategies as it allows instructors to capitalize on their readiness and the context of concrete experiences. As described in the final section of this chapter, instructors receive guidance on

University 101 Class, Fall 2012

addressing each of the course's learning outcomes at various points in the semester to avoid the tendency to front-load topics.

## ■ Enrollment, Credit, and Grades

Since the course's founding in 1972, more than 110,000 students have taken UNIV 101 on the Columbia campus. From the first cohort that enrolled approximately 250 students, annual student enrollment has risen to around 5,000 students each fall, representing approximately 83% of the first-year class. See Figure 3.1 for historical enrollment trends in UNIV 101.

UNIV 101 is an elective for about 70% of its enrollees; however, selected programs and colleges—such as TRIO, Teaching Fellows, Capstone Scholars (an engagement program for high-achieving students), and Arnold School of Public Health—require their students to take the course. Although it is offered in the fall and spring semesters, the vast majority of UofSC Columbia students take UNIV 101 in the fall. Students with fewer than 30 credit hours and other first-semester students are permitted to enroll in the course. Transfer students may register, but only in their first term of enrollment at the university. Hours earned in UNIV 101 can be applied as elective or required credit toward most baccalaureate degrees offered by the university.

Small class size is vital for a first-year seminar given the reliance on discussion and active learning, the need to build community, and the importance of instructors offering individual attention to each student and remaining

**FIGURE 3.1**

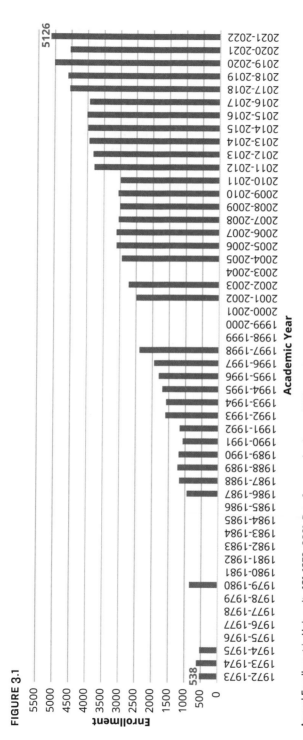

Annual Enrollment in University 101, 1972–2021. Data from academic year 1973–1974 to 1991–1992 only represent fall semester enrollment. Data for 1972–1973 from *The Freshman Year Experience, 1962–1990: An Experiment in Humanistic Higher Education* [Unpublished doctoral dissertation] by E. Watts, 1999. Data from 1974–1975 from "University 101 Evaluation 1974–1975: Research Questions and Findings" [Unpublished report] by P. P. Fidler, n.d., University of South Carolina. Data for 1979–1980 from "A Preliminary Longitudinal Comparison of Retention, Persistence, and Graduation Rates Between University 101 Freshman Seminar Participants and Non-Participants at the University of South Carolina During the Period 1979–1986" [Unpublished report] by M. G. Shanley, n.d., University of South Carolina. Data for 1986–1991 from "A Comparison of Effects of Campus Residence and Freshman Seminar Attendance on Freshman Dropout Rates," by P. P. Fidler and P. Moore, 1996, *Journal of The First-Year Experience & Students in Transition*, 8(2), 7–16. Data for 1991–2020 from unpublished University 101 Programs data tracking documents.

alert for early signals of distress. As such, the UNIV 101 section size is capped at 19 students. Faculty and staff selected to teach the course have expressed a special interest in working with first-year students. A further explanation of these concepts is addressed in Chapter 4.

Course credit is awarded on a letter-grade basis. A key decision in the history of the program was moving from pass/fail to a letter grade in 1990. As Skipper noted in Chapter 2, John Gardner successfully lobbied the Faculty Senate's curriculum committee to change the grading policy based on student feedback indicating they were doing too much work for a pass/fail course and that they would take the course more seriously with the motivation of a letter grade.

## ■ Special Sections of University 101

Special sections of the course for members of various subgroups and majors have been offered since the early 1970s. In recent years, special sections have been offered for majors in business; public health; education; journalism; engineering; hospitality, retail, and sport management; pre-pharmacy; and nursing. Sections have also been offered for students in various programs such as the Honors College, Capstone Scholars, TRIO, Teaching Fellows, and residential learning communities. Figure 3.2 showcases a graphical representation of the section distribution from the fall of 2021. While centrally

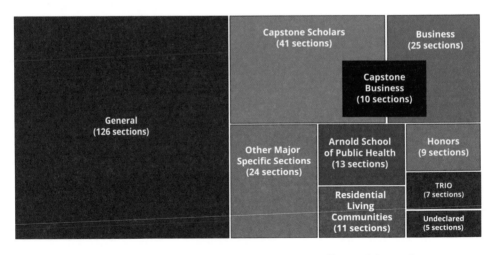

**FIGURE 3.2.** Section type distribution in University 101, Fall 2021. Other major-specific sections include education; hospitality, retail and sport management; journalism; pre-pharmacy; School of Earth, Ocean & Environment; sport and entertainment management; Teaching Fellows; and social work.

administered through the University 101 Programs office, these sections involve significant partnerships with colleges and programs to ensure adequate staffing, enrollment, and relevant customization of the curriculum. These sections allow the course to meet the needs of the colleges while achieving the more universal needs of entering students.

While the learning outcomes remain consistent across all sections, specialized sections may incorporate additional and unique areas of emphasis relevant to the population. Major-specific sections, for instance, allow for greater tailoring of content related to academic advising and employability, given the narrower possibilities of majors and career paths within a specialized section. These sections may also incorporate small projects related to their field, guest speakers, or additional readings related to the population or major.

## ■ Course Content, Philosophy, and Approaches

University 101's current goals and learning outcomes were carefully formulated to ensure a relevant, sustainable, and dynamic course design. Learning outcomes were not developed and instituted until 2009. Prior to that time, instructors were required to "cover a substantial list of essentials" (Jewler, 1989), including 10 hours of community service, six required presentations from campus offices, cultural event attendance, and use of the local newspaper. As the course matured, it accumulated more content. Friedman (2012) has commented that first-year seminars suffer from what may be called the family-attic syndrome:

> As a need arises on a campus, it is often the first-year seminar that gets charged with addressing that particular concern. It goes something like this . . . 'students are drinking too much, we need to talk about that in the first-year seminar' or 'students are struggling with managing their money, so we need to add a financial literacy component.' What results is an attic full of content that needs to be covered without the resulting yard sale to purge items no longer as useful or relevant as the new topics. The rub is that the majority of what needs to be covered in a first-year seminar is important, but there is only a limited amount of time available with our students, so hard choices must be made. (pp. 77–78)

Instructors felt the family-attic syndrome acutely and expressed a desire for more flexibility and fewer required components but also greater clarity and guidance on the aims of the course. A program review process was implemented to respond to these concerns and determine what the seminar should include.

## University 101 Program Review Process

University 101 Programs at the University of South Carolina conducted an internal review of the first-year seminar during the fall 2008 semester. As the new director of University 101 Programs, I coordinated the review process beginning with an exploration of instructor perceptions of the course. During the summer of 2008, I met with 35 UNIV 101 instructors and asked them to identify the strengths of the current model and areas of opportunity for continued growth and improvement. In addition to these interviews, I reviewed several years of course evaluations and noted the areas in which students reported the greatest learning and satisfaction as well as areas for improvement.

Following this initial assessment, I established a Program Review Committee (PRC) to provide recommendations about the future direction of UNIV 101, including what the outcomes should be, how to best achieve them, and how to ensure greater consistency across sections while still giving individual instructors the necessary flexibility to be creative and authentic.

The PRC originally consisted of 10 university faculty and staff members and one graduate student. Members were selected and invited to serve on the committee based on their interest in first-year student success, previous involvement with the UNIV 101 course, and knowledge of building and assessing learning outcomes. To form an objective committee, no university staff member whose department was responsible for a previously required component of the course was included in the membership. The committee met for 10 two-hour sessions throughout the fall 2008 semester.

The first step of this group's work was to better understand the needs of students and how they had changed over the previous decade by reviewing national, UofSC-specific, and course data. This activity's major purpose was to educate members about the UofSC students who took the course and to replace anecdotal assumptions with data and evidence.

The second step involved generating ideas for relevant content to include in UNIV 101. Through a needs-identification activity, each committee member submitted 10 topics or general goals that UNIV 101 should cover. From this list, 26 categories were created, such as academic integrity, campus resources, time management, stress management, and information literacy, among others. All were viewed as important, but they could not all be equally valuable. In asking our instructors to do so much, it would be unreasonable to expect that they could do it all well. We had to start prioritizing what we *could* strive to achieve versus what we *should achieve*. One additional metric to help the PRC set priorities for the course was to consider the areas in which we could reasonably expect to have an impact. Some of the topics were important, but given the parameters under which we operate, which ones were we primed to really do well? The PRC completed a prioritization activity to elevate the most important and relevant possibilities.

The third step involved replicating the needs-identification activity with multiple stakeholder groups on campus, including current and former students, course instructors, and peer leaders. The PRC then reconciled the work of these stakeholder groups with its own deliberations to develop a prioritized master list based on each topic's average ratings. This led to the creation of larger categories and purposes for the course and the articulation of three overarching goals.

Once the goals and essential content for the seminar were determined, the PRC turned the list of topics into a smaller group of learning outcomes. From there, multiple new subcommittees—which in turn were composed of relevant campus partners and instructors—were charged with mapping specific outcomes to the seminar curriculum. They were asked to consider both specific content and the process (or pedagogy) that would facilitate the desired outcomes. At this point, other course faculty members and campus partners with specific area expertise were brought in to offer recommendations or set parameters for achieving the outcomes. Subcommittees were comprised of a diverse membership of individuals committed to student success. The subcommittees met throughout the first half of the spring 2009 semester and were charged with recommending what students should know, the methodologies to help students learn such things, and associated resources needed to support the outcomes. A common template that asked them to articulate the following items guided their work:

1. a statement explaining the relevance of the outcome for first-year students at the University of South Carolina,
2. a description of what students absolutely need to know or be able to do regarding this topic (key objectives),
3. an inventory of good practices and recommendations for covering the topic (methods), and
4. associated campus resources that can help students with this topic or resources for instructors to get help in covering this topic (e.g., presentations, guest speakers).

The product of each subcommittee was a chapter in the *University 101 Faculty Resource Manual* (see Friedman & Sokol, 2021) containing lesson plans, activities, assignments, and talking points for achieving the course learning outcomes. Each instructor receives an updated digital version of the 600-page resource annually.

This review process is repeated every five to seven years, ensuring that the course remains relevant to the needs of students and emerging institutional priorities. The goals and outcomes listed later in this chapter are the result of the most recent review process, which was undertaken in 2015. While modifications to the curriculum at that time were more modest than with the 2008–2009 program review, several important changes were made, including reducing the number of learning outcomes from 13 to 10 to make the curriculum more manageable and to allow a deeper dive into the content.

## Course Principles

Developing the principles for UNIV 101 originated from conversations in the PRC surrounding the goals and outcomes. It became apparent that the course's goals would be broad and encompass a variety of relevant outcomes. Outcomes would be regularly assessed to determine the course's success. While the goals would be revisited based on the assessment of the outcomes, goals would not be assessed individually. In addition, overarching philosophies of the course framed the beliefs of those involved in the UNIV 101 course about approaches to creating an effective first-year seminar. The PRC called these more eternal and timeless elements of the course, rooted in the long and rich history of the program, the course *principles*. While content may vary across sections, the following principles would serve as the common foundation for instructors:

1. Community should be established early to promote a sense of belonging and create an inclusive and welcoming learning environment.
2. Course content should be tailored to the specific needs of the students in each section.
3. University 101 should be an active, engaging, and enjoyable learning experience.
4. Course content, methods, instructional strategies, and assignments should be purposeful and firmly aligned with the common learning outcomes.
5. Each student should receive an appropriate balance of challenge and support.
6. The class should have students reflect on and process course content and their experiences rather than merely distribute information.

## ■ Course Goals and Learning Outcomes

As a result of periodic program review, UNIV 101 currently has three broad goals with 10 learning outcomes (see Figure 3.3). The *University 101 Faculty Resource Manual* (Friedman & Sokol, 2021) has a chapter devoted to each learning outcome. In response to instructors' desire to understand more about the aims of the course, each of these outcome-focused chapters begins with a theoretical or practical discussion of the importance of the learning outcome

| Foster Academic Success | Discover and Connect with the University of South Carolina | Promote Personal Development, Well-Being, and Social Responsibility |
|---|---|---|
| As a result of this course, students will... | | |
| A) Adapt and apply appropriate academic strategies to their courses and learning experiences.<br><br>B) Identify and apply strategies to effectively manage time and priorities.<br><br>C) Identify relevant academic policies, processes and resources related to their academic success and timely attainment of degree requirements. | A) Identify and use appropriate campus resources and engage in opportunities that contribute to their learning within and beyond the classroom.<br><br>B) Develop positive relationships with peers, staff, and faculty.<br><br>C) Describe the history, purpose, and traditions of the University of South Carolina. | A) Clarify their values and identify and articulate how these shape their perspectives and relationships with people who are similar to and different from themselves.<br><br>B) Explore the tenets of the Carolinian Creed.<br><br>C) Examine and develop strategies that promote well-being and explain how their wellness impacts their academic and personal success.<br><br>D) Initiate a process toward the attainment of personal and professional goals and articulate potential pathways to employability. |

FIGURE 3.3. Course goals and associated learning outcomes for University 101 at the University of South Carolina.

for first-year students. The introduction also highlights key objectives (i.e., knowledge, activities, or experiences that will help students achieve the outcome). The remainder of this chapter offers instructors sample lesson plans, assignments, and resource descriptions tied to these objectives. This section is adapted from the introductory material of Chapters 10 to 19 in the *Faculty Resource Manual* (Friedman & Sokol, 2021) and demonstrates how goals, learning outcomes, and key objectives are communicated to instructors.

## I. Foster Academic Success

### a. Adapt and apply appropriate academic strategies to their courses and learning experiences.

The University of South Carolina's first-year students are demonstrably stronger academically than they were just a few years ago. However, many students continue to use the same study strategies they used in high school, even when those strategies may not work very well. Responses to the 2019 Freshman Survey (Bara Stolzenberg et al., 2020) found that entering first-year students were less likely to engage in behaviors associated with academic success, such as taking intellectual risks or asking questions in class. At the same time, more than half of the respondents (56.7%) reported spending less than 5 hours in a typical week studying or completing homework. These data suggest that many incoming first-year students may not be equipped with the proper academic habits and strategies, or they do not fully understand how to apply those strategies to succeed in college-level courses. To achieve this outcome, instructors may address the following key objectives:

- mastering general academic strategies for college success;
- knowing the resources that support academic success, including supplemental instruction, academic coaching, the math lab and writing centers, and peer tutoring;
- writing strong papers;
- developing information literacy skills, including finding and evaluating sources, incorporating them into papers and presentations, and citing them appropriately;
- making effective presentations; and
- working in groups, including strategies for planning, delegation, and integrating multiple viewpoints and materials.

**b. Identify and apply strategies to effectively manage time and priorities.**
One of the greatest challenges for college students is managing time effectively. In high school, students' schedules were set and regular. They often had daily routines that included after-school activities, dinner with family, homework and study time, and a parent-enforced bedtime. In college, students have newfound freedoms that require greater autonomy and responsibility. Distractions and lack of structure often make it difficult for first-year students to juggle all their responsibilities, which can include 12 to 18 hours of class, work, cocurricular activities, and sometimes hours of downtime throughout the week. UNIV 101 provides an opportunity for first-year students to identify their priorities, learn about the benefits of time management, understand their many responsibilities, and develop a plan for how to best use their time. The key objectives for this outcome include:

- helping students understand and analyze how they are currently spending time,
- identifying and applying strategies to better manage time and priorities,
- reinforcing the importance of planning, and
- setting goals and aligning time with priorities.

c. Identify relevant academic policies, processes, and resources related to their academic success and timely attainment of degree requirements.

New undergraduate students at the University of South Carolina face significant challenges that may impact their academic and personal success. Like most large research institutions, UofSC is a complex educational system. The decentralized nature of the university, where individual colleges set college-specific academic policies and procedures, can easily confuse new members of the community, especially first-generation students. We also have an obligation to do everything we can to ensure students graduate in a timely manner. UNIV 101 can help students understand how to take a proactive approach to academic planning and how to seek information that is relevant to their goals. The key objectives related to this outcome include:

- knowing the various academic standards and entities to which they are beholden, such as the university, college, department, program (e.g., TRIO, Capstone), or scholarship and requirements associated with that affiliation;
- understanding key academic policies;
- knowing how to calculate their GPA;
- understanding what constitutes a violation of the Honor Code;
- knowing the elements of a degree (i.e., Carolina Core, major, minor, electives) and the requirements for their major;
- drafting a four-year plan for degree completion and understanding what is needed to graduate, the pathway toward the degree, and necessary prerequisites and corequisites;
- understanding the process for advising, including how and where to get advised, how to prepare for an advising appointment, and department-level advising policies and practices; and
- becoming familiar with key resources including the *Undergraduate Studies Bulletin,* University Advising Center, advisor and dean's office for specific colleges, DegreeWorks, and EAB Pathfinder.

## II. Discover and Connect With the University of South Carolina

a. Identify and use appropriate campus resources and engage in opportunities that contribute to their learning within and beyond the classroom.

The University of South Carolina seeks to create environments where students use their resources and maximize learning through beyond-the-classroom engagement. In assessing the benefits of cocurricular learning, Kuh (1995) noted that "out-of-class experiences presented students with personal and social challenges, encouraged them to develop more complicated views on personal, academic, and other matters, and provided opportunities for synthesizing and integrating material presented in the formal academic program (classes, laboratories, studios)" (p. 146). The concept of student engagement is often realized through students' involvement on campus. While involvement is critical, student engagement goes beyond mere participation in campus organizations or events to a deep connection to the learning experience. Key objectives for this outcome include:

- discovering the myriad opportunities for engagement and involvement, understanding the importance of getting involved, and articulating benefits stemming from their involvement, including how the resulting skills and experiences will enrich their learning and enhance their employability;
- identifying relevant campus resources to support engagement; and
- participating in and reflecting on at least one beyond-the-classroom learning opportunity during the first semester.

**b. Develop positive relationships with peers, staff, and faculty.**

Making new friends and establishing new relationships throughout the campus community are among the most important aspects of developing a sense of belonging and finding a niche in college. Relationships formed in college—both positive and negative—can have a lifelong impact on an individual's development and success and initiate the behavioral patterns of how individuals will relate to others throughout their lives. Further, relationships are important in such facets of life as optimal health and well-being and future employability. This outcome helps students understand the importance of relationships and the changes that are likely to occur in their pre-college relationships while learning skills to develop and nurture new connections. Key objectives relevant to this outcome include:

- learning strategies for developing and maintaining positive relationships;
- valuing a diverse peer group and being a part of more than one group;
- identifying strategies for finding a niche at UofSC;
- finding the person or office on campus that can help with an issue, problem, or question;
- developing appropriate expectations of faculty and learning tips for interacting with them before, during, and after class;
- anticipating changes in relationships with parents and maintaining relationships with high school friends;
- knowing the difference between healthy and unhealthy relationships; and
- developing strategies for managing conflicts.

**c. Describe the history, purpose, and traditions of the University of South Carolina.**

Founded in 1801, the University of South Carolina is home to more than 200 years of unique history and tradition. Each new class is encouraged to leave their individual mark on UofSC history. At the same time, the course strives to help students appreciate the roots, spirit, and purpose of the university. When students develop an understanding of the history and tradition of their new community, it helps them to establish a sense of belonging on campus, connect to their own sense of purpose, and begin to visualize their future at the university. Exploring campus history and traditions can help students develop a stronger sense of belonging and appreciation for their new home. Key objectives include:

- engaging in university traditions that foster excitement and a sense of belonging,
- understanding a few key aspects of South Carolina's rich history that provide context for their current experience,
- articulating the purpose and importance of earning a college degree from the University of South Carolina, and
- developing a sense of what makes this place special and unique to deepen their affinity for UofSC.

### III. Promote Personal Development, Well-Being, and Social Responsibility

**a. Clarify their values and identity and articulate how these shape their perspectives and relationships with people who are similar to and different from themselves.**

College provides students the opportunity to encounter many different people, ideas, and opinions. For many students, college is the first time their values and beliefs are challenged. They may begin to question what they really believe; they "have the opportunity to see the world through their own eyes and develop their own opinions and values" (Mullendore & Hatch, 2000, p. 9). University 101 is the perfect environment for first-year students to continue their value exploration.

The most important part of helping students understand their values is creating a space for reflection. Providing students the time and space to think actively about what is most important to them will help them better understand what they value and where their priorities lie. Values clarification provides the basis for helping students understand others. For many students, entering UofSC is the first opportunity they have had to be exposed to so many different people in one place. Helping students understand who they are will prepare them to get to know others who are different from themselves. Key objectives include:

- determining their values;
- articulating dimensions of their intersecting identities;
- relating to people whose backgrounds, experiences, and beliefs may be different from their own;
- discussing the power of language when interacting with diverse others;
- emphasizing the importance of openness to diverse viewpoints and awareness of privilege; and
- recognizing and confronting instances of individual and structural racism.

**b. Explore the tenets of the Carolinian Creed.**
In October 1990, University of South Carolina students, faculty, and administrators gathered on the historic Horseshoe to formally adopt the Carolinian Creed, an aspirational document that guides the personal, academic, and professional life of each member of the UofSC community (see Figure 3.4). Carolinians pledge to live by those ideals, which include respect, acceptance, concern for others, and dignity for all. University 101 helps students explore the Carolinian Creed tenets and reflect on their role and responsibility in upholding these tenets and contributing to a strong UofSC community. Key objectives include:

- understanding academic and personal integrity, including its importance and what constitutes a violation of the Honor Code;
- defining community and exploring the idea of membership in multiple, intersecting communities;
- identifying actions that support a respectful community;
- identifying strategies for engaging in civil discourse, managing conflict with others, and practicing conversations with people who have different opinions;
- identifying ways to keep self, others, and property safe;
- defining sexual assault, consent, and interpersonal violence, and identifying resources to support survivors of sexual assault and interpersonal violence; and
- defining bystander accountability and understanding their personal role as an accountable bystander and ways to intervene when necessary.

**c. Examine and develop strategies that promote well-being and explain how wellness impacts their academic and personal success.**
There is a strong correlation between personal wellness and academic success. Among undergraduate respondents to the 2019 National College Health

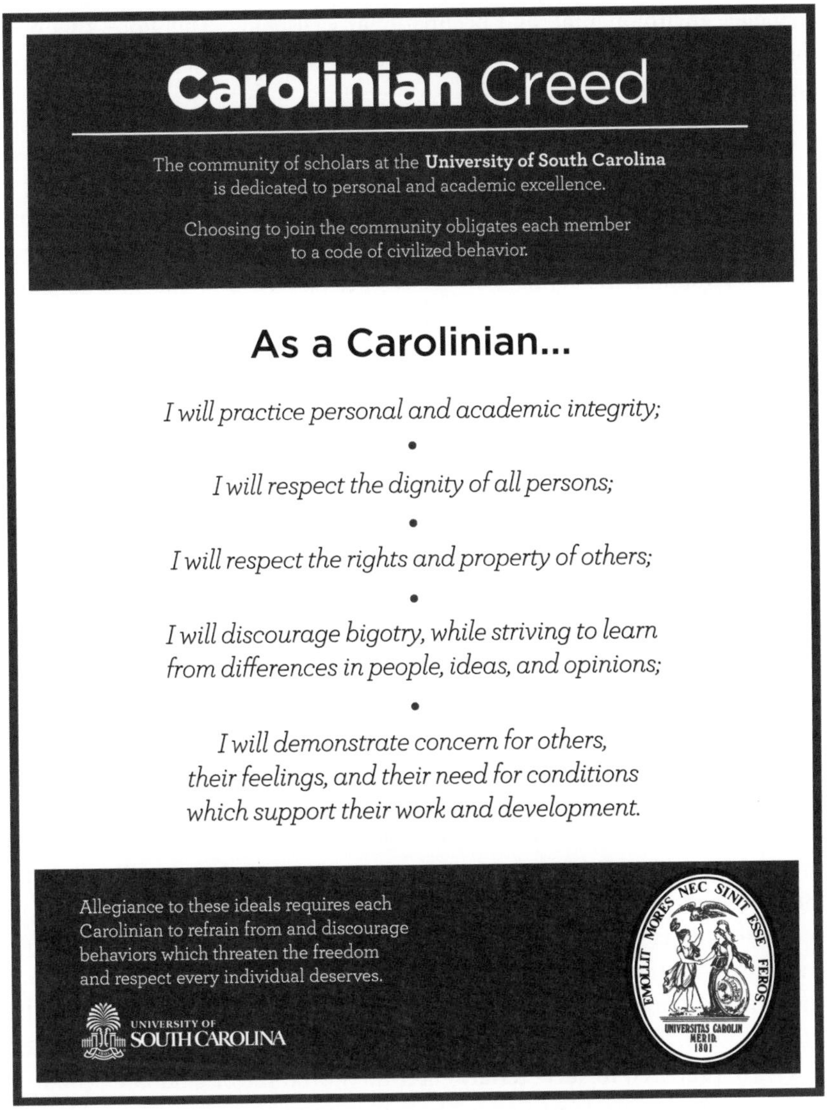

# Carolinian Creed

The community of scholars at the **University of South Carolina** is dedicated to personal and academic excellence.

Choosing to join the community obligates each member to a code of civilized behavior.

## As a Carolinian...

*I will practice personal and academic integrity;*

•

*I will respect the dignity of all persons;*

•

*I will respect the rights and property of others;*

•

*I will discourage bigotry, while striving to learn from differences in people, ideas, and opinions;*

•

*I will demonstrate concern for others, their feelings, and their need for conditions which support their work and development.*

Allegiance to these ideals requires each Carolinian to refrain from and discourage behaviors which threaten the freedom and respect every individual deserves.

UNIVERSITY OF
SOUTH CAROLINA

**FIGURE 3.4.** The Carolinian Creed, a community values statement adopted by the University of South Carolina.

Assessment (ACHA, 2019), students noted stress (36.5%), anxiety (29.5%), and depression (21.6%) as having a negative impact on academic performance (i.e., receiving lower grades on an exam, project, or course; dropping a course; or taking an incomplete). Wellness encompasses more than just emotional and physical well-being; it also includes social, intellectual, spiritual, financial, environmental, and occupational well-being. Therefore, this outcome is interconnected with many of the topics discussed in University 101. The key objectives include:

- understanding the risks associated with alcohol and other drug use;
- understanding what it means to eat healthy, including the importance of balance and mindfulness and identifying healthy eating strategies for on-campus dining;
- understanding the connection between sleep and academic and personal performance and identifying strategies for improving sleep habits;
- finding creative ways to be physically active on campus;
- understanding the importance of making decisions regarding sexual health that are consistent with personal values and knowing the risks associated with unprotected sex;
- gaining awareness of the causes of different types of stress and developing personal strategies for managing stress; and
- understanding the importance of considering the financial implications of personal decisions, using budgeting and financial planning strategies to take responsibility for personal finances, and knowing how to find financial aid information relevant to student loans and scholarships.

**d. Initiate a process toward the attainment of personal and professional goals and articulate potential pathways to employability.**
In today's global economic climate, employability has become a primary concern of higher education's stakeholders. Moreover, 83.5% of first-year students listed getting a better job as a "very important" reason for attending college (Bara Stolzenberg et al., 2020). Yet, employers often note significant gaps in necessary career readiness competencies and the proficiency of new college graduates—most notably in the areas of professionalism and work ethic, oral and written communications, and critical thinking and problem-solving skills (NACE, 2019). To help students make the most of their college experience and leave prepared to successfully enter the workforce or graduate school, it is imperative that students understand what it means to be employable and plan toward that goal. More specifically, key objectives include:

- identifying or solidifying possible career paths based on strengths, values, and interests;
- identifying realities of potential career fields and articulating strategies for pursuing a chosen career path;
- developing familiarity with career planning resources;
- understanding the importance of internships and experiential education; and

- developing a résumé and establishing an appropriate social media presence.

## ■ Course Delivery

As the sheer number of possible key objectives suggests, there is a great deal of content that could be addressed in this course. It is not expected that all sections will incorporate every key objective; however, all learning outcomes must be addressed. Two principles—intentionality and flexibility—define expectations for instructors in designing a course that meets the needs of the students in their section.

### Intentionality and Integration of Course Content

Successful instructors are intentional in all aspects of course planning and design to facilitate student progress toward achieving these outcomes. It is important to note that an outcome is not the same as a daily lesson or topic. Individual lesson plans often touch on numerous outcomes; for instance, an exploration of personality preferences may lead to discussions about academic strategies, time management, diversity, values, stress management, and employability.

University 101 Class, Fall 2018

The course is also more impactful when the content is integrated intentionally and addressed throughout the semester. Thoughtfully sequencing topics allows for more strategic integration. For example, in September, students might discuss and analyze how they are spending their time in one class, followed by an exploration of their core values in the next. The weekly journal prompt could ask students to describe how they spent their time and whether those choices aligned with what is important to them. This brings two different topics together into a more integrated and intentional whole.

Moreover, it is imperative that outcomes be addressed continually throughout the semester rather than simply discussed during one lesson plan. For example, a "diversity day" or "time management day" approach tends to trivialize and silo content. Such approaches would also mitigate the effectiveness of the course since it is unlikely that spending 50 minutes discussing time management or diversity could generate the desired learning gains. Spending a few minutes every few weeks revisiting the content has shown to be an effective approach to achieving our course learning outcomes. Table 3.1 provides an example of how an instructor might approach time management at various points throughout the semester.

TABLE 3.1. Threading Time Management Throughout the Semester

| TIMING | ACTIVITY |
| --- | --- |
| Week 1 | During the second class meeting, students can complete a semester-at-a-glance worksheet in the course textbook, filling in due dates from all their course syllabi for all major assignments, projects, and exams. This activity is designed to challenge students to consider the amount of coursework they will face throughout the semester. The assignment motivates students to successfully manage their time and priorities throughout the year. Students can process the "So what?" and "Now what?" of having this information by discussing the following questions in small groups:<br><br>• How does your workload compare to others in your group?<br><br>• What can you do now to minimize stress later in the semester?<br><br>• How far in advance do you imagine you will need to start each of these projects or begin studying for tests?<br><br>• How might this be different from high school? |
| Week 3 or 4 | An entire class period could be devoted near the end of the term's first month to discussing aspects of time management, perhaps through the lens of personality preference, prioritization, and strategies for |

| TIMING | ACTIVITY |
| --- | --- |
| | overcoming the most common time wasters. As with any UNIV 101 lesson plan, instructors should engage students in active learning and discussion rather than lecturing them about how to manage their time. By focusing on students' lived experiences and actively engaging them in problem solving, students are more likely to identify solutions they are willing to adopt. |
| Week 6 | Students can be asked to track and log their time for a week. This exercise can lead to rich and productive conversations among students. The instructor can create a graph showing the class average and ranges for each category. Results are then debriefed in class, with students reflecting on what was surprising, changes they will need to make, and their biggest time wasters. The instructor can steer the conversation toward motivation and discipline by asking students what they do to stop procrastinating (e.g., watching Netflix) and start studying for their classes. Instructors can put students into small groups to identify their top three strategies and then have the class analyze the various options presented by each group. Students are then asked to commit to trying one strategy. Instructors can follow up a week later to see how successful students were in managing their time. |
| Week 7 | After engaging in a values clarification activity, students can be asked to reflect on the extent to which their values and priorities aligned with how they spent their time in the last week as noted in their time log. |
| End of October | Students learn how to calculate their GPA and can then be asked to project their GPA based on their current progress in all courses. They can also experiment to see what happens to their semester GPA if they are able to improve their performance in one class by a letter grade. For many students, earning an A rather than a B could be the difference between making the Dean's List or keeping their scholarship. Students can then create a plan for using their time over the next month that prioritizes their academic goals. The instructors can send students follow-up emails either congratulating them on doing well or motivating them to buckle down and providing resources on where they can get individualized assistance. |
| End of the Semester | A reflective question about time and priorities could be embedded in the final project, asking students what they have learned this semester about managing their time and what changes they will need to make next semester. |

## *Flexibility Versus Consistency*

Some first-year seminars use a standard syllabus for all sections that prescribes not only the outcomes to be achieved but also the topics to be covered, when they are to be covered, and the assignments to measure what is learned. Yet, flexibility has been built into the structure of UNIV 101 since its origin. In the first major book about the first-year experience, Jerome Jewler, a former codirector of University 101, suggested that the diverse backgrounds of instructors and students demanded a more flexible approach: "[B]ecause no two groups of freshmen have identical needs, it is difficult to imagine a highly structured syllabus as suitable for this type of course" (Jewler, 1989, p. 207). Friedman and Greene (2019) echoed Jewler's concern, noting, "The content, topics, and methods used to achieve outcomes should be tailored to the needs of the students in a given section . . . With such a large enrollment, one size will not fit all" (p. 11).

Capitalizing on instructor buy-in, passion, knowledge, and skill set is equally important. Friedman and Greene (2019) argued that cultivating investment in the course by allowing "instructors flexibility to tailor course material to their interest and expertise" (p. 10) leads to greater enthusiasm and innovation in the classroom. Moreover, it sends the message that there is not a single correct approach to teaching the seminar. Student engagement is positively influenced by instructor enthusiasm for the course. An overly prescribed approach to teaching the first-year seminar may dampen instructor enthusiasm and, ultimately, lead to a less effective learning experience for students. Moreover, Friedman and Greene noted, "Giving instructors autonomy in determining lesson plans and content, if coupled with assessment and faculty development, allows for innovation" (p. 10) while maintaining course quality.

It should be noted that while flexibility for instructors is important, they are not permitted to teach whatever they want. Friedman and Greene (2019) concluded that "we will not mitigate course integrity and efficacy by sacrificing what students *need* to learn to accommodate what faculty *want* to teach" (pp. 11–12). The learning outcomes and common course requirements that the PRC created provide a degree of consistency across sections while also allowing instructors the space to customize their sections in ways that speak to their students' needs and their particular strengths and expertise.

## ■ Required Readings

Since 1990, University 101 Programs has partnered with offices across campus to develop *Transitions*, a custom textbook with content created specifically

Cover of *Transitions,* 2021

for students at UofSC. While it is designed to serve as a resource for incoming students, it is not intended to reflect the entirety of the curriculum. *Transitions* provides a baseline of information students will need to help them make the most of their first-year experience.

From the very first edition of *Transitions* in 1990, each version has aimed to connect students to resources and opportunities at UofSC, provide them with guidance on how to succeed academically, highlight important topics on well-being, and introduce them to what it means to be UofSC students. While the fundamental purpose of *Transitions* has remained the same, the content and topics covered in the textbook have evolved to meet changing student needs. Some topics have appeared consistently over the past 30 years, including time management, academic strategies, Carolinian Creed, library, alcohol, involvement opportunities, academic advising, and campus resources. However, other content has come and gone, reflecting the priorities and needs of the times. Each edition of *Transitions* serves as a time capsule, a window into campus life and the current events of the year it was written. For example, editions from the early to mid-1990s offered detailed overviews of electronic mail and the World Wide Web. The 1996 edition introduced students to terms like *internet, file,* and *window* and instructed them on how to use the web to email and search for resources. Flash-forward to the 2020 edition, and the focus has shifted beyond the basic use of the internet to information literacy and how to critically analyze the vast amount of information available to us. In an ever-changing world, the curriculum and resources of a first-year seminar must also constantly adapt and evolve.

The ability to customize and adapt *Transitions* every year in response to changing student needs has contributed greatly to the success and impact of the textbook. For the last 30 years, *Transitions* has served as a valuable resource for both students and instructors. This textbook is foundational to the course, instrumental in the delivery of course content, and flexible in its ability to integrate a constantly changing and evolving curriculum.

Additional Readings and Resources

University 101 instructors incorporate additional readings and instructional resources in their classes to foster achievement of the learning outcomes, provide context or themes for the course, and offer different perspectives. Most sections incorporate the First-Year Reading Experience selection as an additional text (see Chapter 8 for more information on this initiative). Others include books, articles, or local or national newspapers. These readings are intentionally integrated into the course, helping students achieve multiple learning outcomes rather than serving as a stand-alone component. When selecting readings, instructors are asked to consider the following questions:

- Does the reading address a major theme of my course? Is it tailored to the type of section I am teaching?
- Will it lead to meaningful class discussions that address several outcomes of UNIV 101?
- Am I excited and passionate about the reading? Will my students be interested in or engaged by the reading?
- Is it relevant and accessible to first-year students in an extended orientation course?
- Can I thread the reading throughout the semester rather than simply talking about it for one day?
- Will it provide support, guidance, inspiration, or information to first-year students throughout the course?
- How will I tailor assignments or beyond-the-classroom activities to relate to the themes of the reading?

## Assignments in University 101

As with any academic course, assignments serve varied and important purposes. Angelo and Cross (1993) noted that instructors assess learning to focus the learner's attention; illuminate and undermine student misconceptions; increase student motivation to learn; provide learners with feedback; improve student performance; promote student self-assessment and monitoring; and help students develop independent, lifelong-learning skills.

Instructors can assess student learning in multiple ways, both formally and informally, in and outside of class, and through activities and assignments. Assignments, which are a mix of homework, papers, projects, and presentations, need to allow students to demonstrate evidence of achieving the learning outcomes for the course. Given that the course is not about content mastery, assignments should not ask students to recall information. As such, multiple-choice or true/false exams are not an appropriate measure of student learning for this course. While instructors have the discretion to create their own assignments, they must operate within a similar range. Table 3.2 depicts the required grading components along with the recommended weighting.

TABLE 3.2. Guidelines for Grading Requirements for University 101

| REQUIRED COMPONENT | RECOMMENDED WEIGHT | RECOMMENDED RANGE |
|---|---|---|
| Participation | 15% | 10–20% |
| Papers/essays. This includes both (a) formal essays, which involve more substantial effort and time on task and greater emphasis on good writing, and (b) shorter, less formal writing assignments such as reflection papers. We recommend one formal paper that is 3+ pages in length and two to three other papers that are 1–2 pages in length. | 20% | 15–25% |
| Informal writing (e.g., journals, in-class reflections). | 10% | 5–15% |
| Oral presentation(s) | 15% | 10–20% |
| Midterm (project/paper/presentation) | 15% | 10–15% |
| Final exam or culminating project. The final should challenge students to reflect upon and synthesize the major course goals. Methodologies could include portfolios, take-home projects or papers, presentations, or videos. | 15% | 10–20% |
| Other/homework (e.g., projects, quizzes, daily assignments, time management log) | 10% | 10–25% |

Several best practices for designing UNIV 101 assignments were derived from studying the teaching strategies of current instructors. University 101 programs staff members identified the top-performing instructors on course evaluation questions pertaining to the quality of assignments (i.e., the course included meaningful homework and challenging assignments). These instructors and their students were interviewed to determine how they ensured the relevance and quality of their assignments. In general, these instructors

- provided students with a strong rationale or purpose for the assignments;
- supported higher-order learning tasks (i.e., application, analysis, synthesis, evaluation) with their assignments;

- allowed student choice in how they completed their assignments or encouraged students to develop components of the assignment as a class;
- provided timely, constructive, and meaningful feedback on each assignment;
- built a strong community in their classroom and leveraged assignments to support that community;
- modeled successful work by sharing good examples of student work or examples from the instructional team;
- aligned assignments with a course theme, learning outcomes, or supplemental readings;
- included significant reflection (e.g., informal writing, reflective components in all assignments, reflective and cumulative final projects);
- provided opportunities for students to apply their learning (in particular, to being a successful student at UofSC);
- incorporated beyond-the-classroom expectations or requirements (e.g., engagement experiences, interviews, visiting the library or career center);
- encouraged products students could be proud of or wanted to share with others (e.g., videos, blogs, presentations);
- provided clear structure and support on how to complete the assignment successfully (e.g., rubrics, examples of good work, class time to discuss/develop skills); and
- created opportunities for students to work together and get to know each other (e.g., personality or learning style assessments, opportunities for self-disclosure [e.g., sharing lifelines], assignments that require students to work together in groups in or outside of class).

To help instructors better understand how to create meaningful and engaging assignments, Dan Friedman and Kevin Clarke—a former assistant director for faculty development—created a framework (see Figure 3.5) to illustrate the differences between less engaging and more engaging assignments, particularly related to the content, relevance, choice, and structure of the assignments. In addition, Appendix B contains sample assignments that have received positive feedback from UNIV 101 students and instructors.

## ■ Conclusion

The South Carolina model of first-year seminars has evolved over the past 50 years, continuing to meet the changing needs of students and emerging institutional priorities while also maintaining fidelity to its historical mission and purpose. The extended orientation model has shown to be an adaptive

# Designing Engaging Assignments

(Exams, Projects, Papers, Presentations, etc.)

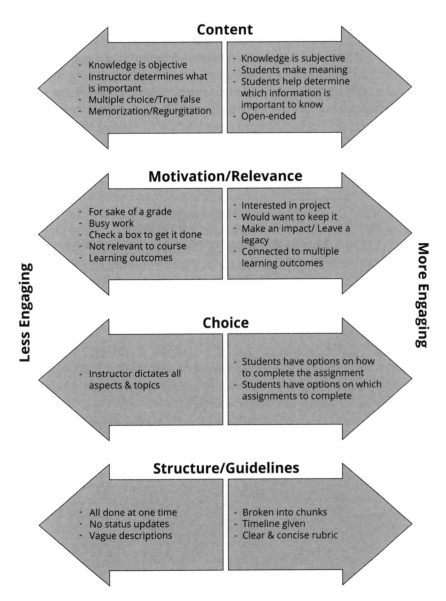

## Content

- Knowledge is objective
- Instructor determines what is important
- Multiple choice/True false
- Memorization/Regurgitation

- Knowledge is subjective
- Students make meaning
- Students help determine which information is important to know
- Open-ended

## Motivation/Relevance

- For sake of a grade
- Busy work
- Check a box to get it done
- Not relevant to course
- Learning outcomes

- Interested in project
- Would want to keep it
- Make an impact/ Leave a legacy
- Connected to multiple learning outcomes

## Choice

- Instructor dictates all aspects & topics

- Students have options on how to complete the assignment
- Students have options on which assignments to complete

## Structure/Guidelines

- All done at one time
- No status updates
- Vague descriptions

- Broken into chunks
- Timeline given
- Clear & concise rubric

Less Engaging

More Engaging

FIGURE 3.5. Guidance for designing more engaging course assignments. Developed by D. Friedman and K. Clarke. In D. Friedman and K. Sokol (Eds.), 2021, University 101 *Faculty Resource Manual,* Chapter 5, p. 7. Copyright 2021 by the University of South Carolina.

educational strategy that can be customized through an intentionally designed approach that assures quality through a flexible curriculum centered on well-crafted outcomes and principles. It is important that courses such as these continue to evolve and that processes are implemented to redevelop or reconfirm the goals and outcomes on a regular basis. The program review process at the University of South Carolina makes clear that course content will undergo modest changes every few years. For example, mental health, antiracism, and reflection—all of which are emerging student needs and new institutional priorities—will likely receive more attention in the near future. Engaging in processes to tailor the curriculum to the needs of the students ensures the continued vitality and relevance of the course. It is through this work that University 101 has continued to support students' personal and academic transition to the university.

## *References*

American College Health Association (ACHA). (2019, Spring). National College Health Assessment II: Undergraduate Student Executive Summary.

Angelo, T. A., & Cross, K. P. (1993). *Classroom assessment techniques: A handbook for college teachers* (2nd ed.). Jossey-Bass.

Bara Stolzenberg, E., Aragon, M. C., Romo, E., Couch, V., McLennan, D., Eagan, M. K., & Kang, N. (2020). *The American Freshman: National norms fall 2019.* Higher Education Research Institute, UCLA.

Fidler, P. P. (n.d.). *University 101 Evaluation 1974–1975: Research questions and findings* [Unpublished report]. University of South Carolina.

Fidler, P. P., & Moore, P. S. (1996). A comparison of effects of campus residence and freshman seminar attendance on freshman dropout rates. *Journal of The Freshman Year Experience, 8*(2), 7–16.

Friedman, D. (2012). *The first-year seminar: Designing and assessing courses to support student learning and success: Vol 5. Assessing the first-year seminar.* University of South Carolina, National Resource Center for The First-Year Experience and Students in Transition.

Friedman, D., & Greene, S. (2019). Increasing first-year seminar quality through greater curricular flexibility. *E-Source for College Transition, 16*(2), 9–12. https://issuu.com/nrcpubs/docs/es_16_2_mar19.

Friedman, D., & Sokol, K. (Eds.). (2021). *University 101 Faculty Resource Manual.* University of South Carolina, University 101 Programs.

Greenfield, G. M., Keup, J. R., & Gardner, J. N. (2013). *Developing and sustaining successful first-year programs.* Jossey-Bass.

Heckel, R. V., Hiers, J. M., Finegold, B., & Zuidema, J. (1973). *University 101: An educational experiment.* University of South Carolina, Social Problems Research Institute.

Jewler, A. J. (1989). Elements of an effective seminar: The University 101 Program. In

M. L. Upcraft, & J. N. Gardner (Eds.), *The freshman year experience: Helping students survive and succeed in college* (pp. 198–215). Jossey-Bass.

Kuh, G. D. (1995). The other curriculum: Out-of-class experiences associated with student learning and personal development. *Journal of Higher Education, 66*(2), 123–155.

Mullendore, R. H., & Banahan, L. A. (2005). Designing orientation programs. In M. L. Upcraft, J. N. Gardner, B. O. Barefoot, & Associates, *Challenging and supporting the first-year student: A handbook for improving the first year of college* (pp. 391–409). Jossey-Bass.

Mullendore, R. H., & Hatch, C. (2000). *Helping your first-year college student succeed: A guide for parents.* University of South Carolina, National Resource Center for The First-Year Experience and Students in Transition.

National Association for Colleges & Employers (NACE). (2019, November). *2020 Job Outlook.*

Shanley, M. G. (n.d.). *A preliminary longitudinal comparison of retention, persistence, and graduation rates between University 101 freshman seminar participants and nonparticipants at the University of South Carolina during the period 1979–1986* [Unpublished report]. University of South Carolina.

Watts, E. (1999). *The freshman year experience, 1962–1990: An experiment in humanistic higher education* [Unpublished doctoral dissertation]. Queen's University.

Young, D. G. (2019). *2017 National Survey on the First-Year Experience: Creating and coordinating structures to support student success* (Research Report No. 9). University of South Carolina, National Resource Center for The First-Year Experience and Students in Transition.

# Chapter 4

# Key Ingredients to a Successful First-Year Seminar

*Daniel B. Friedman*

For the past 50 years, University 101 (UNIV 101) at the University of South Carolina has fostered greater academic achievement and higher first-to-second-year persistence and graduation rates among its participants. Three primary factors contribute to the course-level success of UNIV 101: (a) fostering a sense of belonging, (b) supporting early alert, and (c) including engaging pedagogies. Similarly, several institutional and programmatic characteristics contribute to course success. This chapter explores and explains these factors.

## ■ Elements of a Successful Course

### *Sense of Belonging*

Of all the elements of a UNIV 101 class, building community is arguably the most important. Creating a strong, safe, and inclusive community is essential to a successful seminar, which in turn supports student acclimation and persistence at the university. Community is both the number-one reason students take the course and the top predictor of their decision to remain at South Carolina. Students report their most important reason for enrolling in UNIV 101 is to make friends. With approximately 6,000 first-year students starting each year, UNIV 101 offers a very small class that allows students to make connections with 18 of their peers. They also develop a significant connection to at least one faculty or staff member as a result of taking the course. The peer and instructor interaction within UNIV 101 can make a large research university feel small and personal for many students.

Course evaluation data suggest that UNIV 101 helps most students make friends and establish community. In fall 2020, for example,

- 94.8% of students reported that as a result of the course they felt part of the Carolina community ($M$ = 6.5 out of 7),

- 95.1% said the course helped them get to know other students ($M$ = 6.49 out of 7),
- 94.3% said it helped them meet people who share their interests ($M$ = 6.47 out of 7), and
- 94.5% said it helped them establish friendships with peers ($M$ = 6.49).

This community lasts beyond their first semester. When the 2018 cohort was surveyed a year later in 2019, 72% of students reported they were still in contact with at least one person from their UNIV 101 class. Moreover, 90% said they had felt accepted by other students in their section.

Most importantly, community is the number one reason the course works to foster student persistence to the second year. Padgett and Friedman (2010) used the First-Year Initiative (FYI) data set, a nationally benchmarked instrument, to explore which elements of the course predicted persistence. The data were collected through a web-based survey at the end of the fall 2008 semester from students enrolled in UNIV 101. Of the target population, 2,014 students completed the survey, yielding a response rate of 72%. Responses to the FYI survey were matched with persistence and first-year grade point average from the student data file to explore course impact on these outcomes.

The FYI contains 15 factors, each of which represented a vetted good practice and campus initiative grounded in theoretical and empirical evidence. To predict the effectiveness of these factors on persistence into the second year, a series of logistic regressions were conducted. Several control measures—gender, race, and high school grades—were introduced into the model to isolate the effect of each factor on student persistence. The results of the analysis indicated that the number one variable associated with persistence was Sense of Belonging.[1] In fact, a standard deviation increase in Sense of Belonging increased the odds of persisting into the second year by 38% ($p$ < .001), holding all other variables constant.

This finding is not surprising given the substantial literature attesting to the importance of belonging. People are not likely to stay in any environment for long if they do not feel like they belong. We often tell instructors that if they only do one thing in this course, it should be to help students make friends and build an inclusive and supportive community. Fortunately, we can accomplish this goal while also achieving the other important course learning outcomes.

In addition to positively impacting persistence, research suggests that student learning is at its greatest in an environment that is perceived as "inclusive and affirming" (Kuh et al., 2005, p. 8). Students are more willing to engage with and contribute to a learning environment in which they feel a sense of belonging and where there is mutual respect among classmates and

University 101 Class, Fall 2019

instructors. For a seminar to be truly effective, students must feel encouraged and free to discuss their attitudes, beliefs, and behaviors. Furthermore, according to Howard, "by providing opportunities for students to interact with each other (not merely the instructor), the faculty member is creating bonds of acquaintance and friendship that will facilitate further participation and greater learning" (2015, p. 29).

This is essential not only for helping students establish a sense of belonging and connection with faculty and peers, but also for establishing the classroom as a safe place for honest conversation. This is especially important in a class like UNIV 101 where the content includes topics that are difficult for many of our students to discuss (e.g., diversity, sexuality, substance use, and personal values).

Instructors invest time early in the semester to build community. Teaching practices emphasizing discussion and active learning lead students to have conversations with their peers about important sociocultural and personal matters. Moreover, regular check-ins at the start of class, such as sharing highs or lows for the week, often provide students with much-needed affirmation or validation about their personal experiences.

As Figure 4.1 demonstrates, community building leads to a sense of belonging, which positively impacts student persistence. It also creates an

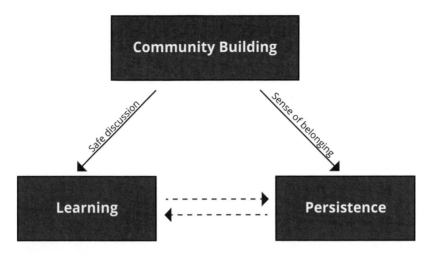

**FIGURE 4.1.** Relationship among sense of community, learning, and persistence in the University 101 course.

environment allowing for safe and robust discussions that foster student learning. The graphic suggests an iterative relationship between learning and persistence. As students continue to learn, they get more excited about their studies, which also leads to persistence. Moreover, if a student does not stay enrolled, the opportunities for learning are diminished.

### Early Alert: UNIV 101 as the Canary in the Coal Mine

Historically, coal miners used canaries as an early warning system for the build-up of harmful gases in the mines. Just as these small birds functioned as "a sentinel species" to safeguard human life (Eschner, 2016), problematic patterns of participation in UNIV 101 can signal larger concerns for a first-year student, allowing issues to be addressed before it is too late. While the University of South Carolina has a wide variety of early-alert initiatives as well as people and programs to support students and their success, the UNIV 101 instructor is arguably in the best position to identify emerging problems and offer assistance. If a student stops going to class, it could be two weeks before a resident mentor notices that they have not left their room recently. Yet, the UNIV 101 instructor would notice the absence immediately. Missing class, not turning in work, and changes in disposition are signs that allow attentive instructors to intervene early before difficulties mount. The relationships formed between the instructor and student not only allow the teacher to identify possible problems but also lay the groundwork of trust and respect, which may make the student more receptive to offers of help or referral.

## Engaging Pedagogy

The third course element impacting the UNIV 101 experience is the quality of teaching or use of engaging pedagogies. This course is not about content delivery or giving students answers. If an institution is interested in a first-year course to simply distribute information, having many small classes is both extremely inefficient and ineffective. Instead, UNIV 101 helps students process their experiences by pulling wisdom from the group (Friedman & Greene, 2020). Thus, the real success of this course is not so much in *what* is covered but rather *how* it is covered.

Like the study by Padgett and Friedman (2010), results from Skyfactor's First-Year Seminar Assessment (formerly referred to as the First-Year Initiative Survey) were used to explore the impact of individual course elements on selected outcomes. These data suggest the number-one predictor of overall course effectiveness[2] is the extent to which an instructor used engaging pedagogies, operationalized as (a) using a variety of teaching methods, (b) fostering meaningful discussion, (c) encouraging students to speak in class, (d) encouraging students to work together, (e) using class time productively, (f) assigning meaningful homework, (g) and incorporating challenging assignments. Thus, given the importance of good teaching to course effectiveness, a significant focus on faculty development is a must for any high-performing first-year seminar. In the end, the process of the course is equally as important as the content.

### Words of Wisdom

*The process of the course is equally as important as the content.*

## ■ Programmatic Elements Associated with High-Performing First-Year Seminars

In addition to the course-level factors, several institutional and programmatic characteristics contribute to the success of University 101. Barefoot and Fidler (1996) observed that successful first-year seminars—defined as those that enjoy strong, broad-based institutional support and longevity—have the following characteristics:

- They carry academic credit and are centered in, rather than tangential to, the first-year curriculum, serving as an integral part of general education, core, or major requirements.
- They include academic content—often extra—or interdisciplinary

content that is woven into essential process elements such as study skills, library use, writing, and so on.

- Faculty and student affairs professionals are involved in all stages of program design and instruction.
- Instructors are trained in basic methods of group facilitation and active-learning pedagogies: Course *process* becomes as important as course *content.*
- Instructors are paid or otherwise rewarded for teaching the seminar.
- Upper-level students are involved in course delivery.
- Courses are evaluated on a regular basis, and results of this evaluation are made available to the entire campus community. (p. 61)

These characteristics provide a useful framework for exploring the structural elements that have made the long-running success of University 101 possible.

### *Academic Credit and Centrality to the First-Year Curriculum*

From the very outset, University 101 has carried three units of credit applicable to most degree programs as elective credit. It counts as a major degree requirement for students in the Arnold School of Public Health and is listed in the degree maps for most majors at the University of South Carolina. According to the 2017 National Survey of the First-Year Experience, 96% of institutions providing first-year seminars offered them for credit, with 32.8% being offered for three credits (Young, 2019).

Credit and grades are a form of academic currency and provide legitimacy for the course. Without academic credit, students would not take the course as seriously and would not have as much incentive to invest time on task. Moreover, seminars with more contact hours have been shown to produce greater learning outcomes than those with fewer contact hours, especially for at-risk subgroups (Swing, 2002; Vaughan et al., 2019).

### *Academic Content*

According to the 2017 National Survey on the First-Year Experience, the most frequently noted course objectives in a first-year seminar include academic success strategies, connection with the institution, knowledge of campus resources, analytical/critical thinking skills, academic planning or major exploration, and self-exploration or personal development (Young, 2019). These objectives fall closely in line with the objectives for University 101 as noted in Chapter 3. However, the specific content and outcomes of a given seminar must be relevant to the needs of the students at that particular institution.

At the University of South Carolina, UNIV 101 focuses on 10 learning outcomes, which are organized into three broad goals (see Chapter 3 for an

University 101 Class, Fall 2019

overview of these outcomes). The extent to which an instructor focuses on each outcome may vary based on the needs of the students in a particular section. Our philosophy is to allow for instructor flexibility and discretion when creating the course and lesson plans. As Friedman and Greene (2019) argued, curricular flexibility increases the quality of the course by allowing for greater creativity and innovation and providing a more tailored experience to students.

## Words of Wisdom

*Consistency is nice, but quality is better. Don't sacrifice the latter for the former. Give seminar instructors flexibility in designing the course experience. A "course in a can" model that is overly prescriptive can stifle creativity and diminish instructor enthusiasm for the course. For students to be excited about the course, the instructor must be excited. The instructor needs the ability to tailor material to their interests and expertise. Be sure, however, not to go too far down this road and let individuals teach whatever they want. Don't sacrifice the integrity and efficacy of the course by sacrificing what students need to learn to accommodate what faculty want to teach. A set of broad common learning outcomes and course requirements can be a nice compromise between flexibility for instructors and consistency across sections.*

Course content, methods, instructional strategies, and assignments should be purposeful and firmly aligned with the learning outcomes. Many institutional leaders are tempted to use a first-year seminar as the cure for whatever ails the institution, leading to the "homeroom syndrome" or the haphazard addition of content and messaging into the existing course. This approach creates a chaotic and fragmented course plan that becomes confusing for students and challenging for instructors to implement. Rather, new components should be purposefully integrated, limiting the amount of content and allowing instructors and students to focus on a few things that really matter— and to do those things well.

### Words of Wisdom

*Components need to be purposeful and integrated.*
*Don't try to do everything. Focus on a few things that matter, and do those well.*

Furthermore, the goals, outcomes, and topics of a first-year seminar must be continually reevaluated. University 101 at the University of South Carolina is redeveloped every five to seven years to ensure that the content is relevant to the needs of students and the priorities of the institution. The course redesign process begins with an analysis of who our students are (and how they have changed over the past five years) as well as an exploration of new and evolving university initiatives and priorities, such as changes to the strategic plan. For an explanation of this review process, please see Friedman's (2012) volume on assessing the first-year seminar.

### Words of Wisdom

*As students' needs and institutional priorities change, so too must the first-year seminar.*

### Broad Involvement in Course Design and Instruction

The course is an important faculty and staff development enterprise. Teaching the seminar provides important benefits to the instructors. UNIV 101 instructors note that teaching the seminar helps them make personal connections with students, get to know students in their major/department, see students in a different way (i.e., in a more positive light), stay in touch with the needs and attitudes of students, and learn more about faculty needs and realities. Teaching a first-year seminar can also improve teaching across the university. Fidler and colleagues (1999) found that faculty teaching a first-year seminar develop new teaching strategies that they apply to other courses they teach, a finding that is reinforced through our local assessment data each year. As Chapter 6 explains, staff who teach the course report greater satisfaction with the university, increased vitality in their work, a larger network of colleagues across the university, greater familiarity with the university and its resources, and improved skills they can apply to their primary roles. Thus, involving staff in seminar instruction is an effective professional development opportunity that allows an institution to attract, retain, and support its human resources.

Engaging both staff and faculty in course instruction is important to leverage all the talents and resources at the institution available to help students succeed academically and personally. It is both possible and desirable to involve faculty and staff in the seminar beyond providing instruction. Faculty and staff should contribute to the creation or reformation of the course content through a course review process, to the development of curriculum and materials, and to the governance of the seminar through participation on a special advisory committee that provides recommendations to the program director.

### Instructor Training

Instructors represent a wide range of backgrounds, professional responsibilities, and teaching experiences. For most instructors, teaching the seminar falls outside their regular job descriptions and disciplinary backgrounds. It also requires the use of engaging pedagogies with which they may not have great familiarity or comfort. Friedman and colleagues (2019) argued that "ongoing instructor development is critical to the success of a first-year seminar as the course is only as good as the person teaching it" (p. 11). Thus, institutions must invest heavily in faculty development. When done well, the investment pays dividends far beyond the benefits to the students in the first-year seminar. Chapter 6 provides a more comprehensive explanation of the University 101 faculty development efforts, which have been a core objective of the course from the outset.

### Words of Wisdom

*The course is only as good as the person teaching it.*
*Invest heavily in faculty development.*

### Compensation and Reward Structure

UNIV 101 instructors at the University of South Carolina teach the course as an additional responsibility for which they are paid $3400. While this is a bit lower than the typical adjunct rate across the university, providing compensation at this level acknowledges the time and commitment involved with teaching the course. The stipend does not appear to be a primary driver of one's decision to teach UNIV 101. Interestingly, many prospective instructors apply to teach without knowing they will be compensated. Most instructors teach because they want to make a difference in the lives of others, desire vitality in their work, and want to grow personally and professionally. As Daniel Pink's (2009) work suggests, intrinsic motivation seems to be a more important driver than the extrinsic rewards we provide. Moreover, instructors are appreciative of the numerous recognition efforts, including thank you emails from students, letters from campus leaders, and nominations for the teaching award.

*Peer Involvement*

The involvement of peer educators is an important course feature gaining prominence in US colleges and universities, with 53.3% of institutions overall (and 63.6% of four-year institutions) reporting the use of student leaders in the first-year seminar (Young, 2019). Involving undergraduate students in UNIV 101 instruction benefits the first-year students served, the institution,

University 101 Class, Fall 2019

and the peer leaders themselves. Peer leadership can be one of the most significant leadership and development opportunities that a university can offer to upper-division students. In addition, peers can positively impact the culture of the institution and the efficacy of the first-year seminar. At the University of South Carolina, we found that sections incorporating a peer leader have significantly higher course evaluations and achievement of learning outcomes than sections without a peer leader. Just as with instructors, the key to a successful peer leader program is appropriate recruitment and selection, training and development, and ongoing support. Chapter 7 provides more information about peer leaders.

### Regular Evaluation

First-year seminars have been identified as the most frequently assessed course in higher education (Upcraft, 2005). This perception probably stems from the fact that these courses were among the trailblazers of the higher education assessment movement. When John Gardner and colleagues established the University 101 course at the University of South Carolina, assessment was built into the fabric of the program. As early as 1974, studies were commissioned to assess the effectiveness of the seminar. A strong commitment to assessment continues to this day and is a considerable factor in the course's success.

Assessment is the engine driving a successful first-year seminar. Without assessment, we would know little about whether programs work or what areas need to be improved. Assessment provides valuable feedback about programmatic strengths and weaknesses and can offer evidence of efficacy. To be effective, assessment needs to be integrated into the design of the course and become a continual part of the improvement process. Assessment is imperative for other reasons. Most notably, it demonstrates to others what we are doing, facilitates funding requests, informs planning and decision making, helps us make inferences about the overall quality of a program or educational approach, allows us to celebrate our success, and most importantly, provides a method of continuous improvement. The assessment philosophy of University 101 is that it is not enough to know whether the program works, but to understand why and for whom. It is this type of formative assessment that allows us to improve the experience year after year (Friedman, 2012).

### ■ Conclusion

First-year seminars have been shown to be an effective educational strategy to increase student success and engagement on college campuses around the world. To maximize their potential, institutional and program leaders must understand the key ingredients that will make a first-year seminar successful. The courses' mission and purpose are too important to leave their success to chance. While every institution has its own context and culture, it is quite likely that the principles outlined in this chapter will contribute greatly to the success of first-year seminars at other colleges and universities, regardless of seminar type. Fostering a sense of belonging, supporting early alert, and using engaging pedagogies to teach the seminar, along with aligning practices with Barefoot and Fidler's (1996) characteristics, will lead to a higher quality first-year seminar experience. These foundations, processes, and structures should be intentionally designed to fully leverage the power and purpose of the first-year seminar.

## References

Barefoot, B., & Fidler, P. (1996). *The 1994 National Survey of Freshman Seminar Programs: Continuing innovations in the collegiate curriculum* (Monograph No. 20). University of South Carolina, National Resource Center for The Freshman Year Experience and Students in Transition.

Eschner, K. (2016, December 30). The story of the real canary in the coal mine. *Smithsonian Magazine.* https://www.smithsonianmag.com/smart-news/story-real-canary-coal-mine-180961570/.

Fidler, P., Neururer-Rotholz, J., & Richardson, S. (1999). Teaching the freshman seminar: Its effectiveness in promoting faculty development. *Journal of The First-Year Experience & Students in Transition*, *11*(2), 59–73.

Friedman, D. (2012). *The first-year seminar: Designing and assessing courses to support student learning and success: Vol 5. Assessing the first-year seminar.* University of South Carolina, National Resource Center for The First-Year Experience and Students in Transition.

Friedman, D., & Greene, S. (2019). Increasing first-year seminar quality through greater curricular flexibility. *E-Source for College Transitions*, *16*(2), 9–12. https://issuu.com/nrcpubs/docs/es_16_2_mar19.

Friedman, D., & Greene, S. (2020). A model for pulling wisdom from group discussion. *The Toolbox: A Teaching and Learning Resource for Instructors*, *19*. https://issuu.com/nrcpubs/docs/toolbox_19.1.

Friedman, D., Winfield, J., & Hopkins, K. (2019). Faculty development for the University of South Carolina's first-year experience course. *Journal for Faculty Development*, *33*(2), 11–18.

Howard, J. R. (2015). *Discussion in the college classroom.* John Wiley & Sons.

Kuh, G. D., Kinzie, J., Schuh, J. H., & Whitt, E. J. (2005). *Student success in college: Creating conditions that matter.* Jossey-Bass.

Padgett, R. D., & Friedman, D. B. (2010). *Relationship of FYI factors and persistence for University 101 students.* Unpublished study. University of South Carolina.

Pink, D. H. (2009). *Drive: The surprising truth about what motivates us.* Riverhead Books.

Swing, R. L. (2002). *The impact of engaging pedagogy on first-year seminars* (Policy Center on the First Year of College Report). Retrieved from http://www.sc.edu/fye /resources/ assessment/essays/Swing-8.28.02.html.

Upcraft, M. L. (2005). Assessing the first year of college. In M. L. Upcraft, J. N. Gardner, & B.O. Barefoot, *Challenging and supporting the first-year student: A handbook for improving the first year of college* (pp. 469–485). Jossey-Bass.

Vaughan, A. L., Pergantis, S. I., & Moore, S. M. (2019). Assessing the difference between 1-, 2-, and 3-credit first-year seminars on college student achievement. *Journal of The First-Year Experience & Students in Transition, 31*(2), 9–28.

Young, D. G. (2019). *2017 National Survey on the First-Year Experience: Creating and coordinating structures to support student success* (Research Report No. 9). University of South Carolina, National Resource Center for The First-Year Experience & Students in Transition.

Chapter 5

# University 101's Impact on Students' Transition and Success

*Carrie Van Haren and Sandy Greene*

Over the last 50 years, University 101 has continually evolved to address and support the ever-changing needs of first-year students. As a result, it has profoundly impacted student adjustment and success at the University of South Carolina. This is true for the student body as a whole and for sub-populations of students whose access to pre-college opportunities and preparation indicate they could benefit from a first-year seminar as they transition to the university. In addition to positively impacting student retention, graduation, and first-year GPA, the course continues to increase student satisfaction with the university and help students succeed both academically and socially.

The story of University 101's impact on students' successful transition to and through college is shaped by a number of different sources. Institutional data[1] document student persistence, academic achievement, and progress toward graduation as a function of taking the course. Students' self-reports about their learning, growth, and enhanced connection to the university community are gathered through student focus groups, end-of-course evaluations, national benchmarking surveys like the First-Year Seminar Assessment (formerly First-Year Initiative Survey), and surveys of former University 101 students still enrolled at the university. The data from these sources are brought to life through Impact Stories—short articles guided by one-on-one interviews showcasing the experiences of first-year students and the benefits they received from the course. These stories are typically published on the University 101 Programs website three to four times a semester. Additionally, assessment instruments like the National Survey of Student Engagement (NSSE) and EAB's First-Year Retention Survey are administered to all first-year students, allowing program staff to explore the impact of the course on key engagement indicators for students who take the course compared to those who do not. Viewing student transition and success through these multiple lenses provides a deeper understanding of the impact University 101 has on entering students.

This chapter presents student outcomes data gathered between 2010 and 2020 and contextualizes these findings within more historical assessment data. Several student stories at the end of this chapter provide an individualized perspective on the value of University 101. The data and stories presented here are summative in nature, demonstrating course effectiveness over time. Formative assessment is also an important and regular component of ongoing course improvement, informing decisions about the curriculum, faculty development, and course policies—all of which impact student success. As Friedman noted in Chapter 4 when discussing University 101's assessment philosophy, formative assessment establishes not only that the course works, but why and for whom, leading to an improved student experience each year.

■ **Influence on Retention, Graduation, and First-Year GPA**

Since University 101's inception, students who take the course each fall have consistently earned higher first-year GPAs, been more likely to return for their sophomore year, and graduated at higher rates. These differences occur within the student population at large and often are more pronounced among first-generation college students, federal Pell Grant recipients, students in the lowest predicted GPA quartile, and Black students—groups of students who may need additional guidance and support as they transition to college because of disparities in access to pre-college opportunities and quality education in the United States. It is important to note that these groups are not mutually exclusive, and students in each group are often members of at least one other sub-group. Additionally, as a group, students who enroll in UNIV 101 tend to have a lower academic profile coming into college (i.e., a lower predicted GPA) than nonparticipants, making the difference in academic success and persistence measures among course-takers even more impressive.

*Retention*

University 101's impact on first-to-second-year retention has been documented since the fall of 1973, the second year the course was offered. For nearly 50 years, students who have taken the course each fall have consistently returned to the university for their sophomore year at higher rates than those students who do not take the course, with only two known exceptions in 2001 and 2010 (see Figure 5.1). In fact, from 1973 to 1995, when researchers first recorded participant and nonparticipant retention rates, 15 of the 23 University 101 cohorts were retained at significantly higher rates than students not enrolled in the course (Fidler, 1996). An early study comparing first-to-second-year retention rates of participants and nonparticipants from 1973 to 1988 investigated whether differences in retention were a result of student input variables (e.g., academic ability, race, sex, motivation) or course characteristics. Fidler (1991) concluded the course's content and process (i.e., creation of a peer support group and provision of a faculty mentor), rather than student input variables, explained participants' higher retention rates.

The difference in retention rates between University 101 participants and nonparticipants is even more pronounced when South Carolina Honors

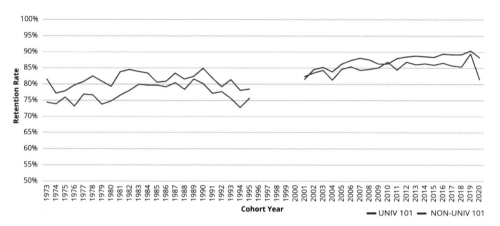

FIGURE 5.1. First-to-Second-Year Retention by University 101 Enrollment (1973–2020). *Note.* Retention data are unavailable for 1996–2000.

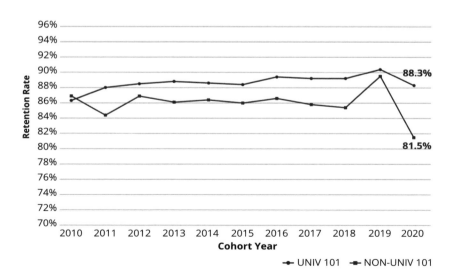

FIGURE 5.2. First-to-Second-Year Retention, All Students (2010–2020).

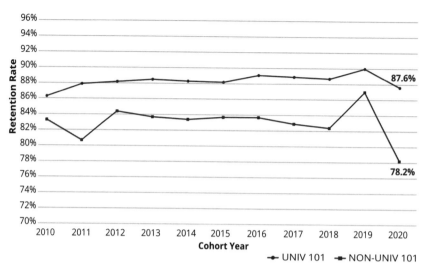

**FIGURE 5.3.** First-to-Second-Year Retention, Without SCHC Students (2010–2020).

College (SCHC) students, who make up a large portion of nonparticipants, are removed from the analysis. SCHC students are in the highest predicted GPA quartile (with an average weighted GPA of 4.68), have high standardized test scores (with the middle 50% scoring between 1440 and 1520 on the SAT), and, on average, graduated in the top 4% of their high school class (SCHC, n.d.). Figures 5.2 and 5.3 illustrate the increased gap between participants and nonparticipants when this group is removed from the analysis.

The course has also shown some promise in improving first-to-second-year retention rates among Black students. In the 1980s and early 1990s, researchers found that Black students who took University 101 were more likely to be retained to their sophomore year than Black students who did not take the course, with course participants achieving higher retention rates in 9 of 13 years studied (Fidler & Godwin, 1994). Figure 5.4 shares first-to-second-year retention data for Black participants and nonparticipants between 2010 and 2020, with Black students who took the course being retained at higher rates for 9 of the 11 years.

Additionally, the course has been effective in retaining first-generation students, federal Pell Grant recipients, and students with lower predicted GPAs. Figures 5.5 to 5.7 show retention rates for these student populations over a period of several years, with UNIV 101 students generally being retained at higher rates than those who did not take the course.

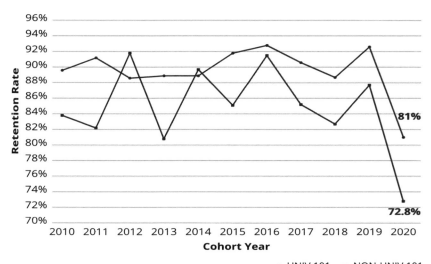

**FIGURE 5.4.** First-to-Second-Year Retention, Black Students (2010–2020).

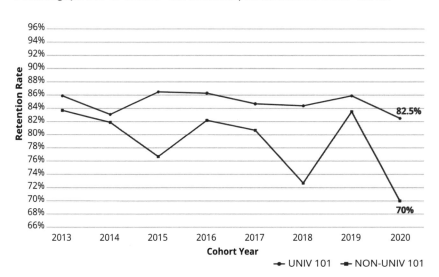

**FIGURE 5.5.** First-to-Second-Year Retention, First-Generation Students (2013–2020).

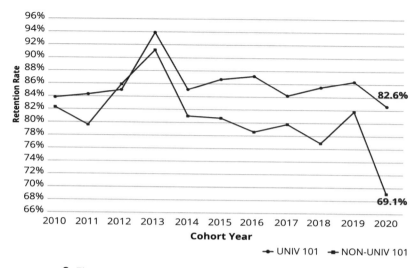

**FIGURE 5.6.** First-to-Second-Year Retention, Pell-Grant Recipients (2010–2020).

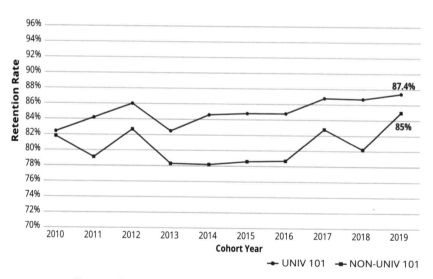

**FIGURE 5.7.** First-to-Second-Year Retention, Lowest Predicted GPA Quartile (2010–2019). *Note.* Data for this subpopulation are unavailable for 2020.

## Graduation

The course's impact is also evident in graduation rates. In a study spanning seven years, from 1979 to 1986, Shanley and Witten (1990) found that the graduation rate for University 101 participants was significantly higher than for nonparticipants (56.2% vs. 50.7%; $p < .01$). Today, University 101 participants are more likely on average to graduate in six years than students who do not take the course. As with retention, the difference is more pronounced when SCHC students are removed from the analysis (see Figures 5.8 and 5.9).

Among those student sub-populations with limited pre-college access and opportunities, the six-year graduation rates of students within the lowest

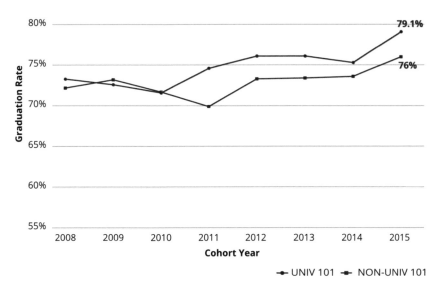

**FIGURE 5.8**. Six-Year Graduation Rate, All Students (2008–2015).

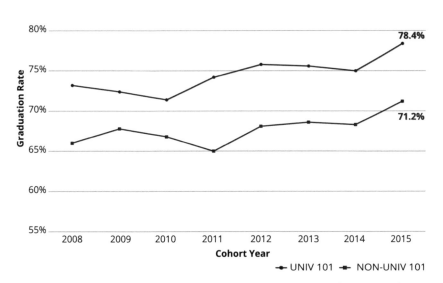

**FIGURE 5.9**. Six-Year Graduation Rate, Without SCHC Students (2008–2015).

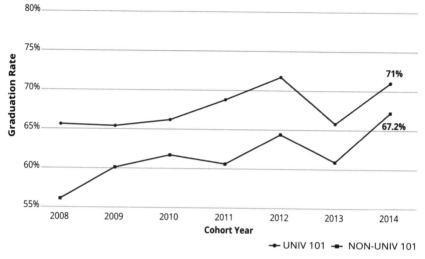

**FIGURE 5.10**. Six-Year Graduation Rate, Lowest Predicted GPA Quartile (2008–2014). *Note.* Data for this subpopulation are unavailable for 2015.

predicted GPA quartile are most notably impacted by course participation. Taking the course had a consistently positive impact on the six-year graduation rates for the most recent cohorts studied, with University 101 participants graduating at substantially higher rates than nonparticipants for all seven years included in Figure 5.10.

### First-Year GPA

Establishing a strong first-year GPA is important not only for students' progress toward degree but also for retaining scholarships and qualifying for involvement opportunities and leadership roles with minimum GPA requirements. Historically, first-year GPAs of students who take University 101 have been higher than those of students who do not take the course. This difference is more pronounced when SCHC students are removed from the analysis (see Figures 5.11 and 5.12).

When the GPA data are disaggregated by student sub-population, taking UNIV 101 is correlated with higher first-year GPAs for first-generation students, federal Pell Grant recipients, students with lower predicted GPAs, and Black students. Students who do not take University 101 are more likely to have GPAs that skim or fall below the 3.0 minimum GPA requirement for state scholarships and many on-campus leadership opportunities (see Figures 5.13–5.16).

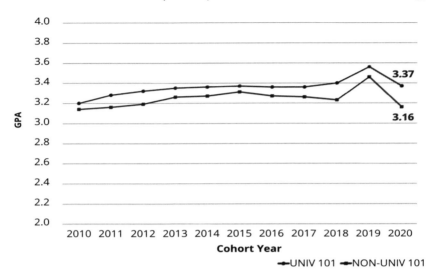

**FIGURE 5.11.** First-Year GPA, All Students (2010–2020).

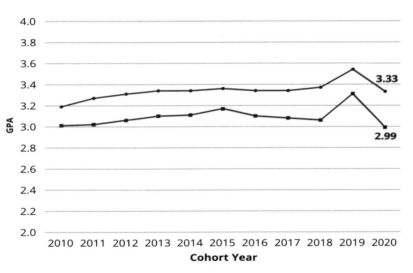

**FIGURE 5.12.** First-Year GPA, Without SCHC Students (2010–2020).

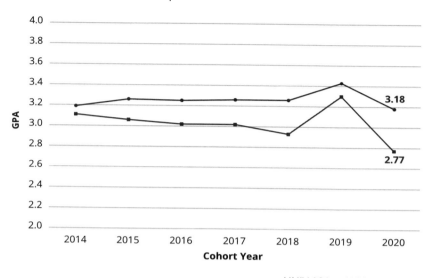

**FIGURE 5.13**. First-Year GPA, First-Generation Students (2014–2020).

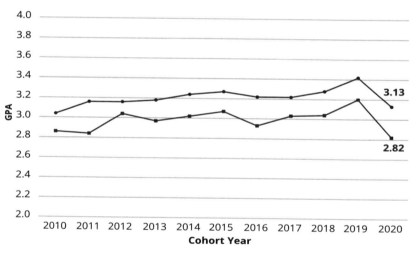

**FIGURE 5.14**. First-Year GPA, Pell-Grant Recipients (2010–2020).

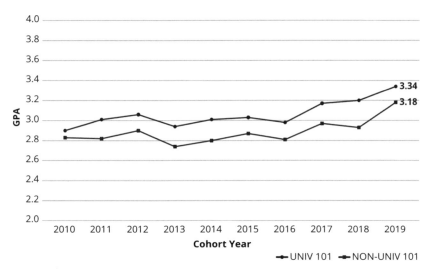

FIGURE 5.15. First-Year GPA, Lowest Predicted GPA Quartile (2010–2019). *Note.* Data for this subpopulation are unavailable for 2020.

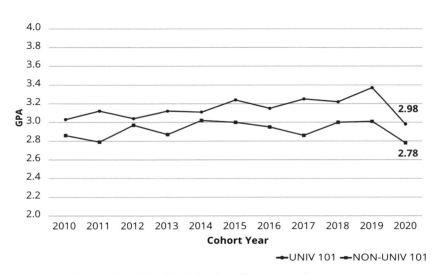

FIGURE 5.16. First-Year GPA, Black Students (2010–2020).

## ■ Student Learning and Connection to the University

Early learning outcomes of University 101 included (a) facilitating students' awareness of the purpose and meaning of higher education; (b) increasing students' self-awareness as it relates to choosing a major; (c) helping students completely realize their role as a student in the university; and

(d) deepening students' familiarity with opportunities, available resources, and course offerings (Heckel et al., 1973). Today, University 101's aim has expanded to include 10 learning outcomes organized under three overarching course goals that honor and include the original outcomes while addressing the needs of today's students. University 101's overall goals are to (a) help students discover and connect with the university, so they develop a sense of belonging and love of the university; (b) foster students' academic success by introducing them to, and encouraging the use of, academic resources and effective study strategies; and (c) promote personal development, well-being, and social responsibility within each student. Table 5.4, located at the end of this chapter, lists the course learning outcomes associated with each goal, maps each outcome to related questions on the end-of-course evaluation, and provides the mean score for each question for the fall 2020 University 101 cohort (most recent cohort for which data was available at time of production).

When considering which course outcomes have had the most consistent impact over the past five decades and those which current students find most valuable, six notable areas emerge: (a) connection to UofSC, (b) connection with faculty and staff, (c) connection with peers, (d) campus involvement and engagement, (e) awareness and use of campus resources, and (f) academic success.

As is true with all University 101 goals, learning outcomes, and course topics, these six areas of impact are not independent; they build on and intersect with one another. Often, student learning and development in one area is the direct result of simultaneous or prior learning and development in another.

## Connection to UofSC

In recent years, students overwhelmingly reported on end-of-course evaluations that the course helped them to feel part of the UofSC community ($M = 6.44/7.0$ in fall 2019 and $M = 6.50/7.0$ in fall 2020). This is consistent with student responses on the First-Year Initiative survey and First-Year Seminar Assessment, in which students were asked to what extent University 101 helped them strengthen their connection to the university. In 2010, the mean response was $5.04/7.0$ and steadily increased over the next five years to a mean of $5.61/7.0$ in 2014, the last year the question was asked.

Connection to the university is also apparent in student responses to the EAB First-Year Retention Survey administered just a little over one month into students' first semester at UofSC. Data collected in September 2020 indicated that students who were taking University 101 were significantly more likely to feel they belonged at UofSC ($M = 5.29/6.0$ vs. $M = 5.11/6.0$; $p = .004$) and to believe that a degree from UofSC was a worthwhile investment ($M$ = 5.31/6.0 vs. $M$ = 5.15/6.0; $p$ = .002). In fact, there were statistically significant differences in favor of University 101 in four of the five years the survey was administered (2016–2020).

## Connection With Faculty and Staff

Since the beginning, University 101 has aimed to help students connect with faculty and staff. Early research on the course conducted by Fidler (1975) found that when University 101 students were compared to students not taking the course, they were more likely to be aware of and seek advice from faculty and staff in various student support positions. For example, University 101 students were significantly more likely to report seeking advice from faculty (33.6% v. 24.2%, $p$ < .05) and residence hall advisors (44.5% v. 35.7%, $p$ < .05) than students not enrolled in the course. Figure 5.17 shares part of Fidler's original research report and shows differences between participants' and nonparticipants' practices of seeking advice from campus faculty and staff. Fidler also reported that students believed University 101 helped break "student–faculty" barriers (20.6% of respondents) and helped them get to know faculty on a personal basis (36.8% of respondents).

Below is a list of some persons available to help students at U.S.C. Please indicate those you are aware of (have knowledge of, have been introduced to, etc.) and also, those you have sought advice from this semester.

| Have you sought advice from: | UNIV 101 | NON-UNIV 101 |
|---|---|---|
| Faculty (currently your instructor) | 73.6 | 71.3 |
| Faculty Advisor | 67.2 | 63.8 |
| Faculty (other) | 33.6* | 24.2 |
| Academic Dean or Dept. Head | 32.3 | 27.8 |
| Residence Hall Advisor (only applies to students living in residence halls) | 44.5* | 35.7 |
| Coordinator of Minority Students | 6.4 | 4.0 |
| Coord. for Off-Campus & Married Students | 4.8 | 3.2 |
| Dean of Freshmen (Humanities Bldg.) | 15.3 | 12.0 |

NOTE: Asterisk shows significance at the .05 level

UNIVERSITY 101   N= 256
NON-UNIVERSITY 101   N= 876
NOT REPORTED   N· 8

FIGURE 5.17. First-Year Students Seeking Advice from Faculty and Staff, Fall 1974. *Note.* From University 101 evaluation, 1974–75: Research questions and findings, by P. P. Fidler, 1975, Table 10. Copyright 1975 by Division of Student Affairs, University of South Carolina.

Today, nearly all University 101 students report that the course helped them identify a staff or faculty member who can assist them with an issue, problem, or question (92.9% and 94.5% in 2019 and 2020, respectively). Students also report that they better understand faculty expectations, are more likely to communicate with instructors outside of class, and are more likely to seek feedback from their instructors as a result of taking University 101. Table 5.1 demonstrates the strides University 101 has made in this area since 2010.

**TABLE 5.1.** Perceived Connection with Faculty as Reported on End-of-Course Assessments

| AS A RESULT OF UNIVERSITY 101 . . . | AGREED (%) | | |
|---|---|---|---|
| | FALL 2010 (*N* = 1,826) | FALL 2015 (*N* = 2,173) | FALL 2020 (*N* = 3,511) |
| I better understand faculty expectations of students. | 71.7% | 84.2% | 94.9% |
| I am more likely to communicate with my instructors outside of class. | 66.8% | 82.7% | 95.4% |
| I am more likely to seek feedback on my academic performance from my instructors. | 64.6% | 79.9% | 94.1% |

*Note.* Instruments used to collect data included the First-Year Initiative survey (2010) and First-Year Seminar Assessment (2015), both national benchmarking surveys, and the University 101 end-of-course evaluation (2020).

While the course encourages developing relationships with faculty teaching other courses, the small, personalized class setting also allows strong relationships to form between UNIV 101 instructors and their students. A fall 2019 survey of former UNIV 101 students found that 90.7% (*M* = 4.49/5.0) of students reported that at least one instructor in their first year made them excited about learning; 79.3% of students indicated that one of those instructors was their UNIV 101 instructor. Additionally, 89.2% (*M* = 4.51/5.0) of students reported they had at least one instructor who cared about them as a person; 94.3% said that one of those people was their UNIV 101 instructor. Furthermore, 72.6% (*M* = 4.10/5.0) of students reported that they had a mentor who encouraged them to pursue their goals and dreams, with 74.3% indicating one of those mentors was their UNIV 101 instructor. Fall 2020 data from the EAB First-Year Retention Survey, administered in late September, further supports the idea that the course makes a difference in students' ability to connect with faculty; 61% of students taking UNIV 101 said at least one UofSC faculty or staff member had taken an interest in their success compared to 39.7% of students not enrolled in the course. While the difference in percentages was more pronounced in the fall of 2020, most likely due to COVID-related restrictions that moved most other university classes online, each survey administration between 2016 and 2020 has revealed a statistically significant difference, in favor of University 101, between the two groups.

### Connection With Peers

Making friends is a top concern for most students when they start college. On end-of-course evaluations, students often report that the relationships they develop with students in their UNIV 101 class are the most valuable aspect of the experience. Additionally, students consistently report that they are more likely to meet and get to know other students as a result of taking University 101. As seen in Table 5.2, students' perceptions of the value of the course with respect to peer connections increased between 2010 and 2020 as continually more focus was placed on building community in the classroom.

**TABLE 5.2.** Perceived Connection With Peers as Reported on End-of-Course Assessments

| AS A RESULT OF UNIVERSITY 101 . . . | AGREED (%) | | |
| --- | --- | --- | --- |
| | FALL 2010 (N = 1,826) | FALL 2015 (N = 2,173) | FALL 2020 (N = 3,511) |
| I am more likely to get to know other students at UofSC. | 78.2% | 84.6% | 95.1% |
| I am more likely to meet new people who share my interests. | 72.8% | 84.3% | 94.3% |
| I am more likely to establish friendships with peers. | 69.7% | 85.5% | 94.5% |

*Note.* Instruments used to collect data included the First-Year Initiative survey (2010) and First-Year Seminar Assessment (2015), both national benchmarking surveys, and the University 101 end-of-course evaluation (2020).

### Campus Involvement and Student Engagement

Fidler's (1975) early research also investigated whether taking University 101 helped students participate more actively in extracurricular activities. He found that course participants were more likely than nonparticipants to know about and engage in campus activities, including noncredit learning opportunities, student organizations, sponsored lectures, and residence hall programs. According to Fidler, students taking University 101 participated to a

Below is a list of activities or opportunities available to students at U.S.C. Please indicate those activities or opportunities which you have knowledge or (have read of or heard about) and also, those you have attended or participated in this semester.

| | Are you aware of? | | Have you attended or participated in? | |
|---|---|---|---|---|
| | UNIV 101 | NON-UNIV 101 | UNIV 101 | NON-UNIV 101 |
| Bell Camp | 74.2* | 64.6 | 18.8 | 16.9 |
| Golden Spur | 92.4 | 90.8 | 54.2 | 47.7 |
| Intercollegiate Football Game | 88.0 | 88.2 | 49.2 | 42.2 |
| Student Government | 92.4 | 92.7 | 11.5* | 7.4 |
| Cockfest | 90.5 | 91.6 | 34.5* | 27.5 |
| Fraternity or Sorority Rush | 89.3 | 91.6 | 29.2 | 23.8 |
| Non-credit Short Courses | 71.1* | 63.2 | 13.4* | 8.9 |
| Chartered Student Organizations | 59.1 | 56.8 | 17.5* | 11.5 |
| Intramural Program | 83.0 | 80.8 | 27.8 | 23.3 |
| Movies at Russell House | 93.7 | 94.7 | 54.2 | 50.8 |
| Concert or Dance sponsored by campus org. | 87.3 | 85.6 | 49.4 | 47.1 |
| U.S.C. Drama Production | 78.6 | 81.4 | 17.1 | 13.6 |
| Music Events at the Coliseum | 92.5 | 93.5 | 50.2 | 52.5 |
| Lectures sponsored by Univ. Union or academic departments | 81.0 | 78.3 | 23.4* | 17.4 |
| U.S.C. Tennis Courts | 90.9 | 91.0 | 29.4 | 28.8 |
| Russell House Game Room | 79.4 | 84.0 | 41.5 | 44.4 |
| Political Rally | 76.7 | 77.4 | 36.8* | 23.2 |
| University Union Cultural Series (Duke Ellington, etc.) | 65.2 | 58.1 | 14.7 | 12.4 |
| Art Gallery, Russell House | 69.0 | 67.4 | 36.8 | 30.0 |
| Opportunity Scholars | 35.2 | 29.9 | 5.2 | 3.7 |
| Honors Program | 75.1 | 76.3 | 7.9 | 7.5 |
| Residence Hall sponsored Programs | 72.9* | 64.6 | 54.2* | 40.0 |

NOTE: Asterisk shows significance at the .05 level.

UNIVERSITY 101        N=256
NON-UNIVERSITY 101    N=876
NOT REPORTED          N=8

**FIGURE 5.18.** First-Year Students' Knowledge of and Participation in Campus Activities and Involvement Opportunities, Fall 1974. *Note.* From University 101 evaluation, 1974–75: Research questions and findings, by P. P. Fidler, 1975, Table 12. Copyright 1975 by Division of Student Affairs, University of South Carolina.

higher degree in 21 of the 22 activities and opportunities listed on the instrument used to gauge student involvement (see Figure 5.18.).

In recent years, nearly all University 101 students agreed that taking the course increased the likelihood that they would participate in student organizations (93.0% in the fall of 2019 and 94.4% in the fall of 2020) and campus activities (92.9% in fall 2019 and 94.5% in the fall of 2020). According to the fall 2020 EAB First-Year Retention Survey, University 101 participants were more likely than nonparticipants to have already become involved in student organizations one month into their first semester at UofSC ($M = 4.12/6.0$ vs. $3.59/6.0$; $p = .000$); this has been true each fall since the survey was first administered in 2016.

Each year, the NSSE asks students about their participation in experiential learning opportunities, several of which are emphasized in University 101:

(a) internships and other career-related field experiences, (b) study abroad, (c) undergraduate research, and (d) formal leadership roles in student organizations. In the spring of 2019, first-year students who had taken University 101 the previous fall were more likely than those who had not taken the course to report that they had already begun engaging in or intended to engage in three of these practices (see Table 5.3).

**TABLE 5.3.** First-Year Student Plans to Participate in Experiential Learning by University 101 Participation, NSSE Spring 2019

| EXPERIENTIAL LEARNING OPPORTUNITY | "DONE OR IN PROGRESS" OR "PLAN TO DO" | |
| --- | --- | --- |
| | UNIVERSITY 101 PARTICIPANTS (N = 189) | UNIVERSITY 101 NONPARTICIPANTS (N = 191) |
| Internship, co-op, field experience, student teaching, or clinical placement | 91.2% | 88.5% |
| Study abroad program | 62.5% | 52.2% |
| Formal leadership role in a student organization or group | 61.0% | 57.2% |

### Awareness and Use of Campus Resources

Fidler's (1975) research also found that students enrolled in University 101 were more likely than nonparticipants to know about or use academic support resources, career services, and counseling and health services, indicating students taking the course were better situated to take advantage of the university's helping resources supporting their academic, occupational, and personal health and success. Fidler reported that UNIV 101 students were significantly more likely than nonparticipants to report being aware of or accessing the career development center, the communications skill development center, the counseling bureau, financial aid, psychological services, religious centers near campus, and the student health center (see Figure 5.19.).

In recent years, when students were asked on end-of-course evaluations what they liked most or found most valuable about their University 101 experience, their introduction to campus resources has consistently been among the top aspects listed. Additionally, students in the 2019 and 2020 cohorts reported that the course significantly helped them identify resources that can assist with their academic success ($M = 6.47/7.0$ and $M = 6.54/7.0$, respectively).

Below is a list of some offices and programs which provide services to students at U.S.C. Please indicate those you are aware of (have read about, seen on campus tour, etc.) and also, those you have used this semester.

| | Are you aware of? | | Have you used? | |
|---|---|---|---|---|
| | UNIV 101 | NON-UNIV 101 | UNIV 101 | NON-UNIV 101 |
| Career Development Center, Pendleton Building | 64.5* | 46.0 | 13.3* | 6.3 |
| Communications Skills Development Center, Pendleton Building | 66.5* | 43.3 | 15.1* | 6.7 |
| Counseling Bureau, Pendleton Building | 75.1* | 57.2 | 12.7 | 9.1 |
| Financial Aid Office, Pendleton Building | 71.5 | 66.8 | 26.5* | 20.3 |
| Legal Aid Clinic, U.S.C. Law School | 50.6* | 38.5 | 6.8 | 4.6 |
| Libraries (McKissick, Undergraduate, Professional) | 94.5 | 95.3 | 87.4 | 83.1 |
| Placement Bureau, Lieber College | 34.4 | 29.0 | 5.2 | 3.7 |
| Psychological Services Center, 1819 Pendleton Street | 41.1* | 32.5 | 5.6 | 3.7 |
| Religious Centers surrounding campus | 84.6* | 78.1 | 24.1 | 18.6 |
| Student Banking Services, Adm. Building | 58.9 | 53.0 | 20.3 | 15.4 |
| Student Health Center, behind Russell House | 90.1 | 88.4 | 44.0* | 36.1 |

| | | |
|---|---|---|
| UNIVERSITY 101 | N= | 256 |
| NON-UNIVERSITY 101 | N= | 876 |
| NOT REPORTED | N= | 8 |

NOTE: Asterisk shows significance at the .05 level

FIGURE 5.19. First-Year Students' Awareness and Use of University Resources and Services, Fall 1974. *Note.* From University 101 evaluation, 1974–75: Research questions and findings, by P. P. Fidler, 1975, Table 11. Copyright 1975 by Division of Student Affairs, University of South Carolina.

## Academic Success

Key objectives of University 101's academic success outcome include help-ing students adapt and apply appropriate strategies to their coursework and identify and apply strategies for managing their time and priorities. In the fall of 2020, students reported the course helped them better understand the study strategies that work best for them ($M$ = 6.06/7.0) and that they were likely to apply academic strategies to their other courses ($M$ = 6.47/7.0). Students also reported the course helped them identify strategies to better manage their time ($M$ = 6.42/7.0) and indicated that, as a result of the class, they were more likely to complete their tasks on time ($M$ = 6.51/7.0).

The spring 2019 NSSE administration gives further insight into University 101's impact on students' academic success. While there were no statisti-cally significant differences between UNIV 101 participants and nonpartici-pants with respect to individual study habits (i.e., students equally reported identifying key information from reading assignments, reviewing notes after class, and summarizing what was learned from class or course materials), students who enrolled in University 101 reported being more collaborative in their learning and were significantly more likely to study with and learn from other students. University 101 students more frequently reported asking other students to help them understand course material ($M$ = 2.77/4.0 vs. $M$ = 2.60/4.0 $p$ = .050) and preparing for exams by discussing or working through course material with other students ($M$ = 2.68/4.0 vs. $M$ = 2.45/4.0; $p$ = .023) than nonparticipants.

### ■ Student Satisfaction with the Course

In the fall of 1972, most students (92.3%) in the pilot section of UNIV 101 indicated they would recommend the course to other students (Heckel et al., 1973). Nearly 50 years later, students still reported that they found the course valuable. On fall 2020 course evaluations, 92.7% ($M$ = 4.68/5.0) of students reported they would recommend future students take University 101, and 91.2% ($M$ = 4.61/5.0) reported that taking the course was a valuable experience. Student perceptions of the course's value steadily increased from 2010 to 2020 (see Figure 5.20).

Of course, each University 101 student has a unique first-year experience and individual reasons for valuing and subsequently recommending the course to others. However, when students are asked what they like most about the course, general themes emerge, many appearing year after year. In the fall of 1972, the first cohort of University 101 students reported that the course supported their adjustment to college by helping them (a) learn how to solve problems related to university procedures, (b) become more confident and aware of themselves, (c) make close friends, and (d) become more open-minded and willing to accept others. The reported strengths of the course were the closeness that developed between the students and faculty, the opportunity to openly discuss problems, and the encouragement for students to take initiative. In recent years, when asked on end-of-course evaluations

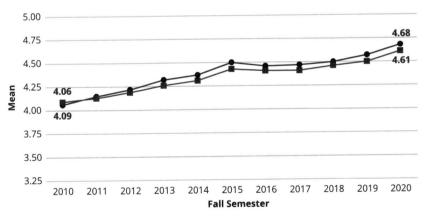

FIGURE 5.20. Students' Perceptions of University 101 (2010–2020).

what they liked most about their University 101 experience, students reported (a) meeting and getting to know other people, (b) developing relationships with their instructor and peer/graduate leader, and (c) learning about the university and its resources and opportunities. They also commented on the environment and the format of the class (e.g., safe, welcoming, discussion-based, laid back, small class size).

■ **Student Stories**

While student success data, student perceptions of their learning, and feedback about the course on end-of-course evaluations allow us to demonstrate University 101's efficacy quickly and easily, individual stories of growth and development are also powerful evidence of course impact. In this section, we share excerpts from three University 101 Impact Stories highlighting students' experiences with the course. Following these stories is a transcript of an interview with a father and son who took University 101 during their first semester at the University of South Carolina, 30 years apart. Their collective reflections on the University 101 experience demonstrate the enduring objective at the heart of the course—helping individual students adjust to and fall in love with the university—and its long-lasting effects.

*Marvin Mitchell, Fall 2017 University 101 Cohort*

Marvin Mitchell

During the first weeks of college, Marvin Mitchell, a first-generation student from South Carolina, considered transferring to a smaller school. "I thought I was going to come to UofSC, have fun, and make a ton of friends, but the first part of the semester wasn't like that at all." Marvin shared his feelings in a journal entry in University 101, and his graduate leader, Tyra Young, pulled him aside to make sure he was doing okay. Marvin says that was the first of many moments in University 101 that made him realize his instructors cared about him as an individual.

It's the simple things that made a difference for Marvin. "U101 pushed me outside my comfort zone. I wasn't a big talker . . . but my instructor pushed us to talk; she wanted to hear our opinions. She would always ask, 'Marvin, how do you feel?' It was the only course where I felt like my opinion mattered. That made me feel valued."

University 101's focus on connecting students with opportunities and resources led Marvin to get involved on campus. "When I met with Tyra, she talked about different leadership roles on campus like being a resident mentor [RM]. She's the one who encouraged me to be an RM, and that position has opened up more and more opportunities." Additionally, a presentation from the Leadership and Service Center led to his involvement as a Service Saturday Site Leader and Gamecock Food Pantry volunteer.

Taking University 101 helped Marvin see how the opportunities at UofSC could help him reach his goals. "My eureka moment was realizing that I can't leave this place that has so many great opportunities for me to grow as a person and as a leader. I remember thinking, if I want to be the best Marvin I can be, I can't leave this University. I love UofSC now. As cliché as it sounds, this is home." (*University 101 Helps First-Generation Student*, 2020)

### *Kate Snelson, Fall 2016 University 101 Cohort*

Kate Snelson

When Kate Snelson was a first-year student, any time she wanted to speak in class, her palms would sweat and her heart would race. In most of Kate's classes, she could sit off to the side and stay silent, but that wasn't the case in University 101. "As a freshman, I was painfully introverted. I was going through so much, but I didn't feel comfortable or know how to speak about it to anyone. I was horribly homesick, I had roommate issues, and I realized that my major wasn't a good fit. There was a lot going on."

"Thankfully, my instructor, Duncan Culbreth, never gave up on encouraging me to speak in class. He never let me shut down." The more Kate talked in class, the easier it got. "Once I started sharing, I realized that other students in the class were going through similar things and that I wasn't alone."

Duncan encouraged Kate to talk by getting her to share one of her passions, photography. "She has a wonderful eye for photography and always had really gorgeous photos in her presentations. I think encouraging her to talk about her photos helped. She became very open about her first-semester struggles, and I would like to think that a lot of the other students in class responded to that."

Kate also credits Duncan with connecting her to on-campus resources that helped her navigate some of her issues. After Kate shared her struggles with her major, Duncan suggested she meet with an exploratory advisor to learn more about the process of changing majors. "At the time, I didn't even know you could change your major, and I definitely didn't realize there was an entire resource for that. If Duncan hadn't pointed me in the right direction, I never would have gone. That changed everything." (*The Courage to Persist*, 2020)

### Issy Rushton, Fall 2017 University 101 Cohort

Issy Rushton

When Issy Rushton arrived at the University of South Carolina from Queensland, Australia, she was alone and nervous about what the next four years would hold. "I was so excited to be at the university. I had all these hopes and dreams, but I was nervous I wouldn't be able to achieve them. I didn't know anybody, and I didn't know what I wanted to get involved in."

Issy's University 101 class gave her the push she needed to go outside of her comfort zone. "I ran for Executive Council in my sorority, and I really do attribute that to my instructor, peer leader, and peers in U101 for believing in me and helping me find a passion for leadership." The class provided her with a much-needed sense of community and helped her feel a lot more at home, because she knew she had a group of students, an instructor, and a peer leader who genuinely cared about her.

The connections Issy developed because of her leadership position in her sorority led to her involvement in Student Government and election as student body president. She was also a university ambassador and a presidential ambassador. She acknowledges University 101 as the first step on her path to success at Carolina. "It really set me on a trajectory to get involved on campus, to meet friends, and to find out what I was passionate about . . . I look back on my time in University 101 very fondly. If I hadn't taken the course, I don't know where I would be today" (*University 101 Helps Student Maximize Her Time*, 2020).

### *University 101's Impact on a Family Across Generations: Jason Heath (Fall 1988) and Tyler Heath (Fall 2018)*

In 1988, Jason Heath was a first-year, out-of-state student at the University of South Carolina. Jason credits University 101 with setting him up for success at UofSC. In 2018, Jason's son, Tyler, enrolled at UofSC and found that University 101 helped him in many of the same ways that it had helped his father 30 years earlier. An interview with Jason and Tyler (personal communication, December 9, 2020) demonstrates the ways University 101 has impacted a family across generations.

Jason and Tyler Heath

**What do you remember about your University 101 class?**

**JASON:** I was a new student from Pennsylvania, so I was 600 miles away from home and didn't really know anyone. I literally knew no one at the school. I felt like it was a great opportunity to meet people in a different classroom setup, to learn about the university, to engage in the university, to have people providing guidance on how to leverage the resources and really get involved. The other thing was that . . . I went to school to get a job, so I felt like U101 would be a great way to have success—it would get me involved, help me learn how to be a college student (which is very different from a high school student) and provide me with the best support system and resources to have a successful first year, and therefore come back and be able to finish my degree in four years, which I was able to do.

I do believe that it contributed to my success. It allowed me to get engaged quickly, to have faculty that I knew and was able to use as a resource, and some other students who I was able to develop relationships with and start the college process.

**Do you remember any specifics of it connecting you to faculty and peers?**

JASON: A lot of my freshman classes were larger classes, and this was a smaller size, so it was more discussion-based versus lecture. I felt like that allowed me to have a connection with my instructor versus in a 200-person lecture hall. While you're able to learn, you're not able to engage and have discussions; it's more one-way learning.

**Did taking University 101 help you develop a sense of community?**

JASON: Definitely. I think it was key. That was my goal as a kid coming from the suburbs of Philadelphia down to Columbia, South Carolina, by myself. It allowed me to engage more quickly; it allowed me to develop some good relationships and learn the resources that the university had to offer. And I don't want to say it forced me to get involved, but it encouraged me.

**Did you encourage Tyler to take University 101?**

JASON: Tyler is a Capstone Scholar so he was required to take it anyway, but it certainly gave me some extra confidence that he was going to be successful, knowing that he would be in a U101 class and get a lot of the same benefits that I did.

**What were the biggest benefits of taking University 101?**

TYLER: Learning about the history and resources available on campus was a big one. I learned about the Student Health Center, the Student Success Center, tutoring, the Writing Center. Similar to my dad, the biggest benefit I gained from the class was a sense of comfort. Coming from very far away in Pennsylvania and not knowing a single person on campus it was a little bit overwhelming going to a large southern university. Being in U101 helped me realize that there were people . . . from all over the country in my class, so I realized that I'm not at all alone in the struggle. At the very beginning of the semester, I thought that every other freshman had it all figured out, but through U101 I learned that was not the case, that everyone was having struggles and that we're all in this together.

**Is there anything else that you want to share?**

JASON: I could tell his first couple of weeks there Tyler was questioning a little bit: Did I make the right decision? Did I bite off more than I can chew moving from Pennsylvania to a school where I don't know anyone at all? But I would say, just a few weeks in I could tell he was really finding himself, really getting involved, getting engaged with the university. And again . . . I feel like part of that was through University 101, just the fact that he had resources available to him, he was meeting people, he was making friends, I think that probably played a role in it.

**TYLER:** I remember the first couple of weeks, you're leaving home, your amazing friends, and being comfortable with everything, for a situation where you know nobody, you're in a brand-new state, it's very uncomfortable, it's a tough situation. But . . . at one point it just clicked, where you start developing a group of friends, you fall into a bit of a routine, you're comfortable with everything going on. U101 wasn't the sole reason, but it certainly was one of the things that helped.

**JASON:** My guess is that U101 isn't intended to be, "hey, take this course, you're going to make friends and love everything," but I think it helped you understand how to do those things, and to your point, let you know that other people are also uncertain and uncomfortable, and missing their friends and wanting to meet new people. I think having that experience and being able to talk about it in a smaller class environment and understand that other people had similar challenges just gives you more comfort in reaching out, trying new things, meeting new people. It's a piece of the puzzle . . . It just kind of gives you a leg up and the confidence and the understanding of resources to take advantage of all of the amazing things that the university has to offer.

## ■ Conclusion

The summative data and student testimonies presented in this chapter, while serving as evidence of University 101's impact on students, represent only part of the course's rich history of student transition and success. Over the last 50 years, each University 101 student has had their own success story, which is imperfectly captured by the aggregate data provided here. In fact, those thousands of unique stories are the true measure of University 101's success as it is the desire to impact individual students—meeting them where they are and providing them with what they need when they need it—that is at the heart of all the course strives to do. Through its small-class environment and cadre of highly trained and caring instructors, University 101 can provide the support, guidance, and content necessary to help generations of students connect to the university and its people, work toward academic and personal goals, and ultimately graduate from the university as more confident, informed, developed, and well-rounded versions of their first-year selves.

## References

*The courage to persist: U101 helps student to feel a sense of belonging.* (2020, August 25). University 101 Programs, University of South Carolina. https://sc.edu/about /offices_and_divisions/university_101/about/impact_stories/thecouragetopersist .php.

Fidler, P. P. (1975). *University 101 evaluation, 1974–75: Research questions and findings.* Unpublished research report. Division of Student Affairs, University of South Carolina.

Fidler, P. P. (1991). Relationship to freshman orientation seminars to sophomore return rates. *Journal of The Freshman Year Experience*, *3*, 7–38.

Fidler, P. P. (1996). *University 101 research summary: Annual update, including profile of freshman class entering fall 1995.* Unpublished research report. Division of Student Affairs, University of South Carolina.

Fidler, P. P., & Godwin, M. A. (1994). Retaining African American students through the freshman seminar. *Journal of Developmental Education*, *17*(3), 34–36, 38, 40.

Heckel, R. V., Hiers, J. M., Finegold, B., & Zuidema, J. (1973). *University 101: An educational experiment.* University of South Carolina, Social Problems Research Institute.

Shanley, M. G., & Witten, C. H. (1990). University 101 freshman seminar course: A longitudinal study of persistence, retention, and graduation rates. *NASPA Journal*, *27*(4), 344–352.

South Carolina Honors College (SCHC). (n.d.). *What are typical test scores and grades for admitted students?* Apply. Retrieved June 14, 2021, from https://sc.edu/study /colleges_schools/honors_college/apply/index.php.

*University 101 helps first-generation student feel at home.* (2020, April 16). University 101 Programs, University of South Carolina. https://sc.edu/about/offices_and_ divisions/university_101/about/impact_stories/impact_first-gen.php.

*University 101 helps student maximize her time at UofSC.* (2020, September 30). University 101 Programs, University of South Carolina. https://sc.edu/about/offices_and_ divisions/university_101/about/impact_stories/Maximizing_Time_at_UofSC.php.

TABLE 5.4. University 101 Learning Outcome Factors and Related Questions from the End-of-Course Evaluation (*N* = 3,511)

| UNIVERSITY 101 COURSE EVALUATION STATEMENTS | FALL 2020 | |
|---|---|---|
| | *M* (7-POINT SCALE) | AGREE (%) |
| **Academic strategies factor** | **6.20** | |
| *As a result of University 101 . . .* | | |
| I better understand study strategies that work best for me. | 6.06 | 87.3% |
| I better understand strategies for giving effective oral presentations. | 6.07 | 87.9% |
| I better understand strategies for completing a college-level writing assignment. | 5.93 | 84.2% |
| I better understand how to determine the quality of information sources. | 6.03 | 85.5% |
| I am more likely to apply academic strategies to my other courses. | 6.47 | 94.7% |
| I am more likely to evaluate the quality of opinions and facts. | 6.40 | 92.9% |
| I am more likely to read critically for information. | 6.29 | 90.8% |
| *To what extent did University 101 help you . . .* | | |
| Work effectively in a group/team? | 6.36 | 92.4% |
| **Time management factor** | **6.49** | |
| *As a result of University 101 . . .* | | |
| I better understand how to set goals (e.g., college, personal, career). | 6.49 | 95.3% |
| I am more likely to set priorities so I can accomplish what is most important to me. | 6.53 | 95.5% |
| I am more likely to complete tasks on time (e.g., assignments, homework). | 6.51 | 94.9% |
| *To what extent did University 101 help you . . .* | | |
| Identify strategies to help you better manage your time? | 6.42 | 94.1% |
| **Academic policies, processes, and resources factor** | **6.48** | |
| *As a result of University 101 . . .* | | |
| I better understand rules regarding academic honesty. | 6.54 | 95.8% |
| I better understand how academic advising works. | 6.51 | 95.6% |
| I better understand how to register for classes. | 6.48 | 94.1% |

Table 5.4 continued

| UNIVERSITY 101 COURSE EVALUATION STATEMENTS | FALL 2020 | |
| --- | --- | --- |
| | M (7-POINT SCALE) | AGREE (%) |
| **Academic policies, processes, and resources factor** | 6.48 | |
| *As a result of University 101 . . .* | | |
| I better understand academic majors that align with my professional goals (e.g., graduate school, employment). | 6.39 | 93.4% |
| I better understand the requirements for completing a UofSC degree. | 6.42 | 93.7% |
| *To what extent did University 101 help you . . .* | | |
| Identify relevant academic policies and procedures related to your academic success (e.g., honor code, academic bulletin, drop/add deadlines, how to calculate GPA)? | 6.47 | 95.0% |
| Identify resources that can assist with your academic success (e.g., SI, peer tutoring, Writing Center)? | 6.54 | 96.2% |
| **Student engagement factor** | 6.48 | |
| *As a result of University 101 . . .* | | |
| I better understand how outside-of-the-classroom learning experiences contribute to my overall learning. | 6.48 | 95.0% |
| I am more likely to participate in student organizations. | 6.46 | 94.4% |
| I am more likely to participate in campus activities (e.g., sporting events, intramurals, Carolina Productions events, lectures). | 6.48 | 94.5% |
| *To what extent did University 101 help you . . .* | | |
| Identify appropriate campus resources/opportunities that contribute to your educational experience? | 6.53 | 96.1% |
| Understand the impact international learning experiences can have on your education? | 6.44 | 94.1% |
| **Positive relationships factor** | 6.47 | |
| *As a result of University 101 . . .* | | |
| I better understand faculty expectations of students. | 6.43 | 94.9% |
| I am more likely to communicate with my instructors outside of class. | 6.51 | 95.4% |
| I am more likely to seek feedback on my academic performance from my instructors. | 6.44 | 94.1% |
| I am more likely to get to know other students at UofSC. | 6.49 | 95.1% |

| UNIVERSITY 101 COURSE EVALUATION STATEMENTS | FALL 2020 | |
| --- | --- | --- |
| | M (7-POINT SCALE) | AGREE (%) |
| I am more likely to meet new people who share my interests. | 6.47 | 94.3% |
| I am more likely to establish friendships with peers. | 6.49 | 94.5% |
| *To what extent did University 101 help you . . .* | | |
| Identify a staff or faculty member who can help you with an issue, problem, or question? | 6.46 | 94.5% |
| **UofSC history & traditions factor** | **6.48** | |
| *To what extent did University 101 help you . . .* | | |
| Understand what it means to be a Carolinian? | 6.48 | 94.4% |
| Articulate the purpose and importance of earning a degree from the University of South Carolina? | 6.48 | 94.4% |
| Understand the history and traditions of the University of South Carolina? | 6.44 | 93.8% |
| Feel part of the Carolina community? | 6.50 | 94.8% |
| **Values & identity factor** | **6.40** | |
| *As a result of University 101 . . .* | | |
| I better understand how a diverse environment contributes to my education. | 6.47 | 94.5% |
| *To what extent did University 101 help you . . .* | | |
| Clarify your values and identity? | 6.34 | 91.4% |
| Explain how your values and identity influence how you relate to others? | 6.38 | 92.9% |
| **Carolinian Creed factor** | **6.49** | |
| *As a result of University 101 . . .* | | |
| I better understand the value of academic integrity. | 6.58 | 96.5% |
| I better understand how to utilize active bystander strategies. | 6.38 | 92.9% |
| I am more likely to appreciate the value of differences between people. | 6.54 | 95.5% |
| *To what extent did University 101 help you . . .* | | |
| Understand the tenets of the Carolinian Creed? | 6.40 | 93.6% |
| Understand how to keep yourself safe on campus and in the community? | 6.53 | 95.8% |
| Understand the University's policies regarding sexual assault and consent? | 6.51 | 94.9% |

Table 5.4 continued

| UNIVERSITY 101 COURSE EVALUATION STATEMENTS | FALL 2020 | |
| --- | --- | --- |
| | M (7-POINT SCALE) | AGREE (%) |
| **Carolinian Creed factor** | **6.49** | |
| *To what extent did University 101 help you . . .* | | |
| Identify strategies to manage conflict with others? | 6.42 | 93.5% |
| Learn from differences in people, ideas, and opinions? | 6.52 | 94.9% |
| **Well-being factor** | **6.35** | |
| *As a result of University 101 . . .* | | |
| I better understand the positive impact of nutrition and exercise. | 6.29 | 90.8% |
| I better understand the importance of good sexual health decision-making. | 6.27 | 89.5% |
| I better understand how to manage my personal finances. | 6.18 | 88.7% |
| I better understand strategies for improving my sleep. | 6.19 | 89.0% |
| I am more likely to manage my stress. | 6.36 | 92.6% |
| I am more likely to apply strategies for reducing risks associated with alcohol. | 6.47 | 94.0% |
| *To what extent did University 101 help you . . .* | | |
| Develop strategies that promote your overall well-being? | 6.51 | 95.0% |
| Understand how wellness impacts your academic and personal success? | 6.54 | 95.4% |
| **Employability factor** | **6.45** | |
| *As a result of University 101 . . .* | | |
| I better understand careers best suited to my interests, values, skills, and abilities. | 6.36 | 92.2% |
| *To what extent did University 101 help you . . .* | | |
| Initiate a process toward the attainment of personal and professional goals? | 6.51 | 95.1% |
| Identify the steps or pathways you need to take to enhance your employability? | 6.48 | 94.7% |

*Note.* Responses on a 7-point scale with 1 = *strongly disagree* and 7 = *strongly agree.*

# Chapter 6

# Faculty Development, Engagement, and Impact

*Katie Hopkins and Sandy Greene*

Placing qualified instructors in the classroom and providing them with high-quality faculty development results in an impactful and transformative experience for both students and instructors (Fidler et al., 1999; McClure et al., 2008; Stassen, 2000; Wanca-Thibault, 2002). The success of the program, in turn, greatly enhances the overall campus climate. In fact, faculty development has been University 101's cornerstone since the program began in 1972. At the time of its founding, President Thomas Jones identified two main goals for University 101: (a) to enhance the academic success of first-year students and (b) to serve as a vehicle for faculty development (Fidler et al., 1999). Similarly, Berman and Hunter (1999) noted, "Although new students are the beneficiaries and focus of the seminar, the origins of the University 101 program at the University of South Carolina have as much to do with faculty development as with student development" (p. 85).

University 101 Programs invests heavily in recruiting, training, and retaining qualified instructors. This chapter provides an overview of the University 101 instructor pool, faculty development efforts, and the impact of those efforts on the course, instructors, and the University of South Carolina.

## ■ University 101 Instructors

Since the course's inception, University 101 instructors have come from all corners of campus, representing every college and school at the University of South Carolina. In the fall of 1972, 20 instructors representing "9 academic disciplines and 4 administrative offices on campus" taught the course (Graham, 1999, p. 12). University 101 has grown substantially since then: 228 instructors from more than 80 offices and eight divisions on campus taught the course in fall 2021 (see Figure 6.1). Between 2010–2021, 766 faculty and staff members served as UNIV 101 instructors.

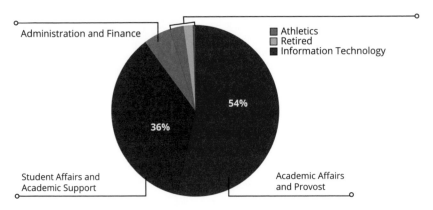

**FIGURE 6.1.** Fall 2021 instructor pool by division home.

The most important requirement for teaching UNIV 101 is the desire to make a difference in the lives of first-year students—a point highlighted by the original proposal for the course (see Atkinson et al., 1972). University 101 Programs prioritizes motivation to teach over employee classification, and a wide range of professionals are selected to teach the course each year. In-structors' primary roles range from faculty and staff who are student-facing to those who are in administrative positions with little student contact (see Figure 6.2). A research study on teaching effectiveness conducted at Stephen F. Austin State University found no differences in first-semester grades, stu-dent persistence, or scores on the College Learning Effectiveness Inventory when comparing sections of a first-year seminar taught by faculty, student affairs staff, and other institutional staff members (Smith, 2012). These

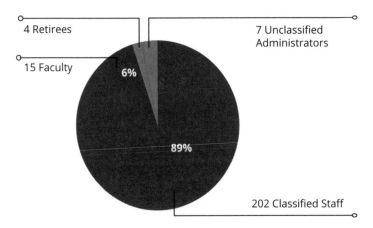

**FIGURE 6.2.** Fall 2021 instructor pool by classification.

findings are in line with unpublished research from University 101 Programs at the University of South Carolina, which found no differences in overall course effectiveness based on instructors' classification or the division in which they worked.

Only looking to one group of professionals on campus would severely limit the ability to identify those who are best suited to serve in the classroom. It would also mitigate the benefits of teaching and the improved campus culture that can come from involving a wide range of qualified professionals. Additionally, broadening the instructor pool increases the university's capacity to serve a growing number of students while simultaneously keeping section size low.

Beyond the motivation to teach, individuals wishing to serve as a UNIV 101 instructor should

- hold a master's degree or higher from an accredited postsecondary institution,
- have status as a full-time university employee or retiree of UofSC Columbia,
- complete a three-day instructor training workshop,
- receive approval from their supervisor or department chair,
- receive approval from the executive director of University 101 Programs, and
- participate in regular professional development opportunities offered by University 101 Programs.

University 101 requires instructors to be full-time UofSC employees or retirees to increase the likelihood that instructors are available to serve as mentors to students beyond their first semester. Retirees have a history of teaching and often have more time to commit to students and the course than those who are currently employed. That multiple retirees choose to teach the course each year suggests how many instructors find this to be a fulfilling experience.

### Instructor Recruitment

More than 250 sections of University 101 are offered each fall, and it is critical that each section is staffed by a qualified and enthusiastic instructor. Fortunately, this is possible due to high instructor retention and effective recruiting of new instructors. Each year, roughly 75% of instructors return to teach. Often, there are more applicants to fill the remaining spots than needed, which leads to a selective instructor recruitment process.

Application information is distributed through two university-wide listservs and on social media each fall. Beyond that, word of mouth is the strongest driver of instructor recruitment. Instructors share stories about their experience with colleagues, who in turn become interested and decide they want the opportunity to get to know and support a group of first-year students. A comment on the fall 2020 faculty survey demonstrates the role of current instructors in program recruitment: "Teaching U101 was a highlight of my semester . . . I have recommended several colleagues apply to teach U101 because you get to see the students in a different setting, and you get to learn and grow with them throughout the semester."

Prospective instructors submit a new instructor application, résumé, and cover letter explaining their motivation, fit, and teaching experience to the University 101 Programs office. Competitive applicants then participate in a group information session with the executive director and, if selected, complete one of the Teaching Experience Workshops offered in the spring semester. The executive director then makes the final hiring decisions.

## ■ Faculty Development

Though instructors bring diverse backgrounds, perspectives, and experiences to the classroom, they are united in their desire to serve first-year students. The diverse institutional backgrounds of instructors contribute to the need for faculty development. While some instructors have backgrounds in teaching and education, many do not have prior teaching experience. Given that teaching falls outside most instructors' disciplines and backgrounds (Groccia & Hunter, 2012), it is critical that first-year seminars invest in faculty development emphasizing active learning and engaging pedagogies.

Additionally, given that instructors have the freedom and flexibility to tailor their syllabus, lesson plans, and assignments, faculty development is especially important to ensure quality. Over the last 50 years, the faculty development model has evolved but continues to be foundational to the success of University 101. Two of the most significant changes include increasingly differentiated training and support tailored to the diverse needs of instructors and the implementation of a year-long training model anchored in assessment findings. In addition, the Graduate Leader Program (see p. 140) represents a pre-service professional development initiative for future student affairs administrators.

### *Differentiated Training and Support*

First-time instructors' needs differ significantly from those of instructors who have been teaching for 10 years or more. For example, first-time instructors need additional support in the mechanics of teaching the course that more experienced instructors do not typically need, such as building the syllabus and setting up the learning management system. As seen in Figure 6.3,

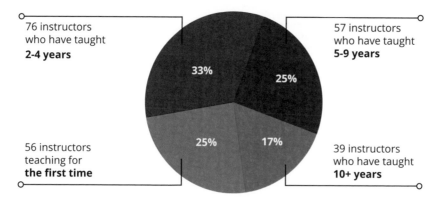

76 instructors who have taught **2-4 years**

57 instructors who have taught **5-9 years**

56 instructors teaching for **the first time**

39 instructors who have taught **10+ years**

33%  25%  25%  17%

FIGURE 6.3. Fall 2021 instructor cohort by number of years teaching University 101.

University 101 Programs hosts a large contingent of instructors with varying levels of teaching experience. As such, it is critical that faculty development events and resources are both relevant and useful for all instructors, especially for those teaching the course for the first time.

Two examples serve to illustrate the targeted support new instructors receive leading up to and during the fall semester. First, while all instructors submit their syllabi to University 101 Programs for review in August, new instructors receive more extensive feedback on their syllabi. This is intended to both reassure instructors and ensure that course requirements are effectively embedded into the syllabus. Second, at the midpoint of the semester, a member of the University 101 Programs staff calls each new instructor to see how their class is going and if they need any help. In many cases, instructors have questions that they may not have thought of before. As one new instructor noted on the fall 2020 faculty survey, "While there were many challenges faced in my first semester teaching . . . the office staff was incredible in the support and guidance that was provided." In addition to these two formal points of outreach, there are several other opportunities throughout the semester for University 101 Programs staff to connect with new instructors.

## Ongoing Faculty Development

University 101 Programs supports instructors through a cycle of ongoing professional development opportunities. Much like the extended orientation model used with first-year students in UNIV 101, the faculty development model is designed to give instructors what they need, when they need it, and when they are ready to receive it (see Figure 6.4). Facilitating faculty development throughout the year ensures that instructors are not only prepared to teach but also have the context needed to fully understand and apply the

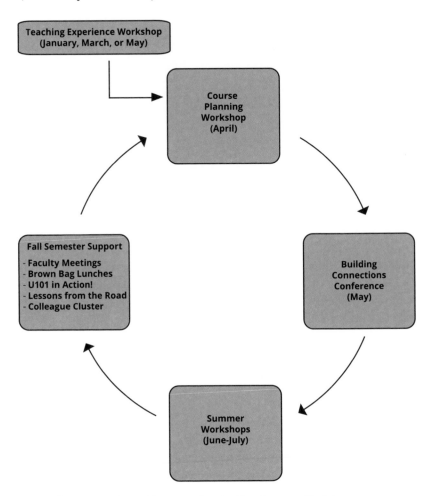

**FIGURE 6.4.** University 101 Programs Faculty Development Model.

content of training to their teaching practice. Groccia and Hunter (2012) argued that "an extended training program exposes instructors to a broader and richer range of topics and perspectives enabling them to provide the best quality teaching to first-year learners" (p. 13). The faculty development model's ongoing nature means that assessment findings can guide training and support. The annual faculty survey and various training evaluations highlight remaining instructor needs and areas for improvement that can be applied to future faculty development events. Moreover, data from course evaluations and other assessments reveal areas that are working well and those that need improvement. High-performing instructors are identified and tapped to lead sessions at various faculty development events.

Each of the following sections provides a description of the history, purpose, and principles that guide the individual components that make up the faculty development model.

### Teaching Experience Workshop

The Teaching Experience Workshop (TEW) is "the central and most critical component" (Berman & Hunter, 1999, p. 85) of University 101 instructor support and development at UofSC. In addition to the content knowledge gained by prospective instructors, the TEW serves to ignite community and collegiality. The TEW provides the foundation for the relationships between the University 101 Programs staff and new instructors—relationships that help instructors feel more comfortable reaching out and asking for help.

Supported originally by a Ford Foundation Venture Grant, the TEW was first created in 1972 to prepare faculty and staff to teach University 101 and has since been held more than 100 times. When the workshop was first launched, it was 45 hours long and focused on defining student needs and characteristics, describing campus resources, and teaching communication skills (Berman & Hunter, 1999). The training was experiential in nature, and Berman and Hunter (1999) noted that it "provided the setting for a substantial human growth experience for the participants" (p. 85).

Instructors after the 2019 Teaching Experience Workshop

Although the length and content of the workshop have evolved since 1972, the spirit of the original workshop goals remains. Today, the TEW is a 3-day workshop offered three times during the spring semester, placing greater emphasis on specific pedagogical styles and strategies than in the initial iteration. One feature that has remained since the first TEW is that the workshop is open to participants from other institutions. As mentioned in Chapter 2, many campuses have sent representatives to participate in the TEW so that they could take knowledge of the South Carolina model back to their home institutions. Since 1983, UofSC has hosted more than 150 attendees from 86 different colleges and universities.

Each TEW is capped at 20 participants to replicate a UNIV 101 class environment. During the workshop, facilitators model activities and strategies that instructors can use with their students. The TEW follows a four-step model for designing a learning environment and is designed to provide a solid foundation for new instructors. Below is an overview of the current approach.

## Step 1: Understand the Audience

The workshop opens with a discussion of community-building principles and best practices. Instructors learn that facilitating relationships among their students is one of the biggest benefits they offer because it will lead to a sense of belonging—a key factor in student retention and success (see Baldwin et al., 2020). In addition, participants spend time discussing incoming students' potential needs, demographics, attitudes, and backgrounds, as well as how that information will inform approaches in the classroom.

## Step 2: Seek Greater Clarity about Goals and Learning Outcomes

As discussed in Chapter 3, the course goals and learning outcomes are consistent across all sections of UNIV 101; therefore, it is critical that instructors understand what each outcome entails. To accomplish this, instructors participate in an activity where they identify lesson plans and activities from the *University 101 Faculty Resource Manual* (Friedman & Sokol, 2021) that they can incorporate into their classes to help students achieve the appropriate learning outcomes.

## Step 3: Discuss How to Accomplish the Outcomes

Once instructors are familiar with the intricacies of each learning outcome, the facilitators discuss the "theories, methods, models, and strategies relevant to teaching a seminar course" (Friedman et al., 2019, p. 13). Kolb's (1984) model of experiential learning is presented as a framework for constructing sound lesson plans. Instructors then work in small groups using Kolb's model to create a lesson plan. This activity not only serves as a helpful practice but also provides participants with a handful of lesson plans they can use in their own classes. In addition, content is frequently covered through participation in active-learning strategies. This practice illustrates how instructors can use active-learning strategies as a vehicle to cover course content and as a method for weaving community building throughout all that they do in University 101. Finally, time is spent on helping instructors master the art and science of meaningful discussion.

### Step 4: Assess Student Learning

In the final step of the framework, the facilitators discuss grading and assignments in UNIV 101. Rather than presenting instructors with a list of do's and don'ts, participants grade a sample assignment and discuss the reasoning behind their grading process. Through this discussion, the group creates a list of recommended practices and things to consider when grading assignments. At the beginning of the workshop, student evaluation is one of the topics about which instructors express concern. This activity not only satisfies an expressed need but also decreases variance in grades across sections, which is important.

In addition to these four steps, four current instructors serve on a panel, answering questions submitted by the participants and sharing advice and lessons learned from their time teaching UNIV 101. The panel is carefully constructed to include instructors with varying years of experience so that participants can gain answers from multiple perspectives. Following the panel, participants discuss the UNIV 101 syllabus components, as well as strategies as they begin building their course plan over the summer. The training ends with a group picture and a community-building activity that gives instructors the opportunity to reflect on what they have learned and what they are looking forward to in the fall. Not only does this activity model the importance of closure activities as a community-building strategy to use with their students, but it also allows them to reflect on their community as a cohort of instructors.

### *Course Planning Workshops*

Course Planning Workshops are held in April and are the first time in the training cycle that instructors and peer or graduate leaders come together to discuss effective strategies for achieving the course learning outcomes and to start planning their courses. Topics discussed range from mutual expectations to ideas for using course resources like *Transitions*, supplemental texts, and campus partner presentations. Instructors and peer or graduate leaders also benefit from brainstorming, collaborating, and exchanging ideas and resources with other teaching teams. While the purpose of these workshops is consistent from year to year, the content changes and adapts in response to anticipated student needs and findings that have emerged from more recent course assessments.

## Building Connections Conference

The annual Building Connections Conference (BCC), first held in May 2009, is a critical component of the faculty development model. The goals of BCC are for participants to identify new strategies for achieving course learning outcomes, share ideas and successful practices, understand campus trends and issues, reconnect with colleagues, and renew enthusiasm for teaching UNIV 101. The daylong event features a keynote address from an expert related to our work and concurrent sessions from instructors and campus partners.

One benefit of this required event is the opportunity it creates for instructors to learn from one another. Through concurrent sessions, instructors share ideas, best practices, and teaching strategies. Two methods are used to elicit conference session proposals. First, three months before the conference, organizers send a general call for proposals to instructors and campus partners. Second, University 101 Programs staff identify high-performing instructors by reviewing the previous year's end-of-course evaluations to see who was most successful in each content area. They invite these instructors

Instructors at the Building Connections Conference

to develop a conference session for sharing strategies that have been successful in their classes. Such examples include strategies for building community, approaches to developing a successful teaching team relationship, and methods for integrating the *Transitions* textbook into the course plan. This process allows University 101 Programs to leverage the wisdom and expertise of a community of instructors.

### Summer Workshop Series

During the summer, University 101 Programs implements a series of optional workshops targeted at the varying needs of instructors. The goal of the Summer Workshop Series is for instructors to receive the information and support they need, when they need it, and when they are ready for it. The series has four major programmatic benefits. First, many of the conference sessions originally presented at the Building Connections Conference are repeated, so instructors who were not able to attend a specific session at the conference have another opportunity to do so. Second, the number of workshops offered and the range of topics covered ensure that instructors receive support in areas where they most need it. Third, these workshops give instructors the opportunity to network with one another and continue to build a community. Finally, the Summer Workshop Series gives the University 101 Programs staff the chance to interact with many instructors, helping them gain a sense of the training and support instructors might need in the fall semester.

### Fall Opportunities and Support

During the summer, faculty development efforts help instructors design course plans and envision their ideal class. At that point, instructors are planning in the abstract. In the fall, training shifts to help the instructor teach the 19 complex individuals in their class and navigate classroom dynamics. Faculty development initiatives also provide instructors with support, validation, and a sense of community. Much like the way University 101 is designed to provide a space for first-year students to normalize their experience and receive support from their peers and instructor, the approach to faculty development follows the same guiding principles. Most challenges that instructors face are not unique to them; it is critical to provide a space to normalize the teaching experience, receive support from other instructors, and brainstorm possible solutions. Additionally, through their classroom experience, instructors develop creative and innovative teaching strategies. Many of the events throughout the fall give instructors the opportunity to share ideas and approaches with each other. Fall faculty development initiatives include the following:

- *Brown bag lunches* are typically held once a month and aim to create a space for instructors to support one another through their successes and challenges. While brown bag lunches are facilitated by a member of the University 101 Programs staff, the content is guided by the instructors who are present. Some lunch sessions focus on themes or challenges that arise during the semester.
- *Colleague clusters* are groups of five to seven instructors who meet throughout the semester to brainstorm, provide support, and come together as an academic community. Colleague cluster participation is voluntary, and groups are assembled in late July. About one third of instructors participate each year, and the composition of each cluster is intentionally designed to include instructors with different years of teaching experience and from different departments on campus. Colleague clusters meet either in person or virtually and communicate consistently through email and group-messaging apps. While many of the faculty development events are formal and agenda-driven, it is also important to create an informal environment for instructors to network, build community, and support one another. Gillespie et al. (2010) suggested that a strength of instructor-driven small groups is that they "are inquiry-based and collaboratively organized rather than led by an expert" (p. 121).
- *Faculty meetings* occur two to three times throughout the fall semester and are an opportunity to share important information, set and reset expectations, and brainstorm ideas or strategies to navigate issues and challenges as a community of instructors. Faculty meetings are also venues for instructors to participate in the governance of University 101. From a programmatic standpoint, it is critical that instructors' voices are heard when new initiatives are being considered. Instructors have a wealth of helpful knowledge for envisioning policy directions and decisions. When instructors have the opportunity to provide feedback and discuss ideas related to governance, it increases feelings of ownership, belonging, and commitment (Gillespie et al., 2010).
- *Lessons From the Road workshops* feature high-performing instructors who have been asked to demonstrate lesson plans and activities, with participants taking the role of students. For instructors, reading a lesson plan that someone else wrote and participating in a lesson are very different experiences. One strength of these workshops is that they give participant-instructors an understanding of pace, tone, facilitation style, and potential challenges. Additionally, these workshops provide instructors the opportunity to feel what their students might feel when they facilitate the lesson plan.

Instructors participating in the Teaching Experience Workshop

- *U101 in Action,* like Lessons From the Road workshops, gives instructors the opportunity to see lesson plans play out in real life. The difference is that rather than watching a high-performing instructor facilitate a group of instructor-participants, U101 in Action allows instructors to see an actual UNIV 101 class facilitated by an experienced instructor. The observing instructors are encouraged to bring questions and make a note of practices they can use in their classes. According to Gillespie et al. (2010), instructor-driven presentations provide "not only examples but [are also] a wonderful way for outstanding faculty members to give back" (p. 120) to the larger program.

### ■ Instructor Resources

Print and electronic resources like the *University 101 Faculty Resource Manual*, SharePoint, the Campus Resource Guide, and the Weekly Newsletter are shared with instructors to ensure high-quality teaching.

### Faculty Resource Manual

The *University 101 Faculty Resource Manual* (FRM) (Friedman & Sokol, 2021) is a 600-page binder first developed in 2009 by committees of faculty and staff who had expertise related to the UNIV 101 learning outcomes. These committees provided guidance and direction on the content of each chapter. The FRM is a constantly evolving document guided by assessment findings. Every year, results from the end-of-course evaluations help staff identify successful teaching strategies and high-performing instructors who were successful in achieving specific learning outcomes (Friedman & Greene, 2019). University 101 Programs staff interview these instructors and integrate the strategies they share into the FRM (Friedman, 2012). The FRM is sold through the National Resource Center for The First-Year Experience and Students in Transition as an institutional license. To date, more than 500 institutions have purchased a license to use this valuable resource.

## SharePoint

University 101 Programs uses an online intranet called SharePoint to share resources, including an electronic version of the FRM, lesson plans, syllabi, activities, assignments, articles, and videos with instructors. University 101 Programs staff vet all resources on SharePoint and post them in editable formats so instructors can modify resources for future class use. As the home of a vast number of resources, SharePoint has two major benefits. First, it can be updated quickly to ensure that materials are relevant and accurate. Second, it is searchable so that instructors can find what they are looking for quickly. In essence, it becomes a one-stop shop for all the resources an instructor needs to teach this course.

## Campus Resource Guide

Every year, University 101 Programs partners with approximately 30 offices, departments, or services on campus to create the Campus Resource Guide, an online tool highlighting information about services relevant to first-year students. The guide's purpose is to ensure that instructors can share timely, accurate, and pertinent information about campus resources with their students. Each page of the guide is broken into three different sections:

- *What instructors should know:* an overview of each service and the components of the service most relevant to University 101 instructors and their students.
- *Tell your students:* information intended for instructors to share with their students, including information about how students should use services and opportunities offered from each office.
- *New for this year:* information about how a particular service has changed within the last year to ensure that instructors are aware of the most recent changes or programmatic developments.

## Newsletter

Each week in the fall semester, instructors, peer leaders, and graduate leaders receive a newsletter via email that highlights upcoming events on campus, reminders, and curricular resources. The newsletter's frequency ensures instructors are up to date and that their students can take full advantage of the resources and opportunities at UofSC.

## ■ Quality of Instruction

The role instructors play has always been important to the success of UNIV 101, and the quality of teaching and student perceptions of instructors has steadily improved. Course data have consistently found that students report that the opportunity to develop relationships with instructors is a key strength of UNIV 101. Table 6.1 shows student mean scores for instructor performance measures on the end-of-course evaluation. Every improvement made in the realm of faculty development has tremendous implications for student satisfaction and success. Therefore, it is critical to continue investing in faculty development.

**TABLE 6.1. End-of-Course Evaluation Means, 2010–2020**

| INSTRUCTOR | 2010 M | 2012 M | 2014 M | 2016 M | 2018 M | 2020 M |
|---|---|---|---|---|---|---|
| I would recommend this instructor for future University 101 classes. | 4.55 | 4.65 | 4.70 | 4.73 | 4.77 | 4.83 |
| The instructor was well prepared for class. | 4.73 | 4.75 | 4.79 | 4.81 | 4.83 | 4.85 |
| The instructor encouraged meaningful class discussions. | 4.63 | 4.72 | 4.77 | 4.79 | 4.81 | 4.84 |
| The instructor showed enthusiasm for the course. | 4.69 | 4.76 | 4.82 | 4.83 | 4.86 | 4.88 |
| The instructor gave useful feedback on assignments. | 4.60 | 4.62 | 4.65 | 4.70 | 4.70 | 4.74 |
| The instructor presented material in an interesting or interactive way. | 4.54 | 4.61 | 4.68 | 4.72 | 4.73 | 4.78 |
| The instructor treated students with respect. | 4.73 | 4.79 | 4.84 | 4.84 | 4.88 | 4.90 |
| The instructor was approachable. | N/A | 4.77 | 4.83 | 4.83 | 4.87 | 4.89 |

*Note.* Responses on a 5-point scale with 1 = *strongly disagree* and 5 = *strongly agree.*

## ■ Impact on Instructors

Instructors serve as an invaluable resource to students and are motivated by the desire to serve students, but they also benefit from teaching the course. Teaching UNIV 101 enhances instructor satisfaction, vitality, and efficacy as members of the university community.

## Professional Development and Vitality

Teaching University 101 helps instructors gain a better understanding of first-year students and develop skills and perspectives they can use in their primary roles on campus, whether as a faculty member, staff member, or administrator. In the fall of 2020, 99.5% of instructors agreed or strongly agreed that teaching University 101 positively impacted their understanding of first-year students. This finding is representative of University 101 assessment from previous years and is mirrored in the broader literature on first-year seminar instructors (Fidler et al., 1999; Stassen, 2000; Wanca-Thibault, 2002).

One of the long-standing goals of University 101 Programs is to help faculty develop new teaching skills that they can use in other courses. Fidler and colleagues (1999) studied the impact of teaching University 101 on 68 faculty members. Participants reported "direct influences on their teaching such as using a wider array of teaching strategies, lecturing less, facilitating discussions more, and modifying the content of their syllabi" (p. 70). Other positive impacts of teaching the course included improved "faculty attitudes and morale, a better understanding of the students they teach, and being more open to spending time with students" (Fidler et al., 1999, p. 70). In fall 2020, slightly less than one third of UNIV 101 instructors taught other courses at UofSC. Of those instructors, 86.7% indicated that the experience helped them improve their teaching ability in other courses.

The story of one instructor illustrates the impact of teaching UNIV 101 on professional development for faculty at UofSC. Dr. Joe Jones, former faculty principal of the Green Quad living-learning community and assistant research professor in the Environmental Health Science program, credits UNIV 101 with a substantial impact on his teaching. During the TEW, he considered for the first time how active-learning strategies might enhance the learning environment within his classroom. Since then, one strategy in particular—classroom discussion—has been prominent in both his UNIV 101 and marine science classrooms. Jones shared,

> I firmly believe students are trained to sit there and say nothing. When we first have a discussion, there is awkward silence. By the end of the first month, there is active discussion about topics from the class. University 101 has made me realize that engaging the class in discussion is important in all of my classes. (Foster, 2018, para. 2)

Regardless of whether University 101 instructors have student interaction in their primary positions, teaching the course enhances their skills and performance in their professional roles. In fall 2020, 94.8% of all University 101 instructors indicated that teaching University 101 helped them learn things they could apply to their other professional responsibilities. Teaching University 101 has helped Tawana Johnson, manager of Faculty HR and Academic Support in the Darla Moore School of Business, hone her public speaking skills and increase her confidence in conducting and facilitating training in her primary role. As a self-proclaimed introvert who has not always been comfortable getting in front of groups, teaching UNIV 101 helped Johnson feel more at ease facilitating training and gave her tools to enhance those experiences for participants. "Now I'm able to get up in front of a large group and engage and get them to reciprocate . . . I've picked up tactics that we use in University 101. For example, now I do check-ins first to help participants open up" (Teaching University 101 Leads to Personal and Professional Development, 2019, para. 7). Johnson also recognizes that teaching University 101 has helped her stay focused on what matters.

> In my primary job as the HR manager, I have very little interaction with students, so teaching is a breath of fresh air . . . at the end of the day, we're all here for the students . . . we get so overwhelmed in paperwork and different policies, and seeing what we're all here for, the students, is a great reminder of our purpose. (Teaching University 101 Leads to Personal and Professional Development, 2019, para. 8)

### Satisfaction, Commitment to UofSC, and Sense of Belonging

Chapter 4 details the important role that University 101 plays in helping students develop a sense of belonging at the University of South Carolina—a benefit not exclusive to students. Instructors develop a network of colleagues, learn more about the university, and experience an enhanced satisfaction and commitment to UofSC, which contribute to sense of belonging.

In addition to interacting with students and peer or graduate leaders, University 101 instructors develop relationships and community with other instructors through both formal and informal faculty development initiatives. The development of community begins immediately as instructors go through the initial Teaching Experience Workshop with 19 other new instructors from across the university. In addition to the TEW, ongoing faculty development creates a space for instructors to share thoughts, ideas, and advice about teaching the course and helps them build relationships with colleagues from outside their campus units. In fall 2020, 84.4% of instructors agreed that teaching UNIV 101 increased their network of colleagues within the institution.

For many instructors, teaching UNIV 101 helps them learn about UofSC and feel more connected to the institution. Mike Lagomarsine, former assistant director of fitness for Campus Recreation, decided to accept a position at

UofSC, in part, because of the opportunity to teach University 101. "I realized what a great impact I could have in addition to my 9 to 5 job. I would have this other opportunity to interact with students and help them become comfortable at UofSC" (University 101 Instructors Find Connection, 2020, para. 5). When Lagomarsine was a first-time instructor, he understood the importance of learning about the university alongside his students: "Teaching University 101 is like an extended orientation as a staff member. As I learn more about the university, I feel more connected to the university, and I care more about the university" (University 101 Instructors Find Connection, 2020, para. 3). Now a seasoned instructor, he continues to find meaning in his role: "Teaching gives me a sense of pride. I'm doing more than just my job; I'm going above and beyond" (University 101 Instructors Find Connection, 2020, para. 5).

## ■ Instructor Recognition

Serving such a large number of students would not be possible without the dedication and commitment of instructors, and it is important to the UNIV 101 staff that instructors recognize the significant impact they make on the program as a whole. In addition to the compensation for teaching the course, instructors are recognized in other important ways, such as an annual teaching award, Impact Stories, and committee service.

### *M. Stuart Hunter Award for Outstanding Teaching in University 101*

At the end of each fall semester, students enrolled in UNIV 101 are invited to nominate their instructor as an outstanding teacher. Selection criteria include the use of engaging and interactive methods to facilitate student learning; enthusiasm for the course and students; and the promotion of an inclusive, enjoyable, and welcoming environment. The executive director of University 101 Programs sends a copy of the nomination and a letter congratulating the instructor on this achievement to both the instructor and their supervisor. This simple process allows the instructor to be recognized by their full-time supervisor and reminds the instructor that their commitment to teaching is valued by their students and the larger program.

Next, a group of 10 to 12 finalists is selected, and each finalist is asked to submit a statement of teaching to be reviewed along with their end-of-course evaluations, student nominations, and syllabus. These materials are reviewed by a committee consisting of the previous year's award recipient, a peer leader, and University 101 staff members. The recipient is announced at the annual Building Connections Conference and has an opportunity to share remarks at the conference. They receive an honorarium, a plaque, and a brick on UofSC's historic Horseshoe customized with their name and award recognition.

### Impact Stories

Impact Stories are short articles published three to four times a semester on the University 101 Programs website that highlight the impact the course has on students, peer and graduate leaders, and instructors. These stories stem from one-on-one interviews and aim to both tell the story of University 101 and to recognize the work of instructors. There are two main strategies used to select instructors to be highlighted. First, ideas emerge from assessment data, as do the names of high-performing instructors whose work illustrates those themes. Second, instructors are highlighted when compelling and powerful stories emerge anecdotally. These stories demonstrate the impact that teaching has on instructors and students; and when these stories are shared broadly, they give instructors a sense of pride.

### Additional Involvement with University 101 Programs

As mentioned in Chapter 4, involving instructors in University 101 governance helps create a stronger program, but it also serves as a form of recognition. Each time an instructor is asked to serve on a committee, participate in the Teaching Experience Workshop panel, or contribute their ideas to curricular resources, it reminds them that they are valued and appreciated. At the same time, it benefits the University 101 staff greatly because the program is improved, and the instructors feel ownership in the course's administration.

The personal relationships developed by the University 101 Programs staff with instructors drive the recognition efforts. They serve to reinforce the sense of belonging cultivated through the faculty development initiatives. Recognizing instructors for the work they have done conveys that they are valuable members of the University 101 team and motivates them to continue teaching and supporting first-year students.

### ■ Conclusion

In 1973, the authors of *University 101: An Educational Experiment* wrote, "It is anticipated that University 101 will never become a static, unchanging course. As student needs change, as faculty needs emerge, the training program in University 101 will inevitably change . . . It is only through growth and change that University 101 will continue to be meaningful and viable (Heckel et al., p. 67).

For 50 years, faculty development has been the cornerstone of University 101, continually changing to meet student and instructor needs and ensuring both groups are receiving what they need when they need it. Guided by assessment findings, faculty development offerings have expanded from a one-time workshop to year-round learning opportunities addressing the diverse needs of a growing body of instructors with various levels of classroom, mentoring, and leadership experience. University 101 invests heavily in the recruitment, training, and retention of qualified instructors. Looking to the future, it is imperative that the program continues to prioritize growth, evolution, and innovation that will lead to improved student and instructor satisfaction and success.

## References

Baldwin, A., Bunting, B., Daugherty, D., Lewis, L., & Steenbergh, T. (2020). *Promoting belonging, growth mindset, and resilience to foster student success.* University of South Carolina, National Resource Center for The First-Year Experience & Students in Transition.

Berman, D., & Hunter, M. S. (1999). The teaching experience: A faculty development workshop series at the University of South Carolina. In Hunter, M. S., & Skipper, T. L. (Eds.), *Solid foundations: Building success for first-year seminars through instructor training and development* (Monograph No. 29, pp. 85–90). University of South Carolina, National Resource Center for The First-Year Experience & Students in Transition.

Fidler, P., Neururer-Rotholz, J., & Richardson, S. (1999). Teaching the freshman seminar: Its effectiveness in promoting faculty development. *Journal of The First-Year Experience & Students in Transition, 11*(2), 59–73.

Foster, R. (2018). Teaching University 101 Enhances Teaching in Other Courses. University 101 Programs. https://sc.edu/about/offices_and_divisions/university_101/about/impact_stories/teachinguniversity101enhancesteachinginothercourses.php.

Friedman, D. (2012). *The first-year seminar: Designing and assessing courses to support student learning and success: Vol. 5. Assessing the first-year seminar.* University of South Carolina, National Resource Center for The First-Year Experience and Students in Transition.

Friedman, D., & Greene, S. (2019). Increasing first-year seminar quality through greater curricular flexibility. *E-Source for College Transitions, 16*(2), 9–12. https://issuu.com/nrcpubs/docs/es_16_2_mar19.

Friedman, D., & Sokol, K. (Eds.). (2021). *University 101 Faculty Resource Manual.* University of South Carolina, University 101 Programs.

Friedman, D., Winfield, J., & Hopkins, K. (2019). Faculty development for the University of South Carolina's first-year experience course. *Journal for Faculty Development, 33*(2), 11–18.

Gillespie, K., Robertson, D., & Associates. (2010). *A guide to faculty development* (2nd ed). Jossey-Bass.

Graham, M. R. (1999). *University 101: Education's Aladdin's lamp at the University of South Carolina 1972–1999* [Unpublished report]. University of South Carolina.

Groccia, J. E., & Hunter, M. S. (2012). *The first-year seminar: Designing, implementing, and assessing courses to support student learning and success: Vol. II. Instructor training and development.* University of South Carolina, National Resource Center for The First-Year Experience & Students in Transition.

Heckel, R. V., Hiers, J. M., Finegold, B., & Zuidema, J. (1973). *University 101: An educational experiment.* University of South Carolina, Social Problems Research Institute.

Kolb, D. A. (1984). *Experiential learning: Experience as a source of learning and development.* Prentice-Hall.

McClure, A., Atkinson, M., & Wills, J. (2008). Transferring teaching skills: Faculty development effects from a first-year inquiry program. *Journal of The First-Year Experience & Students in Transition, 20,* 31–52.

Preparing graduate students to be extraordinary student affairs professionals. (2020, February 11). University 101 Programs. https://sc.edu/about/offices_and_divisions /university_101/about/impact_stories/graduateleaders.php.

Smith, H. (2012). *A comparative analysis of factors promoting academic and social integration in first-year seminars at three regional institutions in Texas* (Publication No. 3511659) [Doctoral dissertation, Texas A&M University-Commerce]. ProQuest Dissertations.

Stassen, M. L. (2000). 15: "It's hard work!": Faculty development in a program for first year students. *To Improve the Academy, 18,* 254–277.

Teaching University 101 leads to personal and professional development. (2019, October 1). University 101 Programs. https://sc.edu/about/offices_and_divisions/ university_101/about/impact_stories/BenefitofteachingU101.php.

University 101 instructors find connection through teaching. (2020, December 10). University 101 Programs. https://sc.edu/about/offices_and_divisions/university _101/about/impact_stories/ConnectionThroughTeaching.php.

Wanca-Thibault, M., Shepherd, M., & Staley, C. (2002). Personal, professional, and political effects of teaching a first-year seminar: A faculty census. *Journal of The First-Year Experience & Students in Transition, 14,* 23–40.

# Graduate Leader Program

Since 1994, the University 101 Graduate Leader Program has given second-year graduate students in the Higher Education and Student Affairs master's program the opportunity to learn how to effectively develop and teach a first-year seminar. University 101 Programs approaches this experience as an early faculty development initiative by preparing graduate students to one day serve as student affairs professionals who may teach first-year seminars and/or advocate for first-year students on their campus.

Graduate leader development comes from two major sources: (a) the mentorship and guidance of a seasoned teaching partner and (b) enrollment in EDHE 834: Internship in College Teaching. As a result of this course, students are able to:

1. articulate and apply the best practices to teaching first-year students;
2. articulate the personal development resulting from the graduate leader experience, including how this experience will be useful in their future professional roles;
3. apply knowledge of first-year students and engaging pedagogies to the development and delivery of an effective lesson plan for use in University 101;
4. develop and share ideas for specific course activities or discussions; and
5. identify strategies to deal with challenges associated with the graduate leader role.

One former graduate leader, Grace Kazmierski, who now serves as a University 101 instructor, shared that the most valuable lessons she learned in EDHE 834 were "how to create lesson plans and engage every person in a class or audience through active-learning strategies. I learned how to mentor and support first-year students, which was valuable because I didn't work with students in my graduate assistantship" (personal communication, February 2020).

The teaching partnership is also influential in graduate leader development both during and after their experience. Through close partnership with a seasoned professional, many graduate leaders gain skills, confidence, and a lifelong mentor. Sonya Singleton's story illustrates these benefits. She notes that her co-instructor offered her constructive feedback, helped

CONTINUED NEXT PAGE

her develop confidence in her skills, and became a mentor to her. Single-ton continues to seek advice from the co-instructor: "When I got the job of assistant dean for students with the College of Social Work, I met with her to help me navigate having a new leadership position. I feel confident our relationship will continue throughout my career" (Preparing Graduate Students to Be Extraordinary Student Affairs Professionals, 2020).

In 2016, graduate students in Dr. Amber Fallucca's EDHE 839: Institutional Assessment in Higher Education class studied the impact of the experience on former graduate leaders. This study found that 94.6% ($n = 104$) of former graduate leaders reported developing skills that they had applied in other settings and 85.5% ($n = 94$) reported applying learned concepts and skills to their current professional roles. On the Former Graduate Leader Survey, one respondent wrote,

> I learned how to be a better facilitator and how to ask effective ques-tions—both of these skills have helped me enormously in my current role. Additionally, in my first job after graduate school, I found that people looked to me as an expert because of my experience working in a nationally recognized program.

The graduate leader experience has a ripple effect on student success. First-year students at UofSC benefit from their presence in the UNIV 101 classroom, and each former graduate leader uses the lessons learned and skills developed through the experience to positively impact students as they assume new roles on different campuses.

# Chapter 7

# Peer Leaders in University 101

*Emma Reabold and Mikaela Rea*

R esearch has consistently shown the significant positive impact students have on their peers' learning and development (Astin, 1993; Chickering, 1969; Newton & Ender, 2010). The use of undergraduates as helpers at colleges and universities has a history spanning many decades (Stone & Jacobs, 2008; Tobolowsky & Associates 2008; Upcraft et al., 2005). Specifically, peer educators are "students who have been selected, trained, and designated by a campus authority to offer educational services . . . [that] are intentionally designed to assist peers toward the attainment of educational goals" (Newton & Ender, 2010, p. 6). Newton and Ender (2010) recognized that "there has been a proliferation in the use of peer educators into nearly every aspect of college academic and support service" (p. 4), including orientation, residence life, and student success programs. They are a prominent component of first-year seminars, with more than half (53.3%) of the institutions responding to the National Survey on the First-Year Experience indicating that they used peer educators to assist in the delivery of the first-year seminar (Young, 2019).

Until 1992, each section of University 101 (UNIV 101) was taught by a single faculty or staff instructor. Recognizing that first-year students need mentoring and support and are more likely to accept it from their peers, upper-level students were added to sections of the course in 1993 to help co-teach and foster community. While not the first, University of South Carolina (UofSC) was certainly an early adopter of peer education in first-year seminars and has become a national leader in the field.

The ultimate purpose of the University 101 Peer Leader Program is to support the successful transition of new students to the university by connecting them with upper-level students who serve as role models and mentors, resources, and facilitators for learning and to optimize the engagement, satisfaction, and leadership development of those upper-level students. Thus, peer leaders not only benefit the students they serve, but they also experience a significant leadership development opportunity.

This chapter offers insight into recruitment and selection practices along with the larger development and training model in which they are embedded. The impact of the peer leader experience on first-year students, the peers themselves, and course instructors are discussed.

## ■ Role of Peer Leaders

Over the past 25 years, more than 2,500 students have served as a University 101 Peer Leader. Placement of a peer leader in the classroom is designed to ensure that new students will

- identify appropriate campus resources and opportunities that contribute to their educational experience,
- develop a connection with the Carolina community and establish a sense of belonging,
- articulate and apply appropriate behaviors inside and outside the classroom,
- have a valuable University 101 experience, and
- make a successful transition to the University of South Carolina.

Additionally, as a result of serving as a University 101 Peer Leader, students will

- develop and articulate transferable skills applicable to the UNIV 101 setting and to their personal and professional goals;
- enhance communication and facilitation skills;
- identify personal leadership styles and strengths; and
- establish positive relationships with students, faculty, and staff.

To achieve these ends, peer leaders serve three primary roles:

- *Role model and mentor:* As upper-level students, it is expected that peer leaders have the experience and knowledge to serve as effective role models and mentors to first-year students. Newton and Ender (2010) suggested that "the goal of a good role model is to emulate the qualities of self-awareness, personal growth, and the ability to self-manage behavior" (p. 17). While perfection is not expected, peer leaders should display "openness to being genuinely human," comfort with making mistakes, and a willingness to understand and develop themselves (Newton & Ender, 2010, p. 17). Peer leaders should model appropriate behaviors in and out of the classroom, while effectively communicating any mistakes made and lessons learned throughout their college experience. This transparency builds trust with students, making the peer leader seem more approachable and able to help with varying issues throughout the semester. Other ways peer leaders serve as a role model or mentor include being available to students; meeting outside of class to help students solve their problems; upholding the tenets of the Carolinian Creed; modeling an appropriate balance between academics and involvement; helping students engage in healthy and responsible decision making; demonstrating empathy toward students' needs and problems; and setting the example of a successful student by having a positive attitude, regularly attending class, and actively participating in all class activities and discussions.

- *Resource:* Peer leaders play an important role in connecting students to both academic and social resources on campus and in providing the student perspective on what it means to be a Carolinian. Additionally, peer leaders serve as an important resource to their teaching partner, bringing innovative ideas for course content, knowledge of campus culture and current events affecting the student population, along with other unique perspectives that an instructor may not have. Peer leaders use a range of strategies to fulfill the resource role, such as creating a

New Peer Leaders at Fall Training

GroupMe, a group messaging app, or a class hashtag on Instagram or Twitter to facilitate community development outside the classroom; sharing information about upcoming events and opportunities at the beginning of class periods and through social media or email; promoting the relationship between students and instructor; and providing feedback to their teaching partner on assignments and lesson plans.

- *Facilitator for learning:* Because of their unique perspective, peer leaders are trained to play a key role in the facilitation of student learning. They often lead community-building activities, read and respond to student journals, facilitate class discussions, and lead engaging class activities, often on topics such as alcohol and drugs, academic advising and registration, Carolina traditions, and student involvement. As noted by Latino and Ashcraft (2012), many peer leaders come into the role with the desire to improve their facilitation and communication skills (p. 10). Therefore, serving as a facilitator for learning benefits both the first-year students and the peer leader.

## ■ Recruiting and Selecting New Peer Leaders

Recruiting and selecting a robust group of applicants ensures that University 101 Programs can assign a peer leader to each course section. Peer leader recruitment is a process that begins in September and extends through January. Recruitment efforts include social media posts, targeted emails to all students who meet the GPA requirement, announcements in broadcast emails, and tabling events around campus staffed by current peer leaders. Word of mouth and nominations are consistently the most effective recruitment tool. Often, students apply for the position after having a positive experience with their own UNIV 101 peer leader. In fact, anecdotal data from interviews suggests this is the case for most applicants.

Additionally, faculty, staff, and students across campus are invited to nominate students they think would do well in the peer leader position. Students are notified of their nomination and invited to apply. University 101 Programs staff members recognize that "acknowledging a student's capabilities in this way . . . fosters mentorship and positive feedback [and] guides candidates toward a developmental opportunity" (Friedman & Sokol, 2021, Chapter 8, p. 7). In short, students are more likely to apply when they know someone has identified them as being a strong applicant for the role.

### Application and Selection

Each year, two rounds of peer leader selection take place. Early-decision selection, intended for but not limited to students planning to study abroad in the spring semester, occurs in November; and regular-decision selection occurs in February. Spreading the application and interview timeline over the course of a full academic year provides an opportunity to recruit and select a more diverse group of applicants, allows staff and campus partners adequate time to thoroughly review applications, and gives instructors ample time to nominate and contact any student they feel would be a great fit for the position.

The requirements to serve as a UNIV 101 Peer Leader are strategic in that they help ensure peer leaders have the maturity and ability to be a positive and well-informed role model, while balancing their academics with other significant responsibilities. Because of these requirements, University 101 Programs consistently recruits a strong cohort of well-rounded peer leaders each year. To serve as a peer leader, qualified candidates must meet the following requirements:

- be classified as a junior or higher during the semester they serve (i.e., they have completed at least four semesters of coursework while attending a higher education institution),

- have a minimum 3.0 cumulative GPA, and
- demonstrate leadership skills and involvement in other substantive areas of university life.


## Applications

The peer leader application includes four essay questions and a recommendation from a professional or academic reference. Applicants respond to the following questions:

- Tell us about your involvement both on and off campus. How has your involvement prepared you for this role?
- How would you define a University 101 Peer Leader? Describe what you perceive to be the role of a peer leader and how you would perform such a role if you were selected.
- What personal attributes, skills, or qualifications do you bring to the position that would contribute to the success of first-year students and to the University 101 Peer Leader Program?
- What are your personal and professional goals? How do you feel serving as a peer leader will assist you in achieving these goals?

UNIV 101 instructors and current peer and graduate leaders are recruited to assist with application review. Each application is reviewed by an instructor, peer or graduate leader, and a member of the University 101 Programs staff and is rated on the following areas using a five-point scale, where 1 equals *poor* and 5 equals *outstanding*:

- personal attributes and skill sets,
- quality of involvement and experiences,
- understanding of role,
- potential for success in position,
- goal alignment with program, and
- support of recommendation.

In addition to the numerical score, each candidate receives a rating of *do not recommend*, *recommend with reservations*, *recommend*, or *highly recommend*. Each reviewer also can provide comments on the recommendation, allowing the peer leader program team to consider additional factors when deciding whether candidates should be invited to interview for the position. Once all applications have been reviewed and scored, the peer leader program team decides how many candidates to invite for interviews based on the estimated number of sections that will be offered the following fall.

As part of the holistic review of candidates, institutional conduct records are requested to ensure the highest caliber of students serve in these roles.

In collaboration with the Office of Student Conduct, records are reviewed, and decisions about removing an applicant from the pool are made on an individual basis. A conduct record does not automatically disqualify a student from serving; students may be called and given the opportunity to explain the circumstances behind their offense and describe what they learned from the experience. Since peer leaders are expected to be appropriate role models, the goal is to select students who can articulate lessons learned from poor decisions and communicate those lessons to first-year students.

### Interviews

The large volume of applications received, coupled with limited staffing and a compressed timeline, necessitates a group-interview format, which allows many candidates to be seen in a short period of time. Each group interview is conducted with no more than eight applicants and three evaluators—a University 101 staff member, a UNIV 101 instructor, and a current peer or graduate leader.

Interviews use a combination of traditional question-and-answer formats and group-based activities. This structure allows evaluators to assess candidates' interpersonal skills, ability to collaborate, problem-solving skills, approachability, and willingness to take initiative. Evidence of their ability to serve as a positive role model is also gleaned from the interview process.

In the first activity, applicants explain how they might present a randomly selected university resource or tradition to first-year students. Next, applicants respond to questions intended to measure their maturity and ethical decision-making skills. This is followed by a mock panel activity where they are asked questions as a group and respond as comfortable. In the final activity, applicants list topics that should be covered in UNIV 101 and work as a group to determine the top five topics. Those topics are then incorporated into a commercial advertising the course, acted out before the larger group. Here, applicants begin reflecting on the needs of first-year students and how UNIV 101 can cover topics relevant and useful to meet those needs. The group interview activities model engaging teaching techniques, such as role-play and group work, which applicants can replicate in their UNIV 101 class. Providing these developmental opportunities during the selection process differentiates the University 101 Peer Leader Program from other programs that view interviews as only a part of the selection process.

Selection of a robust group of new peer leaders follows the group interview process. Given that attrition over the spring and summer is likely, several students are selected as alternates who can be assigned to a section of UNIV 101 at any point before the start of the fall semester.

### Matching

Once all sections of UNIV 101 have been confirmed, all instructors, peer and graduate leaders, and alternates are asked to complete a matching form. They are asked to describe themselves as a teaching partner, select a few key words for what they look for in an ideal teaching partner, and are given the opportunity to provide additional information—such as preference for class meeting time or section type—to facilitate the matching process. Students have the option to request a specific instructor as a teaching partner or vice versa. If they do not have a teaching partner in mind, University 101 Programs staff will match them with an instructor. Analyses of course effectiveness have found no significant difference in the quality of the teaching experience for teams that self-select compared to those matched by the University 101 Programs staff. In addition, an internal assessment conducted in the fall of 2020 analyzed the overall satisfaction and performance of new peer leaders, returning peer leaders matched with the same instructor as the previous year, and returning peer leaders matched with a different instructor. The results of the ANOVAs showed no significant difference between these three types of teaching teams. The emphasis on communication to help teaching teams prepare for the semester may explain these findings. Additionally, the amount of support and opportunities for feedback provided to both peer leaders and instructors throughout the course of the semester contribute to the overall confidence and success of teaching teams.

### ■ Peer Leader Development Model

Like the UNIV 101 course, it is important to give peer leaders the information and support they need, when they need it, and when they are ready for it. The design of the Peer Leader Development Model was created to mirror this just-in-time delivery concept (see Figure 7.1). Each peer leader training opportunity serves a dual purpose as articulated in the work of Latino and Ashcraft (2012): (a) to help new peer leaders feel comfortable with and prepared for their role in supporting first-year students and (b) to serve as leadership development opportunities for peer leaders.

Each training event has a specific set of learning outcomes that is communicated to peer leaders to help them understand the experience's purpose and serves as a basis for assessing the training (Latino & Ashcraft, 2012). While the general goals of peer leader development have remained consistent over time, the content has changed and shifted to best suit the needs of peer leaders. For example, topics such as lesson planning and facilitation skills used to be included during Spring Orientation. Now, those topics have been shifted to Fall Training and the peer leader seminar, a letter-graded,

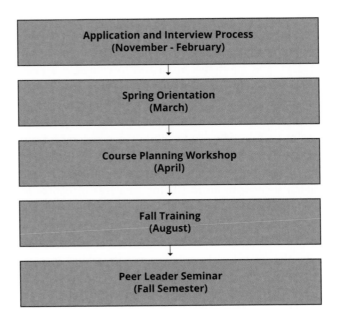

**FIGURE 7.1** University 101 Peer Leader development model.

three-credit-hour course, because these are closer to the time peers engage in lesson planning or facilitating activities in class. As such, the content has more immediate relevance to them. The next several sections outline the major components of Spring Orientation, Course Planning Workshop, Fall Training, and the peer leader seminar and describe how each component fulfills the dual purposes of preparing students for their specific role and providing leadership development opportunities.

### Spring Orientation

Spring Orientation is the first training requirement for approximately 220 new peer leaders and alternates. As the first of many training and professional development opportunities, it sets the expectation of the level of support students will receive as they navigate serving as a peer leader in the UNIV 101 classroom. Groups of 20 to 35 students participate in one of multiple sessions offered, allowing for more effective community building and higher engagement in activities. The peer leader program team facilitates the orientation session. While new peer leaders and alternates have had prior communications with the peer leader program team through the application and interview process, this is an important opportunity for them to get to know the team they will be hearing from and working with throughout the fall semester.

This initial training experience helps lay the foundation for the peer leaders' success in the fall by ensuring they

- understand the history, purpose, goals and success of UNIV 101;
- understand the role, expectations and commitments of a UNIV 101 Peer Leader as it pertains to students, faculty members and the curriculum;
- can articulate desired roles and responsibilities in UNIV 101; and
- develop strategies for working in a teaching team.

Spring Orientation opens with community-building activities to help the peer leaders get to know others in the cohort. As a bonus, peer leaders can replicate these and other activities from training when they are facilitators in their own classrooms (Latino & Ashcraft, 2012). Facilitators then give a brief overview of the history, purpose, goals, and successes of the UNIV 101 course. The overview offers students a glimpse into the impact they will have on students and the legacy of which they are a part and is designed to increase their buy-in to the experience (Latino & Ashcraft, 2012). Next, peer leaders engage in several activities to help them feel comfortable with and understand the expectations of the role, dive into the learning outcomes of UNIV 101 and how they can bring them to life through activities in the classroom, and prepare them to work as part of a teaching team with a UNIV 101 instructor. Working with a faculty or staff member in this capacity is likely a new experience for peer leaders, and it is important for them to be comfortable advocating for their interests and ideas. As explained by Latino and Ashcraft (2012), it is vital to the success of the teaching teams to build this foundation early with peer leaders and continue to weave this content through subsequent trainings.

### Course Planning Workshop

In interviews and applications, peer leaders commonly express a desire to build relationships with faculty or staff members as motivation for taking on the role (Latino & Ashcraft, 2012). Research also emphasizes the importance of relationships with faculty to student success and retention (Astin, 1999). Therefore, developing and supporting this teaching relationship from the very beginning is crucial.

The Course Planning Workshop (CPW) held in April is the first formal opportunity to encourage dialogue between teaching partners and promote a good working relationship. The direction and emphasis of each year's workshop is driven by the themes that emerge from assessment findings. Topics include updates on policies and requirements, lessons learned from assessment, and the best practices for teaching a successful first-year seminar. Time is allotted to allow teaching teams to begin exchanging ideas about their course and laying the foundation for their working relationship. The peer leader role is unique in that peers are mentored by the instructor while also serving as a mentor to first-year students. Therefore, defining roles and setting clear expectations regarding this relationship are critical to the effectiveness of the teaching team (Latino & Ashcraft, 2012). The workshop is offered multiple times over the course of two weeks to accommodate schedules of the peer leaders and instructors.

## Fall Training

Before the start of the fall semester, new peer leaders participate in Fall Training in small groups of up to 20 students who are enrolled in the same section of the peer leader seminar, a required course for first-time peer leaders. The training is facilitated by each peer leader seminar teaching team. Fall Training helps prepare new peer leaders for the first few weeks of class by ensuring participants can

- articulate the role, expectations, and commitments of a University 101 Peer Leader as it pertains to students, faculty, and the curriculum;
- develop methods and ideas for specific UNIV 101 course content and activities;
- develop strategies to navigate challenges a University 101 Peer Leader may face; and
- identify resources that will support success as a University 101 Peer Leader.

Although there are many important topics to cover, the goal is that peer leaders leave Fall Training feeling energized about the start of the fall semester and confident that they will be supported throughout their experience.

Fall Training consists of four major components: (a) community building, (b) discussions about accessibility versus approachability, (c) active-learning strategies, and (d) an overview of resources. Community building serves a dual purpose: to help students become acquainted with other peer leaders in their class throughout the semester and to model activities and facilitation techniques they can use to build community among their UNIV 101 students.

Similarly, facilitators use Friedman and Greene's (2020) discussion model to pull wisdom from the group as to how peer leaders can go beyond being merely accessible to their first-year students to being approachable. After the discussion, facilitators walk peer leaders through the steps of the model, helping them see how they can use this framework to facilitate conversations with their first-year students on virtually any topic.

At the end of Fall Training, facilitators give an overview of resources. For example, peers receive the Peer Leader Toolkit, a pared-down version of the

*University 101 Faculty Resource Manual* (see Chapter 6), created to specifically suit their needs, with activities and lesson plans for class, tips for mentoring first-year students, information on how to market their experience to future employers or graduate programs, and more. The Peer Leader Toolkit continues to evolve as peer leader needs change over time.

## Peer Leader Seminar

When peer leaders were introduced to the UNIV 101 course in 1993, the course staff approached the College of Education about serving as a partner in the training and development of students selected for the role. All new peer leaders are required to enroll in the peer leader seminar, historically known as EDLP 520, during their first fall semester of service. This three-credit-hour course provides ongoing training and development to support new peer leaders in their role. The seminar is a hallmark of the UNIV 101 peer leader experience, not only supporting students in a specific leadership experience but also helping them develop as lifelong leaders.

Like UNIV 101, instructors have the flexibility to tailor the course to fit the needs of their students, but each section of the seminar shares a set of common learning outcomes.

As a result of this course, students will

- articulate the personal development resulting from the peer leader experience;
- apply knowledge of first-year students and engaging pedagogies to the development and delivery of an effective lesson plan for use in UNIV 101;
- develop and apply appropriate transferable skills, such as communication, helping, and leadership skills;
- develop and share ideas for specific course activities/discussions; and
- identify strategies to deal with challenges associated with the peer leader role.

All sections of the course are co-taught to mirror the UNIV 101 course dynamic and to model an effective teaching team (Latino & Ashcraft, 2012). The teaching team consists of a staff member with experience working with student leaders and a senior peer leader (SPL). As described in a later section, students can apply to be an SPL after serving as a peer leader for one semester. As peer leaders serve as role models to first-year students, the SPL serves as a role model for new peer leaders (Latino & Ashcraft, 2012).

As with other aspects of training, the design of the peer leader seminar allows students to "consider and apply information applicable to the peer leader experience, at the times when it is most relevant" and to give peer leaders opportunities for growth and personal development (Latino & Ashcraft, 2012, p. 63). The seminar covers a range of topics, including but not limited to helping skills, giving and receiving feedback, career and leadership development, diversity and antiracism, and lesson planning skills. While instructors have flexibility to design lesson plans and activities to best serve the students in their class, all sections incorporate a set of common assignments:

- *Goals and expectations paper:* Peer leaders can clarify and document the expectations they have created with their teaching partner for their role in the class and to articulate their own goals for the semester.
- *Midterm feedback and analysis:* Peer leaders can foster critical reflection of their contributions to their UNIV 101 class, get feedback from both their teaching partner and students on their role and expectations, and analyze how their UNIV 101 class is going.
- *Final reflection assignment:* The purpose of this assignment is to reflect on the peer leader experience and the ways in which the student has changed, grown, or developed as a result of this experience.

As noted earlier, providing opportunities for lifelong leadership development is an important focus for the peer leader seminar. On end-of-experience evaluations, the vast majority (i.e., more than 95%) of new peer leaders agreed that they developed new skills in this course that they could apply to other settings. Because the peer leader position is not a paid experience, earning course credit can provide an incentive for participation and encourages students to view it as a "service or leadership opportunity, rather than a job" (Latino & Ashcraft, 2012, p. 64). In the absence of financial remuneration, Young and Keup (2018) found that course-based models yielded "the greatest returns for students engaged in these roles" (p. 174) as they appealed to intrinsic motivations. Additionally, this course can count toward a leadership minor or Graduation with Leadership Distinction, a program that encourages students to connect and reflect upon the learning and experiences they have had within and beyond the classroom.

## ■ Returning Peer Leaders

Each fall, a portion of the peer leader cohort is made up of returning peer leaders who go through a brief online application process where they are asked to respond to the following questions:

- What are your strengths in the University 101 Peer Leader role? In what areas would you like to improve in the coming year? What would you do differently next year in this role, and why?
- As a returning University 101 Peer Leader, how will you continue to motivate and challenge yourself for another semester?

In addition to application questions, a peer leader's eligibility to return is based upon their performance in the peer leader seminar and feedback from their UNIV 101 teaching partner. Typically, most students are invited to return for an additional fall semester. For various reasons, not all returning peer leaders teach with the same teaching partner in their second year (e.g., instructor's section time does not work with a student's availability). Therefore, all returning peer leaders participate in the same matching process as new peer leaders.

Support for returning peer leaders differs from that of new peer leaders. They are required to participate in a spring orientation specifically designed for returning peer leaders. The goals of returning peer leader spring orientation are to:

- reflect on their previous peer leader experience and brainstorm ways they can improve as a returner,
- understand the impact of serving as a returning peer leader on first-year students and themselves,
- share ideas for activities and lesson plans with other returning peer leaders, and
- discover ways to continually improve the teaching team relationship.

All returning peer leaders attend the Course Planning Workshop whether they are working with the same teaching partner or someone new. During the fall semester, they receive encouragement and support from one another and the peer leader program team through GroupMe, a group messaging app. They are also encouraged to reach out to their former peer leader seminar instructor for support.

### An Elevated Role: Senior Peer Leaders

Senior peer leaders play a crucial role in new peer leader development by serving as mentors, resources, and facilitators in the peer leader seminar. The role also offers students additional personal and professional development opportunities. SPLs may serve as a returning peer leader for a section of UNIV 101, and most do; however, serving in both roles currently is not required.

To become an SPL, a student must first serve as a new peer leader for one semester, complete the online application, and participate in an individual interview with the peer leader program team. Students interested in being an SPL answer two additional questions on the returning peer leader application specific to that role:

- Why does teaching the peer leader seminar interest you? What do you hope to gain from this opportunity?
- What personal attributes, skills, or qualifications do you bring to the position that would contribute to the success of new peer leaders and to the University 101 Peer Leader Program?

Similar to the returning peer leader selection process, feedback is gathered from applicants' UNIV 101 teaching partners and their peer leader seminar instructors. Following the application review process, applicants are invited to an individual interview with the peer leader program team. During the interview, applicants are asked a series of questions to determine the strengths that they would bring to the role, their ability to mentor students who are very close in age, and their ability to navigate the challenges and sticky situations a senior peer leader might face. It is also helpful to gain an understanding of what they are looking for in a teaching partner since, after being selected, they will be matched with an instructor for the peer leader seminar.

Each year, approximately 10 senior peer leaders are selected to co-teach one section of the peer leader seminar. Upon being selected and matched, senior peer leaders attend a spring orientation session to become acquainted with the role and expectations. Spring orientation also gives newly selected SPLs the opportunity to get to know one another and build community. Following the orientation, teaching teams meet to review expectations, decide on a plan for communication, and prepare for the peer leader seminar.

While senior peer leaders do not enroll in a course, they are required to attend meetings twice a month with the peer leader program team to reflect on their experience, build community with other senior peer leaders, and participate in professional development opportunities. Additionally, throughout the fall semester, senior peer leaders assist with recruitment events, serve as application reviewers and group interview evaluators, and assist with other special projects on an as-needed basis.

## ■ Creating Successful Teaching Teams

As a part of their experience, UNIV 101 peer leaders are matched with a teaching partner with whom they collaborate and support throughout their semester of service. It is important to recognize the added benefit to the instructor of having a peer leader in the classroom. Peer leaders should be treated as teaching partners and share in all aspects of course planning and implementation (though the degree to which they are involved in each aspect can be determined by each teaching team).

Throughout their training, instructors are given multiple opportunities to hear and reflect on best practices regarding working with a peer leader. To facilitate the formation of effective teaching teams, the University 101 Programs staff shares the following set of expectations.

All instructors who work with a peer or graduate leader are expected to

- establish and maintain a plan for open and consistent communication with the teaching partner upon being matched and continuing throughout the partnership,
- serve as a mentor to the teaching partner by providing opportunities that both challenge and support their personal and professional development,
- allow the teaching partner to share responsibility in course planning and implementation based on agreed-upon roles and responsibilities,
- provide practical and reflective learning opportunities for teaching partners to connect skills and theories learned through their classes to experiences in University 101,
- provide constructive feedback and guidance to teaching partners to improve facilitation and communication skills, and
- submit an end-of-semester evaluation of teaching partner to the University 101 Programs office. (Friedman & Sokol, 2021, Chapter 8, p. 12)

UNIV 101 Teaching Team at the Course Planning Workshop

Instructors are also encouraged to set aside time each week to meet with their teaching partner. Dedicated time ensures adequate opportunity to plan for upcoming class meetings and communicates an interest in and concern for the peer leader's personal and professional development. To facilitate effective meetings, Friedman and Sokol (2021) offer a template to instructors, suggesting that weekly check-ins include time for the following:

- touching base on what's happening in the peer's personal life and sharing appropriate information from the instructor's life,

- reviewing previous classes and offering the peer leader praise and constructive feedback to improve future performance, and
- planning for future classes and reviewing what resources the peer leader may need to be successful.

## ■ Impact of Peer Leaders on the University 101 Program

The approach to assessing the Peer Leader Program is multifaceted and seeks to understand the overall value of the program to the UNIV 101 course and constituents. This section explores selected findings related to the effect of the peer leadership experience on students in the course, the peer leaders themselves, and their instructional partners.

### *Impact on First-Year Students*

These student leaders make a significant impact on the entering students and campus culture. At the end of each semester, all first-year students enrolled in UNIV 101 complete an end-of-course evaluation, where they answer questions about all aspects of the course, including the effectiveness of their peer leader. As seen in Table 7.1, first-year students consistently report their peer leader is a valuable part of their experience, helpful in making a successful transition to the University, serves as an appropriate role model and valuable resource, and makes important contributions to the class.

TABLE 7.1. Perceived Impact of Peer Leaders on First-Year Students

| PEER/GRADUATE LEADER EVALUATION ITEM | M | | |
|---|---|---|---|
| | 2010 | 2015 | 2020 |
| My peer/graduate leader was a valuable part of my University 101 experience. | 4.46 | 4.82 | 4.83 |
| My peer/graduate leader helped me make a successful transition to the university. | N/A | 4.73 | 4.78 |
| My peer/graduate leader was an appropriate role model. | 4.55 | 4.85 | 4.88 |
| My peer/graduate leader made important contributions to our class. | 4.48 | 4.81 | 4.87 |
| My peer/graduate leader was a valuable resource. | N/A | 4.82 | 4.86 |

*Note.* Data from UNIV 101 end-of-course evaluation presented on a 5-point scale, with 1 = *strongly disagree* and 5 = *strongly agree.*

Moreover, research conducted by UNIV 101 staff indicated that having a peer leader significantly improves the overall UNIV 101 experience for students. Prior to 2014, the use of peer leaders was not universal in all course sections. Data from the 2013 First-Year Seminar Assessment (FYSA) were analyzed to determine the impact of peer and graduate leaders on the UNIV 101 course, as measured by the FYSA's Overall Program Effectiveness factor. The instrument was sent to 3,848 students, yielding a 59% response rate ($n$ = 2,272). The dataset was coded to include a variable that indicated whether a section was assigned a peer leader. An independent samples $t$-test yielded significant differences in overall program effectiveness for sections of the course with a peer leader ($M$ = 5.49, $SD$ = 1.56) compared to sections without a peer leader ($M$ = 5.14, $SD$ = 1.78); $t$(2270) = 9.46, $p$ = .01. As a result of these findings, peer leaders were assigned to all future sections of UNIV 101.

In addition to quantitative data that points to the effectiveness of having a peer leader, open-ended responses from the end-of-course evaluation also speak to the value of peer leaders. Representative comments from the fall of 2018 to the fall of 2020 course evaluations include the following:

> My peer leader was extremely outgoing and genuinely wants to see us succeed which was very encouraging. She was also really good at trying to relate to us and make us feel better if we had a problem and keeping in touch to make sure the problem would get solved.

> [She] has been a wonderful resource and someone to look to for advice. Not only does she understand the transition, but she is there to offer her advice and support for first-year students. One of the best aspects of this course is the addition of a peer leader because it gives students another resource during their transition.

> He was very relatable with the students. This allowed for many students to approach him with any of their concerns, and I feel that it helped encourage students to participate in the class because they felt more comfortable. He was open in sharing his past experiences and giving real life advice to the students.

## Impact on Peer Leaders

As part of the University 101 Peer Leader experience, students develop transferable skills for many settings outside the classroom. As seen in Table 7.2, peer leaders consistently report high scores in their perception of improved transferable skills, thus suggesting that the program is successful in achieving the stated learning outcomes. These findings are consistent with those reported in the literature on peer leadership. For example, Newton and Ender

(2010) noted, " . . . college students who participate in peer education display significant improvements in leadership, gain interpersonal communication skills, increase peer-education relevant knowledge, develop higher levels of self-esteem, and create better personal health behaviors when measured on assessments before and after their peer education experience" (p. 13).

TABLE 7.2. Peer Leader Transferable Skills

| AS A RESULT OF THE UNIVERSITY 101 PEER LEADER EXPERIENCE (INCLUDING TRAINING AND EDLP 520), I IMPROVED MY | M | | |
| --- | --- | --- | --- |
| | 2010 | 2015 | 2020 |
| Interpersonal communication skills | 4.38 | 4.73 | 4.90 |
| Facilitation skills | 4.40 | 4.79 | 4.92 |
| Helping skills | 4.40 | 4.68 | 4.86 |
| Leadership skills | 4.43 | 4.79 | 4.89 |
| Self-awareness/understanding | N/A | 4.65 | 4.88 |

*Note.* Data retrieved from EDLP 520 end-of-course and end-of-peer-leader-experience evaluations and presented on a 5-point scale, with 1 = *strongly disagree* and 5 = *strongly agree.*

Throughout the course of the semester, instructors can highlight the work of their peer leader in a Peer Leader Spotlight shared on social media. Additionally, selected peer leaders are interviewed about the impact of their experience, and their stories are featured on the University 101 website. For example, these two peer leaders reflect on how the experience helped them develop valuable workplace skills:

> The ability to seemingly "go with the flow" while adjusting to plan B, that I honed as a peer leader, helps me remain professional when I am feeling frazzled on the inside.—Maya Sabbagh (Former Peer Leaders Bring Transferable Skills, 2020).

> I'm a little more subdued and passive, but I care about people. There is no right way to be a leader, but I saw that I was able to lead in the classroom and to connect to each student. I learned that leadership is about listening.—Ore Oluwole (Former Peer Leaders Bring Transferable Skills, 2020).

The profound impact of peer leadership on student development is also evident in a letter written in support of the program's nomination for the 2018 NASPA Gold Award. Jory Fleming is a 2017 graduate of the University of South Carolina, a Rhodes Scholar, and the author of *How to Be Human: An Autistic*

*Man's Guide to Life* (2021). Reflecting on his service as a UNIV 101 peer leader and senior peer leader, Fleming described what he had learned and how he saw being a peer leader shaping his future:

> *To Whom It May Concern,*
>
> *It is my great pleasure to support the University 101 (U101) Peer Leader program for an excellence award in higher education. As a recent graduate from the University of South Carolina (UofSC), I have had some time to reflect on the past four years, and my interactions with U101 were some of the biggest and brightest experiences I had in college, fitting for a program that hammered home for me the value and utility of experiential and interactive learning! I hope that my shared perspective serves as a window into the program's students: both in the class and co-leading the class, and what that meant for me and how it will impact others going forward.*

Jory Fleming and Daisy

> *Without U101 I would not be the student, or indeed the person, that I am today. It is a powerful program, and I hope to give you a glimpse into why. My first interaction with U101 was as a freshman my very first semester. While home-schooled I took classes at UofSC, and I could skip orientation as a result. However, I could not skip U101, and had minimal expectations. The class surprised me by teaching me things about the university that I didn't know despite already being on campus for a year. I also did not expect to develop any new relationships in the class, and I was surprised at the connections I made to both students and my instructors. I made several friends in U101 that lasted throughout college. Someone also in my major became a good friend over the years, and another friend who I kept in touch has plans to visit me while I attend graduate school in Europe. I also developed a relationship with my instructor and my peer leader, an upperclassman who was preparing for medical school. Their cohesion and teamwork made all the difference in the classroom environment, but it was their mentorship which meant*

most to me. *My peer leader led his own research project at the local hospital, which I admired. Seeing my interest, he encouraged me to visit the Office of Undergraduate Research where he first got involved. Every class period he would follow up, even offering to walk me there at one point! Scheduling that visit was the beginnings of a formative part of my college experience, and without my peer leader I may not have stepped outside my comfort zone. It was through our conversations that he listened and noticed a spark, even before I had, and his gentle and persistent encouragement helped me through a daunting process.*

    *Towards the end of my sophomore year my advisor and former peer leaders encouraged me to apply to be one myself. I was unsure about the role because of my disabilities, one of which is autism. Some of the hallmarks of autism are difficulty in social situations, including communicating and reading body language. Thinking back on my own peer leader, I decided that if I could impact a single student like he did for me, then it would be worth it. I ended up impacting several students, and I feel that this outcome was achieved by the program's investment in me through training. Several all-day orientations before the start of the semester had all the peer leaders practice speaking to a group of complete strangers, and the frameworks we would need to be successful in the class. Skills like active listening, encouraging group generated knowledge, and fostering conversations were emphasized and practiced. I was initially unsure if I could implement them well, due to lack of experience and how being autistic impacts my communication. The peer leader handbook I was sent home with was invaluable because of the specificity of its advice: down to specific signs or body language to indicate potential problems, or neutral words & phrases I could use to let my students direct the conversation. Further, the peer leaders' weekly seminar class (EDLP) was a valuable learning laboratory where we gathered to brainstorm class challenges and learn activities. On several occasions, I applied activities or frameworks from EDLP the very next class period for my U101 class. We learned how to listen, and how to use frameworks like "what, so what, now what" to guide debriefs and reflections that helped us and our students grow from having fun together. There was also a senior peer leader for my EDLP class, who was a great mentor for me. My senior peer leader helped me think through the design of a beyond the class experience, where my U101 class restored a zen garden outside the biology building. By the time the end of year banquet rolled around, EDLP had become a community bonded by shared trials and successes.*

*The following year, I in turn was a senior peer leader for a new cohort of peer leaders taking EDLP. Besides simply having more fun, becoming involved with the program as a student leader allowed me to develop more professionally. Designing lesson plans that fully integrated frameworks and learning outcomes into every 10 minutes was eye-opening*

*for me, and allowed me to see the classroom as a place that I could construct and an experience I could craft for my students. I also was able to assist in conducting peer leader interviews and orientations, where I could integrate specific goals and see how a larger program becomes self-sustaining. From participating in and leading peer leader training, I learned that leadership is individually discovered, and that successful frameworks are open to diverse implementations. Listening and guiding students towards these ideas behind U101 allowed me to see them grow and develop in new and different ways. Using the same active listening and mentoring skills I learned from U101, I facilitated a student applying for a scholarship, another speaking to a professor outside of class, and a third joining a student organization. Others that I simply talked with, worked in the class garden with, or baked brownies for told me later how these small moments had helped them in a difficult time or were one of their favorite memories from their first year. These moments solidified for me the simplicity and effectiveness of the U101 strategies I was learning, and allowed me to be the mentor that I always wanted to be.*

*Working every week in the U101 and EDLP classroom as a peer leader resulted in so much change for me. Being a peer leader brought out a quirky and fun side of myself that I didn't know I had. My favorite course evaluation from a student said simply "he is awkward and fun." I developed so much in my communication, and was surprised at how much I enjoyed getting to know my students and seeing them grow. My students commented that as their peer leader I was "approachable," "caring," "insightful," "accessible," and "encouraging." These did not always describe me before U101, and several are antithetical to how autism is typically described. Looking back, I am unsure which were dormant traits empowered by U101, and which were taught in trainings or EDLP community development.*

*The experiences I had in U101 have helped me develop soft skills and critical thinking frameworks that I have continued to use extensively. I have been told by many (including researchers at international conferences) that I am an effective and engaging speaker, which stems from my time in the U101 classroom. Working off a lesson plan and then engaging a class is remarkably like thinking through a speech framework and*

*impromptu speaking! U101 gave me the skills and techniques I needed
to engage with others, and guided me through developing values and
character. Effective communication, caring, openness, and a leadership style which unlocks and empowers the ideas present in a diverse
group are all U101 values that I fully intend to implement in my future
career in public service, where these skills will be extremely valuable to
me in a position as I seek to create change for the public good. However
valuable these skills are though, U101 has taught me that change that
affects people is far more powerful than any skill or technique, something I witnessed multiple times: It is the power of a conversation to turn
a shy student into a confident researcher. It is the power of finding a
new friend in class who is just as excited about study abroad as you are
(including having your phones in foreign languages!). It is the power of a
student who changes their major to better fit who they are. It is the power
of a student unsure if they can fit into a college campus whose booming
laugh can now be heard throughout the student union. It is the power of
U101, and to me it is truly excellent.*

*Sincerely,*

*Jory Fleming UofSC '17, Geography & Marine Science,
Former U101 Peer Leader & Senior Peer Leader
(personal communication, October 4, 2017)*

## Impact on Instructors

Having a peer leader as a part of the course is also extremely valuable to
instructors who benefit from having someone to share the workload related
to course management. The partnership can also expose instructors to new
ideas, reinvigorating the course syllabus and lesson plans while also helping
the growth and development of an upper-division student leader or future
higher education professional. Because the peer leader is also a student, the
instructor has an added resource connecting them to campus life, student
values, and current trends. As Shook and Keup (2012) noted, "There is insight
to be gained from the student perspective, particularly when it is filtered
through the interpretive lens of a peer leader . . . " (p. 13).

On the Fall 2020 UNIV 101 instructor evaluation of peer leaders, more than
99% of instructors noted their peer or graduate leader was a valuable part of
the UNIV 101 experience. Additionally, more than 98% agreed that their peer
or graduate leader made high-quality contributions to class. These results
indicate the caliber of students recruited for the position and offer evidence

of the thorough training received by peer leaders in addition to the communication and support provided over the course of the semester.

## ■ Looking to the Future

As an innovator in peer education, University 101 Programs continues to advance toward the future. Some current initiatives include:

- engaging returning peer leaders in programming and events,
- recruiting a more diverse body of student leaders,
- enhancing technology infusion in the development and support of peer leaders to meet the needs of a digital generation and a world impacted by COVID-19, and
- streamlining processes to allow more time to be devoted to the developmental needs of a growing cohort of student leaders.

Engaging returning peer leaders in program-level activities, such as recruitment events, is an opportunity to leverage their experience and wisdom while giving them more opportunities to develop personally and professionally. Recruiting a more diverse body of student leaders will contribute to efforts to open the leadership pipeline at South Carolina to previously underrepresented students. A diverse cohort of peer leaders will give underrepresented students the opportunity to see someone who looks like themselves in a leadership role which will, in turn, increase their sense of belonging. It is also important to examine how the structure of the peer leader program (i.e., an unpaid volunteer position that requires students to enroll in a three-credit-hour course) may be a barrier to participation for some students. The University 101 Programs staff is also exploring how to use digital tools more effectively to facilitate the development and support of peer leaders while being mindful of continuing disparities in access to technology. Finally, streamlining processes will allow staff members more time to focus on the developmental needs of a growing cohort of student leaders. Important to this goal is navigating the balance of increasing efficiency while continuing to deliver an individualized experience. One clear measure of the success of the Peer Leader Program is the consistent returning peer leader cohort. Students enjoy and value the experience and are interested in serving another semester with a new group of first-year students. While the University 101 Peer Leader Program is an exemplar of peer support in first-year seminars, as student needs change and evolve, so will the program to maintain a legacy of excellence and success.

## ■ Conclusion

Since its inception, University 101 has helped first-year students transition into and through the University of South Carolina by building connections and fostering a sense of belonging. Beginning in 1993 with a couple dozen high-achieving juniors and seniors, peer leaders became an essential part of the course, providing invaluable support and mentorship to first-year students. The peer leader program has grown to more than 200 peer leaders selected from a competitive applicant pool. By serving in this role, students gain new skills that will have ongoing significance after graduation. As we adapt to the changing needs of students, the UNIV 101 peer leader component continues to evolve, providing holistic support for first-year students, instructors, and peer leaders alike.

### *References*

Astin, A. W. (1993). *What matters in college? Four critical years revisited.* Jossey-Bass.

Astin, A. W. (1999). Student involvement: A developmental theory for higher education. *Journal of College Student Development, 40*(5), 518–529.

Chickering, A. W. (1969). *Education and identity.* Jossey-Bass.

Fleming, J. (2021). *How to be human: An autistic man's guide to life.* Simon & Schuster.

Former peer leaders bring transferable skills into the workplace. (2020, January 14). University 101 Programs, University of South Carolina. https://sc.edu/about/offices _and_divisions/university_101/about/impact_stories/peerleaders_transferableskills .php.

Friedman, D. B., & Greene, S. (2020). A model for pulling wisdom from group discussion. *The Toolbox: A Teaching and Learning Resource for Instructors, 19.* https://sc .edu/nrc/system/pub_files/1598889201_0.pdf.

Friedman, D., & Sokol, K. (Eds.). (2021). *University 101 Faculty Resource Manual.* University of South Carolina, University 101 Programs.

Latino, J. A., & Ashcraft, M. L. (2012). *The first-year seminar: Designing, implementing, and assessing courses to support student learning and success: Vol. IV. Using peers in the classroom.* University of South Carolina, National Resource Center for The First-Year Experience and Students in Transition.

Newton, F. B., & Ender, S. C. (2010). *Students helping students: A guide for peer educators on college campuses* (2nd ed.). Jossey-Bass.

Shook, J. L., & Keup, J. R. (2012), The benefits of peer leader programs: An overview from the literature. *New Directions for Higher Education, 2012,* 5–16. https://doi .org/10.1002/he.20002.

Stone, M. E., & Jacobs, G. (Eds.). (2008). *Supplemental instruction: Improving first-year student success in high-risk courses* (Monograph No. 7, 3rd ed). University of South Carolina, National Resource Center for The First-Year Experience and Students in Transition.

Tobolowsky, B. F., & Associates. (2008). *2006 National Survey of First-Year Seminars: Continuing innovations in the collegiate curriculum* (Monograph No. 51). University of South Carolina, National Resource Center for The First-Year Experience and Students in Transition.

Upcraft, M. L., Gardner, J. N., Barefoot, B. O., & Associates. (2005). *Challenging and supporting the first-year student: A handbook for improving the first year of college.* Jossey-Bass.

Young, D. G. (2019). *2017 National Survey on the First-Year Experience: Creating and coordinating structures to support student success* (Research Report No. 9). University of South Carolina, National Resource Center for The First-Year Experience and Students in Transition.

Young, D. G., & Keup, J. K. (2018). To pay or not to pay: The influence of compensation as an external reward on learning outcomes or peer leaders. *Journal of College Student Development, 59*(2), 159–176. https://doi.org/10.1353/csd.2018.0015.

# Chapter 8

# Campus Partnerships

*Catherine S. Greene and Catherine Flowers*

n identifying institutions of excellence in the first-year experience, the Policy Center for the First Year of College (now the John N. Gardner Institute for Excellence in Undergraduate Education) laid out five criteria for evaluating highly successful first-year programs. One of these was the "involvement of a wide range of faculty, student affairs professionals, academic administrators, and other constituent groups in the design and delivery of first-year initiatives" and "evidence of meaningful partnerships rather than different groups working essentially in isolation" (Barefoot et al., 2005, p. 25). The University of South Carolina was identified as 1 of 13 institutions that fit this criterion for excellence in the first year of college—a selection no doubt due, in part, to a long-standing history of collaboration with partners throughout campus.[1]

University 101 is successful, in large part, because it unites offices across the institution in one shared commitment: to support students through the transition to college and beyond. Over the past 50 years, University 101 Programs has become central to a network of connections across the institution—not only through its diverse faculty but also through the inclusion of numerous campus offices and personnel in the design and implementation of the course itself. Through its committee structure, collaborative development of the course textbook, *Transitions,* and the delivery of campus partner presentations, University 101 Programs has created a campuswide investment in the first-year seminar. At the same time, the course has been instrumental in supporting critical student success initiatives at the university. This chapter explores how campus partnerships enable UNIV 101 to support students throughout their first year and beyond and how those partnerships lead to a sustainable first-year seminar and promote an institutional focus on student success.

## ■ A History of Collaboration

Through a harrowing experience in which protesting students barricaded President Thomas Jones in his office, he realized a disconnect was widening between students and the university. In an article from *The Daily Gamecock* outlining the program's history, executive director of University 101 Programs Dan Friedman reflected that "students were not coming to the university angry, but something about the experience was causing them to get angry . . . faculty didn't understand students, and students didn't really understand faculty" (Sullivan, 2020). In the aftermath of the 1970 campus riots, Jones reasoned that the best way to prevent future disquiet was to teach students to love the university.

When he submitted the proposal for the experimental University 101 course in 1972, he identified four goals, one of which was "to orient the student to the University and its resources" (Jones, 1972). University 101, even in its earliest imaginings, was dependent on a foundation that extended throughout the university's administrative structure. A list of faculty attached to the proposal shows instructors from virtually every department on campus. Although the course was created as a faculty development initiative, staff members were brought in early on as instructors. According to former director John Gardner, "Jones's vision was that having student affairs professionals intimately involved in the course would be good for student affairs, but it would also be very good for students, and it would be good for faculty, because it would be getting faculty and student affairs [professionals] to interact" (Gardner, personal communication, March 17, 2021). In fact, Jones agreed to create a new position for the fledgling Division of Student Affairs in exchange for student affairs staff teaching 16 sections of University 101 each year (Gardner, personal communication, March 17, 2021). The logistical need to fill instructor spots was certainly a driving force behind the staffing decision. Yet, incorporating staff as instructors marked an intentional choice to bring together the three major constituent groups at the university—faculty, staff, and students.

The idea behind University 101, then, was to build understanding between students and the university on multiple levels. Most immediately, students would build personal connections with their instructors. In a classroom model like no other, students and instructors would learn about each other as people and develop mutual respect they could carry with them beyond the class. University 101 would also orient students to campus resources through tours of offices and presentations from campus representatives. In a period in which the university was deeply divided between students and administration, the

University 101 classroom would provide common ground to share both grievances and values.

The importance of connecting students to the university is evident in John Gardner's 1973 UNIV 101 syllabus. He invited representatives from 25 campus offices into the classroom, and he required students to leave the classroom to explore campus resources and offices. From the beginning, Gardner recognized that University 101 would not be successful in a vacuum. Rather, its success would depend on connections throughout the university.

### ■ Committee Service

University 101 involves several dozen faculty and staff across the institution each year in the governance, service, and development of the course. The most direct way that University 101 Programs interacts with colleagues across campus is through regularly convening committees and task forces to foster the program's improvement.

University 101 Programs supports a wide range of committees. The groups collaborate on responses to institutional changes (such as the implications for UNIV 101 of a university-wide attendance policy introduced in 2020), but they also provide direction on the program's response to larger emerging issues (e.g., calls for racial justice). These committees—some permanent and others convened in response to changing needs—work to align UNIV 101 curriculum with the priorities of University 101 Programs and the university.

Collaboration between University 101 Programs and other university entities serves a dual purpose: (a) shaping program decisions with stakeholder input and (b) creating buy-in from all corners of the UofSC campus. When numerous stakeholders have seats at the table in the development of all aspects of the program, UNIV 101 becomes a product not just of a single office but of diverse perspectives across campus. As a result, faculty and staff share pride in the course.

### *Committees on Governance and Structure*

Several committees focus on the governance and structure of the course and are convened to respond to major changes in the program. The University 101 Special Advisory Committee provides guidance and counsel to the executive director of University 101 Programs on issues concerning curriculum, faculty recruitment and development, and policies. The group also serves as the hearing committee for student grievances and petitions. In addition, the committee reviews and approves new courses as necessary. The committee consists of representation from tenure-track faculty, UNIV instructors, campus administrators, and at least one undergraduate student.

Other committees function on an ad hoc basis to address new programmatic challenges. In 2010, for example, the Communication Task Force gathered in response to two challenges with regards to communication and collaboration: (a) a concern about instructors being overwhelmed with requests each week to make announcements, give surveys, and host guest speakers; and (b) a strategy for effectively communicating with instructors. The group was charged with identifying what information would be most beneficial to instructors—from the program itself and from others on campus—and the most effective methods for delivering that information. Similarly, the Course Attendance Policy Committee worked to align UNIV 101 attendance policies with institutional attendance policy changes in 2020. Other groups, like the Instructor Advisory Council, bring UNIV 101 instructors together to discuss challenges, course requirements, and professional development.

University 101 regularly adapts to meet the needs of students and the institution through these committees. Every five to seven years, University 101 Programs convenes the Program Review Committee. Through this committee, University 101 collaborates with departments across campus to review the students' emerging needs and make recommendations to the common course requirements and curricular support materials.

The program review process allows University 101 to adapt to the changing climate of the university and further develop strategies to support first-year students' needs. The Program Review Committee is comprised of a diverse group of instructors, UNIV 101 staff members, and representatives from offices and departments across the university. Including a range of disciplines and departments enables the committee to reflect diverse perspectives and campus expertise.

### Committees on Resources and Curriculum

Committees of instructors and University 101 staff work together to author and enhance curricular resources like the *University 101 Faculty Resource Manual* (Friedman & Sokol, 2021) and the Campus Resource Guide (a resource updated annually to highlight important information about university services relevant to first-year students). Staff and instructors also assemble to develop materials to address emerging challenges facing first-year students. For example, the Antiracism Lesson Plan Committee convened in response to racial violence and calls for justice in 2020. The result of this committee was a comprehensive curriculum guide for addressing topics of racism and discrimination. Involving campus partners in the development of curricular materials creates more well-rounded resources and a better course overall.

This shared commitment is particularly evident in the course textbook, *Transitions*. The text—a reference guide and workbook—covers topics relevant to the first-year experience, from academic integrity to employability, from mental health to off-campus living, and from healthy relationships to study skills. The book serves as a comprehensive resource to students as they navigate their first year at the university.

What makes *Transitions* truly special, though, is that it is the product of a year-round development process across numerous offices on campus. Each year, departments author and update their own chapters, providing crucial context and resources for instructors and students who use the text. Through an ongoing editing process with University 101 Programs, departments develop content immediately relevant to first-year students about their resources, services, and guidance. In 2020, 17 departments contributed chapters, which they wrote and edited to ensure information was accurate and current. The textbook evolves along with the services offered by offices on campus and serves as the central reference for students finding their way through their first year.

### ■ Campus Partner Presentations

The most visible connection University 101 Programs has with other campus departments is through campus partner (CP) presentations. Each semester University 101 coordinates approximately 15 presentations from 10 to 12 campus departments. Altogether, CPs typically offer more than 1,200 presentations to UNIV 101 students each fall semester. This section describes why campus departments choose to dedicate considerable time and resources to presentations in the course and how University 101 Programs and CPs mutually benefit from the process.

University departments and offices that support University 101 course goals and learning outcomes develop and offer CP presentations each year. These presentations provide an opportunity for students to hear directly from campus offices that provide valuable information and resources related to the needs of first-year students, such as financial literacy, mental health services, bystander intervention, and many other topics. In bringing these departments into the classroom, UNIV 101 connects students with various campus resources while helping the campus partner fulfill their department's mission.

Although UNIV 101 has always welcomed outside presenters into the classroom to share their knowledge, the process has evolved over the years to better serve students, instructors, and campus partners. As UNIV 101 refined its mission and goals through the years, so too did CP presentations. In its earliest years, the course's mission was to build relationships between students and campus offices. Exposing students to an abundance of campus

Leadership and Service Center facilitating a campus partner presentation

resources within the course seemed the best strategy to achieve that goal. And so, at first, UNIV 101 sections brought in all the campus representatives they could accommodate. The 1991–1992 strategic plan for University 101 Programs points to a shift in focus away from quantity of presentations to their quality. That year's plan aimed to establish more consistency among University 101 sections, including CP presentations, and identified key issues relevant to student success: "drug/alcohol abuse, cultural diversity, racial and gender tolerance and understanding, sexually transmitted diseases, acquaintance rape, campus safety, stress management." Weekly presentations for University 101 sections devoted to those issues were proposed. By 2008, all University 101 sections had six required pre-scheduled presentations on the Carolinian Creed, sexual health, alcohol and drugs, diversity, academic integrity, and library resources.

As a result of the 2009 program review process (described in Chapter 3), University 101 Programs decided to offer instructors more flexibility and creativity in developing course curriculum and responding to the changing needs of first-year students. University 101 Programs empowered instructors to select the presentations for their classes. The move from required presentations to elective ones pioneered a path toward more meaningful CP presentations. Instructors now had the opportunity to select the presentations they felt would be most valuable and relevant to their students and incorporate them more intentionally. Alongside that curricular flexibility, University 101

Programs also recognized the need to support instructors through their use of these presentations. The next section of this chapter highlights how University 101 Programs selects, supports, and evaluates CP presentations.

## Campus Partner Task Force

In 2012, University 101 Programs convened a task force to explore issues and challenges around the process for supporting CP presentations in the classroom. The task force was composed of 15 stakeholders, including University 101 instructors, campus partners, and individuals who serve in both roles. Several factors led to the development of this task force, which ultimately improved and refined the presentation process for both instructors and campus partners. First, the number of UNIV 101 sections increased by more than 80% between 2009 and 2019. Limited staffing and resources complicated the partners' collective abilities to serve an expanding cohort of UNIV 101 students. At the same time, an increasing number of departments and groups wanted to deliver their message to UNIV 101 students. It was important that UNIV 101 not become the "homeroom" for the university, delivering messages for other departments, units, and student groups. University 101 Programs needed a process for selecting and prioritizing content that would balance support for campus offices and the integrity of the UNIV 101 experience, purpose, and goals. Finally, many sections of UNIV 101 were relying too heavily on the use of CP presentations in the classroom and thereby reducing the overall quality of the classroom experience by disrupting the course flow and community development important for fostering persistence.

The task force was asked to develop processes and criteria for approving new presentations, evaluating presentations and sharing feedback with campus partners, renewing presentations each year, and scheduling presentations. This task force's work was instrumental in laying the foundation for much of the process University 101 Programs uses to support the delivery of CP presentations. Key action items included:

- building a structured proposal form that included criteria to increase consistency in submissions and the review process,
- requiring campus partners to participate in the renewal process on an annual basis, using the proposal form as a template for renewal with an additional question about what was learned from the assessment data,
- expanding and standardizing presentation evaluation efforts across all course sections,
- providing additional training opportunities for campus partners focused on topics ranging from best practices in active learning and facilitation to using technology to support the sign-up process, and

- creating more support materials for instructors and campus partners, including documents that highlight which course learning outcomes are supported by presentations and best practices for using CP presentations.

## Presentation Criteria

A key development from the CP Task Force was implementing criteria to help maintain consistency across all presentation offerings. All presentations for University 101 must meet the following criteria:

- The presentation is sponsored by a UofSC office or agency.
- The presentation addresses at least one UNIV 101 learning outcome.
- The topic is critical to student success in the first year of college or is connected to a major university priority or initiative.
- The topic and material are relevant and of interest to all first-year students and section types.
- A presentation is the most appropriate method to address the topic without duplicating or overlapping with the scope of other presentations.

These criteria help ensure that University 101 Programs can continue to guarantee high-quality, valuable presentations in the University 101 classroom while meeting its goal of connecting students to resources on campus that support their success in and beyond the classroom. All presentations, new and returning, are evaluated against these criteria annually to guarantee they continue to be meaningful resources for students.

## Proposal and Approval Process

University 101 Programs ensures the CP presentations' effectiveness in the first-year seminar through the CP proposal process. Any department wishing to offer a new presentation or renew an existing one must participate in this process. In the proposal process, campus partners provide an outline of their presentation, clarify which University 101 course goals and learning outcomes their presentation supports, and provide an overview of the training their presenters go through to prepare them to deliver presentations in the classroom. If the presentation is being renewed from the previous year, then campus partners must also discuss any challenges the presentation encountered in the previous year, as well as how they plan to address those challenges moving forward. The proposal includes student and instructor data on two prompts from the assessment of the previous year's presentation: "This presentation was valuable," and, "I would recommend this presentation for other University 101 classes."

Once submitted, the CP Review Committee evaluates the presentation proposal each spring. University 101 staff, instructors, students, and orientation staff gather to offer feedback on presentation proposals and ensure there is no duplication of content with New Student Orientation. Each of these groups offers valuable perspectives on the alignment of CP presentations with UNIV 101 course outcomes and student needs. The proposal review process, which typically lasts two months, asks committee members to assess the learning outcomes of the presentation and the value of the content to the first-year experience. The committee is tasked with answering key questions about the presentation proposal:

1. Is the content relevant and appropriate for a first-year experience classroom?
2. Are the learning outcomes of the presentation achievable?
3. Is this information going to be presented at orientation? If so, how does this presentation differ?
4. What will first-year students glean from this presentation?

With all members' feedback assembled, the committee meets to synthesize their comments and offer recommendations for the proposals. University 101 Programs then works with campus partners to incorporate changes and address any issues raised by the committee. In subsequent semesters, campus partners may renew their presentations with alterations to meet changing first-year student needs. The Campus Partner Review Committee is another testament to the goal of bringing together a variety of perspectives and expertise to contribute to the development of the University 101 course curriculum.

### Signing Up for Campus Partner Presentations

At one point, University 101 Programs scheduled all CP presentations for UNIV 101. This led to several challenges, the most significant being the impact on the instructor's ability to create a meaningful course plan. Presentations were scheduled at times that did not make conceptual sense based on the other content the instructor had planned for the course. In 2009, University 101 Programs realized a more meaningful approach would be allowing the instructors to schedule presentations based on the way they fit within their syllabus, thus allowing them to integrate the content throughout the semester. While this new model allowed instructors greater flexibility and choice in presentations for their class, it came with logistical challenges. Decentralized communication between individual instructors and various departments—all of which had their own systems for scheduling presentations—could be difficult for instructors to navigate. As the number of UNIV 101 sections grew from 145 sections in 2009 to 271 sections in 2020, the burden of scheduling presentations became even more challenging. Streamlining the scheduling of CP presentations became a critical goal.

Throughout the years, a variety of strategies emerged to support scheduling CP presentations, including a resource fair at the annual Building Connections Conference and repurposing other scheduling software for this task. By 2019, each participating department was offering between 50 and 200 CP presentations during the fall semester, and it was imperative to find a process that worked well for both campus partners and instructors.

In collaboration with IBM, University 101 Programs developed a customized online scheduling platform, ScheduleCenter, specific to the process for signing up for presentations. This system simplified a complex problem, and over the years, has been expanded to house all the major aspects of CP presentations, including the proposal and evaluation processes. The search for a solution highlights University 101's interconnectedness not just to other departments but to technological innovations on campus.

### Presentation Assessment

Assessing the CP presentation effectiveness is critical to their ongoing success and development, University 101 measures this in a variety of different ways, including ongoing conversations with campus partners throughout the year.

Students complete a survey at the end of each presentation, and these data are compiled by the campus partner. Similarly, instructors complete an electronic survey at the end of the presentation. These data are compiled in a database accessible by both University 101 Programs and the campus partner. Formative and summative data, gathered throughout the semester, allow campus partners and UNIV 101 staff to continuously monitor presentation effectiveness. Student and instructor feedback also informs the committee's evaluation of the presentation for the upcoming fall semester and sheds light on any changes necessary to improve the content or structure of the presentation. Data are compiled at the end of the semester into a longitudinal report comparing the data from previous years. This report serves as the jumping-off point for University 101 Programs and campus partners to discuss the presentation.

CP presentations are also assessed to determine the degree to which they support the course outcomes. This is done by comparing students' perceptions of learning on the end-of-course evaluations in sections that hosted a presentation compared to those in sections without the presentation. These reports, known as the CP presentation impact reports (see Table 8.1 for one example), provide another opportunity to understand how presentations contribute to the overall learning in the course.

**TABLE 8.1.** Financial Literacy Campus
Partner Presentation Impact Report

| QUESTION | PARTICIPATION | | NONPARTICIPATION | | |
|---|---|---|---|---|---|
| | *N* | *M* | *N* | *M* | *P-VALUE* |
| *As a result of this course, I better understand . . .* | | | | | |
| How to set goals (e.g., college, personal, career). | 211 | 6.27 | 1,924 | 6.10 | .024 |
| How to manage my personal finances. | 213 | 5.96 | 1,864 | 5.30 | .000 |
| The impact of credit on my life (e.g., credit cards, loans) | 216 | 5.91 | 1,888 | 5.33 | .000 |

*Note.* Responses on a 7-point scale with 1 = *strongly disagree* and 7 = *strongly agree.*

## Using Campus Partner Presentations

Over the years, it has become critical to support campus partners in their development of presentations and instructors in their use of those presentations. Through the Teaching Experience Workshop for new instructors and ongoing faculty development efforts, University 101 Programs imparts best practices for intentionally incorporating CP presentations in class.

### Selecting Campus Partner Presentations

CP presentations are most successful when instructors intentionally select and incorporate them into the course schedule, setting aside time for students to reflect on them. CP presentation assessment has shown four to six presentations per section to be the optimal number in UNIV 101 related to overall course effectiveness. This range allows instructors and students to benefit from the expertise of campus partners without eclipsing the class community. Just as important as the number of presentations scheduled are which presentations instructors choose to bring into class. In making that decision, UNIV 101 encourages faculty to consider the profile of their class (Is it a section of first-generation college students, for example?) as well as their own strengths and expertise. Some instructors may feel comfortable facilitating a discussion with their students around financial literacy, while others may feel they lack the expertise to do so. Similarly, some instructors will feel comfortable discussing sexual decision making with their students, while others would prefer having a staff member from Campus Wellness guide the conversation.

### Incorporating Campus Partner Presentations

CP presentations are most valuable when they enhance the content of the course and fit seamlessly into the instructor's course calendar. If an instructor schedules the Career Center to facilitate the Super Strong Assessment with their students, for example, students will garner more from the presentation if they have already spent time reflecting on how their values might impact their major or career choice.

### Reflecting on Campus Partner Presentations

Presentations will also be more effective if students have an opportunity to reflect and make meaning of them. We encourage instructors to use the presentation as a catalyst for further discussion. After the Super Strong Assessment, for example, instructors can help students discover how their interests translate into academic and professional success through a follow-up assignment or class conversation. Campus partners provide sample assignments and supplemental lesson plans to facilitate further conversation on presentation topics. University 101 Programs also provides instructors additional resources to supplement and support CP presentations.

### *Impact on Departments*

Campus partners dedicate considerable time and thought to developing and facilitating presentations to hundreds of University 101 students each year despite managing a full suite of services and programs. The presentations benefit the departments by generating student traffic to their offices. As such, one of the primary goals of having these presentations, introducing students to campus resources they can use throughout their time at the university, is accomplished. On the University 101 Former Student Survey administered in 2019, 61% of respondents indicated that as a result of hearing a guest speaker or visiting a campus office during their UNIV 101 class, they later used that campus resource or service. Hearing from a representative of the Student Success Center, for example, leads students to feel more comfortable accessing the office's resources in the future. Lauren Brown (personal communication, March 22, 2021) of the Student Success Center commented on the benefit of partnering with University 101:

> Through our partnership, we're able to get additional face time with students to provide them with both academic and financial information necessary for their transition while also supporting instructors in satisfying their course learning outcomes. We recognize both of our departments cannot accomplish all their goals alone. Therefore, we've become

part of a working entity with a shared purpose—student success—that ultimately creates a win-win situation.

Similarly, Jason Halterman (personal communication, March 23, 2021) of Sexual Assault and Violence Intervention and Prevention noted:

> Being a campus partner has been a tremendous help and experience professionally. The obvious component is getting out of the office and interacting with a new set of students and professionals; it has helped us build connections with new offices, student organizations, instructors, and residence halls. It also helps give us a pulse of what is happening in the campus community and how we need to adapt our programming to better serve the needs of students. The experiences and interactions we have as campus partners truly enhance our professional work and are an exceptionally valuable development opportunity. I'm very thankful to be a partner with U101!

CP presentations benefit students, instructors, and campus departments for many reasons that extend far beyond University 101's original intent to give students "a broader and deeper acquaintance with the university's offerings and resources" (Atkinson et al., 1972). When campus partners and instructors work together, students feel empowered to seek out the resources they need to be successful. When students feel empowered, they positively impact other students to seek their own success. When campus partners enter the UNIV 101 classroom, they open the door to a supportive relationship with students that will extend far beyond their first semester.

### ■ Support for University Initiatives

This chapter has explored the many ways UNIV 101 draws on the support and expertise of educators and departments across the campus to build a strong course. University 101 is equally important in supporting key university initiatives. Two highly visible examples of UNIV 101's support of other initiatives is its contributing role in the First-Year Reading Experience and in the university's Quality Enhancement Plans, USC Connect and Experience by Design.

#### First-Year Reading Experience

According to the 2017 National Survey of the First-Year Experience, 38.3% of institutions offer a common reading initiative as part of the first-year experience (Soria, 2019). While the University of South Carolina is far from the only institution to offer a first-year reading experience, it stands apart in the longevity of this initiative. For 27 years, University 101 Programs, in partnership with the Office of the Provost, has steered the First-Year Reading Experience (FYRE). The program has been a valued tradition at South Carolina since its inception. FYRE annually selects a book to serve as a common reading experience among first-year students. With its partners, UNIV 101 develops programming and curriculum centered on the book's themes. While the events that support FYRE have evolved throughout the years, it continues to provide opportunities for collaboration among campus departments and for common curricular experiences among incoming students.

FYRE began in 1994 with four goals in mind. First, Associate Provost and Dean for Undergraduate Affairs Donald Greiner wanted to begin the university's Welcome Week with an academic focus. Second, FYRE would allow students to participate in a college-level academic discussion in a nonthreatening, ungraded atmosphere. Faculty-led small groups would serve as first-year students' introduction to the academic give-and-take that they could expect to experience in their college courses. Third, the program would create a common academic experience for the university's incoming students. Students from all over the country, from varying academic and social backgrounds, would bring their insights to the table in their discussion of the text. Finally, FYRE would give students an opportunity to interact with faculty outside class. Through this experience, students would see that relationships with professors can extend beyond the doors of a classroom; that professors could be approachable, supportive, and—ultimately—human. This aim mirrors Jones's goal in his original conception of UNIV 101: to bring staff, faculty, and students together on common ground.

What grew from those original goals is an experience that inspires collaboration across multiple departments on campus. For example, students in the School of Visual Art and Design create an alternate cover as an assignment for a graphic design course, and the winning design is often used as the custom cover for the books distributed to the UofSC community. University Libraries have also been a key collaborator, curating exhibits related to the FYRE text and the author.

The program grew from 300 students and 30 faculty members in 1994 to include the entire first-year class in 2005. FYRE's growth meant it required additional support and a larger venue. A joint effort with University Conference Services moved the experience to the Carolina Coliseum and eventually the Colonial Life Arena, with 250 discussion groups facilitated in classrooms across campus.

Now, FYRE is incorporated throughout the entire first semester rather than as a single event during Welcome Week. A committee of faculty, staff, and administrators read and select a book whose topics they deem particularly relevant to the incoming class. Past years' texts have centered on information literacy, sustainability, and racism, among other topics. Under the model in place since 2016, the university distributes books to all incoming first-year students and invites them to attend the author's lecture. The mode of discussion has evolved over the years but now takes place primarily in UNIV 101 classes and through a one-day event.

A second committee, consisting of University 101 Programs staff, instructors, and university staff, develops a FYRE curriculum guide. This instructor guide contains activities and assignments relevant to the book. University 101 Programs provides sustained support for the book through faculty development workshops. Many UNIV 101 instructors select the FYRE book as their supplemental text for the course because of the robust curricular support University 101 Programs provides around it.

### Quality Enhancement Plans

The Quality Enhancement Plan (QEP) focuses on improving student learning or success and is connected to the Southern Association of Colleges and Schools accreditation process (SACSCOC, 2020). University 101 has been a key partner in two QEPs: USC Connect, established in 2011, and Experience by Design, launched in March 2021. Both efforts are led by the Center for Integrative and Experiential Learning (CIEL). USC Connect "focused on integrative learning in the context of making connections within and beyond the classroom and emphasizing this learning to solve problems through solution-oriented thinking" (University of South Carolina, 2021, p. 12). Experience by Design builds on USC Connect, focusing on beyond-the-classroom engagement and reflection for all students, with an emphasis on supporting student populations with lower-than-expected retention and graduation rates and who have been less engaged in cocurricular learning historically. University 101 partners with CIEL to introduce engagement opportunities and critical reflection in the first-year course. Because UNIV 101 enrolls nearly 80% of the first-year cohort on the Columbia campus and a very high percentage of students on the Palmetto College campuses,[2] CIEL identified the course as the ideal support for new students seeking connections beyond the classroom.

Student engagement and meaningful reflection are an integral part of UNIV 101. The *Transitions* textbook includes a chapter about student engagement, opportunities for reflection underpin the course structure, and each section of UNIV 101 engages in a beyond-the-classroom experience, either as a class or individually. University 101 faculty development initiatives also support the goals of engagement, integrative learning, and reflection. As noted in the Experience by Design QEP, "This training appears to be highly effective as 87.8% of U101 students indicated that their instructor encouraged them to participate in beyond-the-classroom learning experiences, and 89.5% said that the course helped them to understand how outside-the-classroom experiences contribute to their overall learning (2018 end-of-course evaluation survey)" (University of South Carolina, 2021, p. 50).

University 101 and CIEL believe the course is a good venue for teaching students the basics of reflection and the value of and strategies to pursue engagement opportunities.

University 101's role in the FYRE and initiatives around integrative learning underscore the program's respect and value on campus. It is often sought out as a key partner for major initiatives and understood to be a leading voice on the first-year experience. University 101 frequently contributes to other university initiatives in the same way other departments offer the UNIV 101 course their consistent support. In identifying programs and initiatives that share a mutual commitment to positive first-year experiences for students, University 101 bolsters its own mission, the missions of other offices, and the mission of the University of South Carolina.

## ■ Conclusion

This chapter has described a long history of collaboration between University 101 and partners on campus that share a commitment to enriching students' first-year experience. From its inception, the UNIV 101 course invited historically siloed groups to gather on common ground: a classroom where all views would be heard and the transition to college would be supported. The UNIV 101 classroom established a community for students to connect with faculty, staff, and each other. An essential part of President Jones's legacy in establishing the program—and John Gardner's contribution in implementing it— is UNIV 101's knowledge that its success is wholly dependent on connections throughout the university.

True to its roots, UNIV 101 continues to invite many voices to the table. Through committee service, presentations in UNIV 101 classrooms, collaboration on the course textbook, and support of key university initiatives, University 101 centers itself in a web of connections that fortify the first-year experience. It is a network that benefits all involved. University 101 is reinforced in its mission to foster student success. Departments who contribute their expertise to *Transitions* or campus partner presentations see deeper meaning in their work as they guide students through their first-year experience and to their resources. Instructors hear student perspectives and adapt their own work to fit these perspectives. The University of South Carolina benefits from first-year students driven to love the university, to lead it, and to continue their growth.

Perhaps most importantly, because of UNIV 101's connections with campus partners, students leave their first semester with the knowledge that a support network exists far beyond the UNIV 101 classroom. Through the offices and departments that generously share their resources and expertise in the classroom, students connect their first year with the remainder of their time at the University of South Carolina. Integrating campus partners in the UNIV 101 classroom plays a critical role not only in the transition to college but also in the transition from the first semester to the remainder of students' undergraduate experiences.

University 101 opens the door to meaningful first-year experiences for students. Campus partners ensure that when they leave the community of their UNIV 101 classrooms, students will find many more doors where they are welcomed and supported throughout the semesters that follow.

## References

Atkinson, F., Caldwell, W., Heckel, R., Hiers, J., Mulvaney, R., Rempel, R. (1972). *Proposal for an experimental freshman program.* University of South Carolina.

Barefoot, B. O., Gardner, J. N., Cutright, M., Morris, L., Schroeder, C. C., Schwartz, S. W., Siegel, M. J., & Swing, R. L. (2005). *Achieving and Sustaining Institutional Excellence for the First Year of College.* Jossey-Bass.

Friedman, D., & Sokol, K. (Eds.). (2021). *University 101 Faculty Resource Manual.* University of South Carolina, University 101 Programs.

Jones, T. (1972). *Original course proposal for University 101.* University of South Carolina.

Soria, K. M. (2019). Common-reading programs. In D. G. Young (Ed.), *2017 National Survey on the First-Year Experience: Creating and coordinating structures to support student success* (Research Report No. 9, pp. 45–52). University of South Carolina, National Resource Center for The First-Year Experience & Students in Transition.

Southern Association of Colleges and Schools Commission on Colleges (SACSCOC). (2020). *The quality enhancement plan.* https://sacscoc.org/app/uploads/2020/01/Quality-Enhancement-Plan-1.pdf.

Sullivan, N. (2020, August 13). Rooted in riots: USC's nationally recognized University 101 program was born out of student rebellion. *The Daily Gamecock.* https://www.dailygamecock.com/article/2020/08/history-of-u101-sullivan-news.

University of South Carolina. (2021, March 22–25). Experience by design (Quality enhancement plan). https://sc.edu/about/initiatives/center_for_integrative_experiential_learning/documents/about/experience_by_design_qep.pdf.

University 101 Programs. (1991–1992). *University 101 course strategic plan.* University of South Carolina.

# Chapter 9

# The South Carolina Model

**Lessons Learned and
Recommendations**

*Daniel B. Friedman and John N. Gardner*

We wrote this book in part to appropriately mark the passage of exactly a half century of the University 101 course and all its integral components. As such, it is an opportunity for us to encourage our university community to reflect on this journey and the significant lessons learned and to provide a baseline for moving forward over the next 50 years. This book also provides the most complete compendium of the University 101 story, preserving our historical record for future practitioners and scholars at the University of South Carolina and elsewhere. Finally, we wrote this book to inspire others, especially those who are good enough to be "retained" to this point in our project. Our narrative is a hopeful one, produced during the height of the COVID-19 pandemic and during a time of significant economic disruption, political upheaval, and long overdue attention to racial injustice in the United States. The South Carolina model was designed to meet the needs of entering college students during a similarly tumultuous time. And, we believe its long history signals its continuing promise both at our institution and others.

This work has made us optimistic about what can be done both despite and because of all the forces that could have a far greater negative impact on our students were we not engaged in this work. This book's earlier chapters have described four significant outcomes—what we might also see as legacies—of UNIV 101 at the University of South Carolina. First, the course has improved the beginning college experience for thousands of students on this campus. By encouraging educators at campuses around the world to explore the transition to college for their own students, it has undoubtedly reshaped higher education for millions of others. Second, the course has focused on improving student learning for the sake of learning. The student experience has always been the primary content of UNIV 101, with a process-driven instructional model focused on helping students make sense of that experience and find the tools and strategies to facilitate their success in college and the world beyond. Third, decades of course assessment have demonstrated UNIV 101's efficacy in improving students' academic performance (i.e., grades), their retention, and ultimately, their graduation rates. Moreover, we know that the course structure—specifically, a reliance on engaging pedagogies to help students develop a sense of belonging and connect them to support resources in a timely way—contributes to these outcomes. Finally, we know that course has served the equity agenda at the heart of President Thomas Jones's educational experiments in the late 1960s and early 1970s. It has been incredibly effective in supporting academic performance, retention, and graduation for Black students, students with a lower SES, and those who are the first in their families to attend college.

In this concluding chapter, we look back over the last 50 years to highlight some of our most significant takeaways from directing this course with the hope that these lessons learned will offer insights to practitioners on other campuses who are launching, evaluating, or reviving a first-year seminar. Then, looking beyond our own campus experience, we briefly describe what we believe the promise of the extended orientation course model to be. In closing, we reaffirm the values that have successfully guided this course for half a century.

## ■ 50 Years of University 101: What We've Learned About Improving the College Experience

As unacademic as it may sound, UNIV 101 was developed by a college president who believed students could and should be taught to love the university. After the campus unrest of May 1970, Thomas Jones concluded the students had not entered college as angry rioters ready to burn down his office building. Something had happened to them, alienating them from their professors, from learning, and the university. They had become angry. Then, as now, we sought to give the students a reason to love the university and their place in it. Or, as the course purpose states, University 101 is designed

> to help new students make a successful transition to campus, both academically and personally. The course aims to foster a sense of belonging, promote engagement in the curricular and co-curricular life of the university, develop critical thinking skills and help to clarify purpose, meaning, and direction. (https://sc.edu/about/offices_and_divisions/university_101/courses/)

University 101 is not a cure-all, of course. Some students still struggle to find their place or make a successful transition, and yes, there have been a few student protests in the last 50 years. But no rioting and no attempts to burn down the administration building. We believe the course's remarkable and enduring success is due to several key factors, which we present as lessons learned.

### The Central Role of Course Leadership

For any initiative to stand the test of time, attention to its leadership is vital. We have been remarkably fortunate to enjoy high-level institutional support and stable course leadership throughout the course's history. Our history suggests the critical roles to be played by institutional leaders at all levels—from senior administrators and faculty senate to department heads and current student leaders. Selecting and supporting outstanding course and program leaders is tremendously significant. For 50 years, University 101 has been a priority for all University of South Carolina presidents and its Board of Trustees.

Mentoring has been a consistent theme of our leadership history—and one of the ways that senior administrators and others have communicated the value of the course director role. Our directors have been mentored in the course leadership role by various institutional leaders: presidents, provosts, senior faculty, a preceding course leader, and others. The first executive director was mentored by the founding president from 1972 until three weeks before he died in 1981, seven years after he had departed from the university. Our leaders have never outgrown their need for mentoring—the continuing recognition for and drive to foster their own learning and development may be a factor in our remarkable stability of course leadership.

We have learned that securing the right leadership is critical, as is retaining and supporting that leadership. Since the first permanent appointed leader for University 101 in 1974, only four individuals have led the course. Given the more normative administrative leadership turnover in higher education, this history indicates extraordinary stability and continuity. Undoubtedly, part of the course's success is due to its ability to attract proven leaders who have already demonstrated a high level of institutional commitment. Other institutions can model this success by creating sufficiently attractive positions—both in terms of compensation and the symbolic and real value accorded to the role—to incentivize just that.

### Institutional Ownership for The First-Year Seminar

University 101 is owned by the entire university—faculty, administration, staff, and students. The course has had several administrative homes over the past 50 years, and our experience has been that it has never been associated primarily with its place on the organizational chart. Instead, it has always been a university-wide effort. University 101 is not, after all, just a course for first-year students. Yes, it is a learning experience for first-year students. But it is also a transformative experience for full-time faculty and staff, upper-class student peer leaders, and the entire institution.

University 101 is an entire institutional ecosystem focused on facilitating successful adjustment and learning of new students—and many new faculty and staff need to learn about their new university to teach new students about it. Faculty development has always been one of UNIV 101's core components. Participating in the training and teaching the course help faculty and staff learn more about the university and its students. These experiences also transform the way faculty and staff teach and serve students elsewhere on campus.

Understanding this ecosystem's dynamics can all be reduced to one word: partnerships. We believe that no one program alone can adequately address the plethora of student needs. Instead, colleges and universities need an ecosystem that unifies and coordinates the delivery of institutional resources and services to first-year students. University 101 has both depended on those partnerships to support its own growth and development and served as a key partner in helping others achieve goals related to the first college year at the unit and institutional level.

Decades of research on college student development have pointed to the formative influences of peers on undergraduate students during their college years. In short, peers can be, in many cases, more effective transmitters of institutional norms and values than faculty and staff. Building on that knowledge, we combined in UNIV 101 a seminal learning opportunity for entering students and a significant personal and leadership development experience for our most able cohort of future leaders—a win/win for all students. Since we introduced peer leaders as co-teachers of UNIV 101 in 1993, more than 2,500 upper-level students have participated in this role, taking ownership of and providing leadership for the course.

The interest the Board of Trustees takes in University 101 is further evidence of institutional ownership of the course. In many cases, individual trustees are elected by the state legislature to represent their home districts. As such, they want to communicate institutional efforts to support student success to their constituents back home. Thus, the board has requested updates on the course on several occasions over the past 50 years. One trustee (a former chairman) taught a section of University 101. Another participated in instructor training to understand the value of this voluntary professional development opportunity for teaching faculty and staff about the university they serve.

Other University 101 constituents highlight the extent to which the course has become embedded in the university's fabric. We know through anecdotal feedback, for example, that parents who took UNIV 101 or were simply at the university when the course was offered make their students take the course. We also know that high school counselors point to UNIV 101 as a symbol of the university's commitment to ensuring new student success and encourage students to apply to this large university without fear of being ignored or treated like a number.

Finally, the high enrollment levels among first-year students in what is still primarily an elective course speak to its place as a university-wide initiative. The proportion of the first-year cohort that takes UNIV 101 has steadily increased to 83% in the fall of 2021. Beyond that, we recognize that what we call the critical mass theory is in play with UNIV 101. In short, we believe if enough students (i.e., a critical mass) do anything and if that something has value, they will share it with their roommates, classmates, and friends. Thus, the actual impact of University 101 very likely reaches beyond the 83% of the students who enroll in the course.

The strong identification of an initiative with a campus does not happen overnight, and it is not the work of a single inspirational leader. Instead, it takes focused, intentional effort and involves identifying and cultivating the constituencies both on and off campus to support program sustainability for the long term. Those constituencies and the strategies needed to cultivate their support will vary by institution.

## Adopting a Growth Mindset About Student Success

University 101 has continuously operated with what has been variously called a talent-development or strengths-oriented perspective (Schreiner et al., 2020). We contend that for courses like University 101 to succeed, program administrators, instructors, and others involved with the course must both like college students and believe that they can be taught college success. Specifically, this means we affirm there is a body of information, knowledge, skills, attitudes, and values that can be taught in a course like UNIV 101 by individuals who have been intentionally trained to teach such content and who then hold students accountable in an academic, credit-bearing course for learning and using such material, the mastery of which can be measured empirically. When institutions and their agents approach student success in this way, they foster growth or learning mindsets among students, faculty, staff, and administrators (Baldwin et al., 2020).

## Responsiveness to Changing Needs of Students

We believe perennial, consistent, and predictable truths define the beginning college experience. Students will always need to make friends. They will always need help adjusting to faculty expectations. They will always need help developing specific academic skills. Some of them will always be homesick. Most of them will always need help in making better decisions. But some of the support and knowledge that they will need will change as society, the institution, families, and the students themselves change. So, while University 101 powerfully illustrates the need to remain committed to and consistent with institutional and course traditions, the course also demonstrates the power of constantly assessing student needs and therefore redesigning course goals, content, faculty training, and pedagogies. Thus, any course of this kind must remain dynamic, simultaneously reflecting and shaping its host culture.

## Grading and Academic Credit Drive Student Engagement

We have learned over 50 years that our model of awarding three credits for an extended orientation course is essential for achieving the desired outcomes. The value of the credit hour as a measure of learning or content mastery has been widely debated. It is a measure of one thing only: the amount of time spent in instruction per week. This amount of credit is tremendously important to UNIV 101, as it gives us time to engage with content and experiences the students would probably not have otherwise. Perhaps equally important, the course looks and feels like the other courses students take in the first year, for which students' efforts are rewarded and for which they receive credit toward a degree.

While credit amount is significant to achieving the course objectives and desired outcomes, we have also found that the grading method is critical. For more than 15 years, UNIV 101's grading structure was pass/fail, which reflected the pedagogical ethos of the early 1970s, when credit/no credit courses came into vogue. For years, students told us if only we would give them letter grades, they would take the course more seriously and do more work. And the instructors told us the same thing. They found it much harder to meaningfully evaluate the quality of coursework when the only options were satisfactory or unsatisfactory. The decision to assign letter grades for the course has been unquestionably one of the most significant changes we have made during its history. The three-credit-hour designation is a motivator and a reward, especially when combined with the traditional letter grading system. In general, through our experiences working, consulting, and talking with other seminar leaders, we have found that when institutions require students to take an extended orientation seminar but do NOT offer credit, such courses are not typically sustainable long term.

## Establishing the Value of the Course to Students and the Institution

Without a doubt, the most significant contributor to the long-term success of University 101 has been ongoing assessment efforts and how we use what we learn from the assessment. As noted in Chapter 2, assessment was essential for the course's initial survival, mandated by President William H. Patterson, who was skeptical of his predecessor's experiment. To his credit, Patterson turned to a highly esteemed faculty member and student affairs administration, Dr. Paul P. Fidler, to conduct that first assessment. The findings were so robust and affirming of the course's ability to support greater success among less-well-prepared first-year students that Patterson declared, "University 101 will continue as long as there is student and faculty interest." And here we are 50 years later.

What was established here was not the precedent of a one-time assessment on the laurels of which we would coast for the next half century. Instead, ongoing, annual assessment became an essential component of the course. More important than simply conducting the assessment was that course leadership shared results university-wide and made decisions for course refinements and improvement based on the results of those assessments. Equally important was that Fidler never had any official responsibility for the administration of UNIV 101 and hence was perceived to be objective and acting only in the university's larger interests to monitor and enhance its student support initiatives. Fidler remained active in the performance of assessment studies of the course until he retired in 1999 and passed the baton to Dr. Phil Moore, an institutional researcher Fidler mentored and who later became the university's chief IR officer. Assessment now largely falls to the course director, but this early independence helped protect the course from being dismissed as a pet project or educational fad.

In addition to affirming the course's impact on students and instructors, programs like University 101 may also be asked to demonstrate their impact on the institutional bottom line. We discovered at the University of South Carolina as far back as the late 1970s that some senior administrators saw one of the purposes of University 101 to be an efficient generator of surplus revenues over and above the actual cost of delivering course instruction. Our efforts to document the return-on-investment (ROI) of University 101 included examining how improving first-to-second retention and graduation rates affected overall revenues. We also reviewed the cost of instruction versus the allocation of university resources based on formula funding levels for 100-level courses. This kind of analysis, if appropriately refined and systematized, could prove very useful to other institutions attempting to build the case for launching and sustaining an extended orientation seminar. For a more thorough discussion of first-year seminar assessment, see Friedman (2012).

## ■ Recommendations From Our Experience

This seems like an appropriate place in our reflections on lessons learned to distill a list of recommendations for designing a first-year seminar to support student learning and success.

- Design the first-year seminar for the students you have, not the students you *think* you have or those you would rather have, or those you think are like you as a college student. All students are capable of success; the first-year seminar serves to level the playing field.
- Course components should be purposefully integrated into the broader first-year experience for students on the campus. No single course or instructor can be all things for all students. Instead, focus on a few things that matter in your particular context and for your students and do those well.
- The course is only as good as the person teaching it. Therefore, invest heavily in faculty development. We apply the same growth mindset to course instructors that we do to students. Of course, the best instructors are not born that way, but ordinary individuals can become great instructors with exposure to good pedagogical training and opportunities for practice and feedback.
- Instructors should be selected based on their qualifications, not their classification. Thus, there must be an explicit set of criteria for teaching the first-year seminar.
- The process of the course is equally as important as the content. The content is the process, and the process is the content.
- As students' needs and institutional priorities change, so too must the first-year seminar.
- Similarly, as our country's priorities change, so too must the first-year seminar. For example, the widespread recognition that our institutions must make a significant commitment to and take more action to promote equity for all students should prompt us to explore to what extent the first-year seminar promotes or diminishes historic achievement gaps tied to race/ethnicity, class, gender, or other marginalized identity categories.
- Consistency is nice; quality is better. Don't sacrifice the latter for the former. Give seminar instructors flexibility in designing the course

experience, allowing them to tailor material to their interests and expertise. Being overly prescriptive can stifle creativity and diminish instructor enthusiasm for the course. For students to be excited about the course, the instructor must be enthusiastic. That said, individuals should not be allowed to teach whatever they want. The integrity and efficacy of the course will suffer if you sacrifice what students *need* to learn to accommodate what faculty *want* to teach. A set of broad common learning outcomes and course requirements can be a nice compromise between flexibility for instructors and consistency across sections.

## ■ The Broader Promise of the Extended Orientation Seminar

Thanks to research by Betsy Barefoot (1992) and our extensive observations of other types of seminars, we recognize that many kinds of first-year seminars exist beyond the extended orientation course popularized by the University of South Carolina's University 101 model. We also acknowledge that any first-year seminar must be consistent with institutional traditions, culture, current leadership preferences, and the wishes of the faculty. Still, we contend that the needs of incoming students are so myriad, complex, and multifaceted that they must be addressed intentionally. And we believe that the structure provided by the extended orientation course is the most comprehensive, efficient, and beneficial way to accomplish this. One way or another, we would argue that once students have been admitted, the institution has an educational and ethical imperative to address their entering developmental needs and help them achieve their academic goals. As the most thoroughly assessed, documented in the literature, and replicated first-year seminar in American higher education, the South Carolina model is ideal for meeting these needs. Here, we highlight several critical issues that we believe the extended orientation model is uniquely designed to address.

### Supporting Students Throughout the Critical First Semester

The first-year seminar would ideally span the entirety of a student's first term in college. This notion is based on the concept of just-in-time learning that we have discussed elsewhere in this book. Quite simply, new students cannot learn something they are not developmentally ready to know or sense a need for in some way. Thus, no matter how good pre-term orientation is, there is no way it can wholly or adequately deliver impactful informational and learning experiences before classes start. This critical content must be presented when students are ready to learn it, as the term gradually and naturally unfolds. Students are not prepared to learn new study strategies until they have received negative feedback on their first graded tests or assignments and, hence, discovered that their college study skills are inadequate. On many campuses, this does not happen until week 3 or 4; on some campuses, it will not happen until week 8. As such, we are skeptical of first-year seminars that are frontloaded into the first few weeks of the term.

### Advancing the Equity Agenda

As the data in Chapter 5 suggest, University 101 has narrowed the achievement gap for Black students, low-income students, and first-generation students on our campus. These findings have been consistent since the first course assessment in 1974–1975. This impact is particularly noteworthy in retrospect, given that President Jones was first inspired to consider how the university could improve its outcomes for Black students by the accomplishments of the university's Upward Bound program. Jones hoped that all entering students could experience a learning model with small classes taught by specially selected faculty and supported by undergraduate peer leaders, where the developmental needs of the students were a primary focus and pedagogies emphasized experiential learning. University 101 picks up many characteristics of this model.

University 101 achieves this vital equity agenda by making higher education's hidden curriculum visible to all students. By helping students who have been marginalized by past participation in educational systems because of their race/ethnicity, class, or parents' educational status gain academic and social capital, the course works to narrow achievement gaps and create a more equitable educational environment.

Another group of students supported by the equity agenda of the extended orientation seminar are transfer students. Transfer between institutions or attending multiple institutions is now the normative experience for students seeking a bachelor's degree in the United States. That is, many of the new students on our campuses each fall are not first-time-in-college students coming directly from high school. Transfer students as a population are much more likely to be nonwhite, to be members of lower SES groups, and to be the first person in their families to go to college (Shapiro et al., 2018, 2020). We also know that transfer students are less engaged in experiential learning on many campuses, may have more difficulty connecting to other students and faculty, and may have lower graduation rates (Shapiro et al., 2020). Many institutions have offered success seminars for transfers, including the University of South Carolina. Given the ethical implications of enrolling these students in our institutions and the potential of the extended orientation seminar to support belonging and engagement, we must consider how first-year seminars can narrow the achievement gap for transfer students and provide more equitable access to education.

The course is also a venue for teaching *about* equity. In the wake of racial unrest in the summer of 2020 and the racial disparities in health care, working conditions, and economic security laid bare by the pandemic, most faculty and administrators would readily agree they need to do more to advance equity outcomes on their campuses. The questions always come down to these: Where in the students' experience will this be done? How can this be integrated into the curriculum? How can faculty development be provided for those educators willing to pursue this aspiration? How can this be accomplished for a critical mass of students, ideally approaching 100% of the entering student cohort?

The extended orientation seminar is a curricular structure that can successfully address all those questions and requirements. University 101 includes an intentional focus on diversity and antiracism and structured conversations about civility that are continuations of the program's historical lineage. First-year seminars are especially suited for these difficult conversations due to the initial and primary focus of building community and establishing a sense of belonging. Students may feel more comfortable being vulnerable and having honest discussions once they know and trust their peers in the class. In the case of University 101, the course instructor and peer leader have the training, tools, and disposition to model walking the talk for entering students. We advocate integrating this material throughout the semester with the existing extended orientation content but do not believe the course should be co-opted as a "diversity course."

### Serving as Change Agent for the Larger Undergraduate Experience

University 101 is about reengineering the beginning college experience. It has caused us to examine the traditions and rituals we use to welcome new students to the university. Who is responsible for those traditions? How long does the welcome last? Which aspects come first? How are students' needs for continuing support and adjustment met? What special programs, services, and units have serving new students as their mission? To whom do they report? How are these efforts coordinated and integrated across the campus? What is the nature of the academic experience for new students? How do institutions ensure students thrive in their gateway courses? What student needs are currently not being addressed satisfactorily? These are just some of the questions an institution might ask to determine whether a first-year seminar is needed and why. But the course alone cannot provide the answer to all these questions.

The beginning college experience can and should be viewed as a complex ecosystem within an even larger and more complex ecosystem. When an institution introduces changes in the foundational ecosystem, it triggers adjustments and thus changes that need to be made elsewhere in the system. When members of the larger institutional community see the experimentation engendered by UNIV 101's developers, it is an incentive and even inspiration to consider and attempt changes elsewhere in undergraduate education.

For example, a successful first-year seminar challenged us to ask whether we shouldn't be paying as much attention to what was happening to students as they left college as when they entered. The course was a model for creating a senior year capstone seminar—University 401—which "helps students bring closure to their college experience through systematic, intentional reflection on both the student's major and their general education" and, thus, prepares them for the transition to career and graduate school (https://sc.edu/about/offices_and_divisions/university_101/courses/). As noted in Chapter 8, University 101 plays a critical role in the broader institutional focus on integrative learning. Partnering with the Center for Integrative and Experiential Learning, the course is the principal delivery vehicle for introducing new students to the importance of integrating within and beyond-the-classroom learning experiences and making meaning of them through intentional reflection. Special sections of University 401 help students connect experiences across the undergraduate curriculum and co-curriculum to one of several experiential learning pathways, including Community Service, Global Learning, Professional and Civic Engagement, Research, and Diversity and Social Justice.

### Providing Access to High-Quality Academic Advising

In a 2017 national survey of the first-year experience (Young, 2019), academic advising was the most identified initiative for first-year students. Nearly 63% of respondents suggested it was the primary first-year program on their campus. The increased focus on academic advising in the first college year and professionalization of advising parallels the rise of several student success initiatives emerging in the 1970s, including the first-year seminar. The first national conference on advising was held in Burlington, Vermont, in October 1977, featuring University 101 founder and UofSC President Emeritus Thomas F. Jones as the keynote speaker. Two years and two national conferences later, the National Academic Advising Association, now based at Kansas State University, was established. The evolution of advising practices understandably has mirrored many other changes in higher education. Unfortunately, increasing student enrollments and shrinking financial resources have led to impossible advising caseloads on many campuses. As a result, students may have limited access to an academic advisor. When they do meet with an advisor, the experience may likely be more transactional (i.e., focused on course registration) with less time available for goal setting and educational planning.

The extended orientation seminar may be a vehicle for providing high-quality advising to first-year students. At the University of South Carolina, robust centralized academic advising is available for first-year students, especially those trying to decide on a major or career path. University 101 provides content-driven support for advising by helping students understand the role of the advisor, asking them to engage in educational planning and goal setting, and helping them prepare for advising appointments. On other campuses, embedding students in seminars with their advisors provides continuous delivery of academic information to advisees in a timely and efficient manner that may not be available elsewhere on campus. It also allows advisors to spend time with students exploring their interests, values, and goals. This model seems common on college campuses, although it may touch only a small percentage of first-year students. In a national survey of first-year seminars (Young & Hopp, 2014), almost 90% of respondents indicated that at least some first-year seminar students were placed in sections taught by their academic advisor. However, only 13.4% of respondents reported placing all first-year seminar participants in sections with their advisors. Whatever the configuration, we believe that the extended orientation seminar plays a vital role in helping first-year students begin the educational planning process for their college careers.

### Responding to a Disappearing "First-Year Experience"

In recent years, there has been an explosion of secondary and even middle school students enrolling in college credit courses. In 2019, more than one third of US high school students took courses for postsecondary credit (NCES, 2019), and in some community colleges, total enrollments of so-called dual-credit students are nearing 50%. Some students will have taken courses for credit on a college campus, but most will complete college coursework without ever leaving high school (NCES, 2019). When they arrive on campus, dual-credit students may enter as sophomores (or higher) but have little understanding of what it means to be a college student. Like transfer students, dual-credit learners are not new to college, but they are new to a specific academic community. Also, like transfer students, they will have less time to establish a connection to campus, develop relationships with faculty, and become involved in experiential learning opportunities. They will have specific advising needs to ensure that they have the prerequisites required for intended majors and to avoid accumulating excess credits toward a degree.

Like other new college students, dual-credit students could be well served by an extended orientation course tailored to their unique transition and developmental needs.

## ■ Closing Thoughts

We realize that it may seem daunting for readers who have not yet developed anything like University 101 to ask, "How in the world could we do anything remotely like this?" Well, that is precisely where we were 50 years ago, except we did not have a concrete vision for this course and where it could take us. We knew that our institution was still reeling from the fallout of student protests within the larger context of an unpopular war and in a state where Black college students faced very real threats to their lives in trying to claim their rights as citizens. We had a supportive president and a faculty senate that had granted us a one-year license to experiment. All we had to do was design the course and prepare the first faculty and staff cohort to teach it. Thankfully, that is not where we are now.

Your institution is perfectly designed to get the outcomes you are getting right now. If you want different outcomes or a changed culture, then you must adjust what you are doing. Your context is different, and your goals are different. But, like us, you have new students who need more attention and support to be successful in their first college year and beyond. You also have talented, thoughtful, and creative faculty and staff who can design an improved overall first-year experience. You are not starting from scratch. The first-year seminar dates to 1882 and the University 101 model to 1972. Admittedly, it is always harder to follow a highly successful initiative or leader. Still, if you attempt to launch a new or revised approach to the first year, we have provided you with an idea of what is possible. Please do not say, "Oh, we could never do that!" Oh, yes you can. If we did this at the University of South Carolina, you can do this, too. You just must give yourself the time, the vision, the leadership, and an enduring focus to build your own course traditions on a foundation grounded in a humanistic educational vision for teaching students to be successful in college and to love it and the experience at the same time—and then do it.

While there is much that we cannot possibly know about what the next 50 years will bring, we do know that we will

- maintain fidelity to our roots;
- continue to focus on identifying changing student and institutional needs and practicing continuous evidence-based improvements related to that;

- stay with what we know, remembering what happened when Coke changed its formula in 1985;
- maintain the core components of the South Carolina model, which include a three-credit, letter-graded extended orientation course supported by robust professional development and training for instructors and peer leaders, a university-wide ecosystem of partnership-driven delivery of services and resources, and program delivery informed by ongoing assessment;
- continue our firm commitment to contributing to the unfinished civil rights movement and the pursuit of social justice; and
- continue to play a leading role in improving undergraduate education in the United States and around the world by sharing the South Carolina model.

At the same time, we will remain open to and constantly explore new ways to serve the university, its students especially, faculty and staff, and American higher education. We invite you to communicate and interact with us. We want to know what you are doing in your own versions of the first-year seminar. We will learn from you, and we will surely do our best to reciprocate.

## References

Baldwin, A., Bunting, B., Daughtery, D., Lewis, L., & Steenbergh, T. (2020). *Promoting belonging, growth mindset, and resilience to foster student success.* University of South Carolina, National Resource Center for The First-Year Experience and Students in Transition.

Barefoot, B. O. (1992). *Helping first-year college students climb the academic ladder: Report of a national survey of freshman seminar programming in American higher education.* [Doctoral dissertation, College of William & Mary—School of Education]. W&M Scholar Works. https://dx.doi.org/doi:10.25774/w4–4p9k-8r77.

Friedman, D. (2012). *The first-year seminar: Designing and assessing courses to support student learning and success: Vol 5. Assessing the first-year seminar.* University of South Carolina, National Resource Center for The First-Year Experience and Students in Transition.

National Center for Education Statistics (2019, February). Dual enrollment: Participation and characteristics (Data Point NCES 2019–176). U.S. Department of Education. https://nces.ed.gov/pubs2019/2019176.pdf.

Schreiner, L. A., Louis, M. C., & Nelson, D. D. (2020). *Thriving in transitions: A research-based approach to college student success* (2nd ed.). University of South Carolina, National Resource Center for The First-Year Experience and Students in Transition.

Shapiro, D., Dundar, A., Huie, F., Wakhungu, P. K., Bhimdiwali, A., Nathan, A., & Youngsik, H. (2018). *Transfer and mobility: A national view of student movement in postsecondary institutions, fall 2011 cohort* (Signature Report No. 15). National Student ClearinghouseResearch Center.

Shapiro, D., Dundar, A., Huie, F., Wakhungu, P. K., Yuan, X., Nathan, A., & Hwang, Y. (2020). *Tracking transfer: Measures of effectiveness in helping community college students to complete bachelor's degrees* (Data update for the Fall 2013 Cohort). National Student Clearinghouse Research Center.

Young, D. G. (Ed.). (2019). *2017 National Survey on the First-Year Experience: Creating and coordinating structures to support student success* (Research Report No. 9). University of South Carolina, National Resource Center for The First-Year Experience and Students in Transition.

Young, D. G., & Hopp, J. M. (2014). *2012–2013 National Survey of First-Year Seminars: Exploring high- impact practices in the first college year* (Research Report No. 4). University of South Carolina, National Resource Center for The First-Year Experience and Students in Transition.

Chapter 10

# Major Figures in
# University 101 History

*Compiled by Tracy L. Skipper*

■ **The Founder**

*Thomas F. Jones, 23rd president of the University of South Carolina*

Jones was president of the University of South Carolina from 1962 to 1974. During his tenure, the university tripled in size, was peacefully integrated, and was the site of historic student protests. He was driven to make the research university a more collegial space for faculty and students and to ensure that the university served South Carolinians, especially those who were socially and educationally disadvantaged. As a result, Jones's presidency was marked by educational experimentation and innovation. His signature and longest-lasting initiative, University 101, was a direct response to the student protests of May 1970. In UNIV 101's early years, Jones played an outsized role in course leadership, assisted by the staff of the Social Problems Research Institute and Dean of Freshmen Edward Beardsley. After the first semester, he began to apply the model to other groups of students, urging the development of the first special sections of the course for pre-education majors and readmitted students. Jones continued to follow the progress of UNIV 101, extolling its virtues to leaders on other campuses and offering advice to course director John Gardner, until his death in 1981.

## ■ University 101 Leadership

### John N. Gardner, Executive Director, University 101 Programs (1974–1999)

John N. Gardner

Gardner led the course during its first 25 years, bringing national prominence to the University of South Carolina and launching a larger international movement focused on ensuring the success of first-year college students. In assuming leadership of the course, Gardner faced a skeptical president (William H. Patterson) and faculty. Among the challenges he addressed were a general lack of understanding of the UNIV 101 concept, the need for more academic content and structure, recognition in the faculty reward system, and the charge to demonstrate its value to the students and the university through credible research. He built a reputation for the course by enlisting the support of external evaluators and by promoting it, with the help of Paul Fidler, Chuck Witten, and the Social Problems Research Institute staff, to national conference audiences. To manage the increasing number of inquiries about UNIV 101 and to support growing interest in the first college year with professional development events, research, and publications, he developed a proposal for a national center. The National Resource Center for The First-Year Experience and Students in Transition, as it is known today, began operations on July 1, 1987. Gardner continues to serve University 101 and the National Resource Center as a senior fellow. Before he retired from the university, Gardner piloted a new course for seniors, University 401, designed to prepare them for the transition to career or graduate school by providing them with the opportunity to reflect on their undergraduate experience.

### A. Jerome Jewler, Co-Director of University 101 (1983–1989)

In addition to his work with UNIV 101, Jewler was a professor of journalism. He added greater structure to the course, elevated the role of writing in the first-year seminar, and helped instructors develop writing pedagogy for UNIV 101. Jewler created the first edition of *Transitions*, a UofSC-specific textbook for students enrolled in the course. He also collaborated with Gardner to produce the first commercial textbook for first-year seminars, which, in turn, helped establish student success as a discipline. Jewler also used his advertising expertise to promote the course and its benefits to incoming students and their parents, resulting in increased enrollment for the course.

### Dan Berman, Co-Director (1989–1999) and
### Director (1999–2007) of University 101 Programs

Dan Berman

Berman and Gardner were undergraduates together at Marietta College in the early 1960s. Gardner credits Berman with helping him get off academic probation by "showing [him] how to take lecture notes, and selecting really engaging professors."[1] When an opening for an assistant professor of English in the College of General Studies became available in 1973, Gardner recruited his friend to come to the University of South Carolina. After earning tenure in the College of General Studies, Berman would later move to the department of Media Arts where he taught courses in film criticism. He was devoted to and loved by students. Gardner tapped him to be the second co-director for the course because of his commitment to the philosophy of University 101. Under Berman's leadership, the course added peer leaders and formed a partnership with the College of Education to provide a training course for peer leaders. Berman also strengthened partnerships with a range of campus constituencies by enlisting their involvement in writing contributions for *Transitions*, the course textbook. Berman became the second director of the course in 1999 and served in this role until his retirement from the university in 2007.

### Daniel B. Friedman, Executive Director,
### University 101 Programs (2008–present)

Daniel B. Friedman

Friedman serves as the current and third director of University 101, and he is the first to come from outside the university since the course's founding. He came to the attention of the University of South Carolina through his leadership of the nationally ranked first-year seminar at Appalachian State University, a program that had been modeled on UNIV 101. He re-envisioned faculty development, grounding it in the just-in-time philosophy that drove the course and reducing the number of participants in the initial training workshop so that it more closely resembled the seminar. Intentional, year-round faculty development initiatives coupled with a robust set of teaching re-sources have led to greater consistency across sections while maintaining instructors' flexibility to deliver an experience tailored to the needs of their students. Friedman also brought a renewed emphasis on assessment to University 101, implementing the first set of learning outcomes in the course's history and using assessment to drive improvement of course delivery and instruction. The assessment focus has led to increased quality in the overall course experience for students even as course enrollments have grown exponentially. In 2020, *U.S. News & World Report* recognized University 101 at South Carolina as the number-one first-year program in a public university.

### *Mary Stuart Hunter, Associate Vice President and Executive Director for University 101 Programs and the National Resource Center for The First-Year Experience & Students in Transition (2007–2015)*

Mary Stuart Hunter

Hunter was affiliated with University 101 since joining the staff at the University of South Carolina in 1978 until her retirement in July 2015. She served as an instructor for the course while working in the Admissions office and developed a section for undecided college students with colleagues in the Center for Undeclared Majors in the early 1980s. In 1984, she joined the staff of University 101 Programs to support the fledgling conference series, later serving as codirector and then director of the National Resource Center for The First-Year Experience in Students in Transition. In 2007, Hunter became associate vice president for student affairs and executive director for University 101 Programs and the National Resource Center. She led the search for new directors for University 101 Programs and the Center. Even as responsibilities increasingly connected her to other areas of the university, Stuart remained deeply invested in University 101, continuing to serve as an instructor and cofacilitator for the Teaching Experience Workshop. Because of her dedication to teaching and faculty development, the University 101 Excellence in Teaching Award was renamed in her honor (now the M. Stuart Hunter Award for Outstanding Teaching in University 101) in 2015.

■ University 101 Supporters

*Social Problems Research Institute*

President Jones's commitment to educational innovation and transforming the university frequently hit roadblocks from faculty. In 1968, he saw an opening to request an appropriation from the state legislature to form an Institute for Research on Problems of the Underprivileged (later renamed the Social Problems Research Institute or SPRI) that could serve as an engine of innovation and an institutional home for some of his educational experiments, such as Upward Bound. Robert Heckel from the psychology faculty served as director until 1984. Along with John Zuidema and Manning Hiers, Heckel was instrumental in developing a proposal for Jones's first-year orientation course, which was grounded in behavioral psychology and the human potential movement, and funded by a Venture Grant from the Ford Foundation. The SPRI staff designed and managed the initial training for University 101 faculty, including John Gardner, in July 1972, and continued to support faculty throughout the first semester. Heckel and his team published a monograph reporting on the initial pilot, *University 101: An Educational Experiment*. The monograph included the first evaluation of the course, based on instructor notes and open-ended questionnaires, and helped secure support from faculty for another year. Because SPRI was so closely associated with his presidency, Jones moved the course to the Center for Cultural Development (under the provost) to insulate it after his departure from the university. Nevertheless, the staff of SPRI remained active in preparing faculty to teach the course and in helping Gardner promote the course nationally throughout the 1970s.

*Paul P. Fidler, University 101 Evaluator*

Paul Fidler joined the UofSC staff in the late 1960s, serving under Chuck Witten in the emerging student affairs division. As an administrator, he helped shape student services, creating the Career Center, the Center for Undeclared Majors, and the Academic Planning Office (later the Office of Institutional Planning and Assessment). He was a pioneer in the higher education assessment and accountability movement. When Gardner needed an outside evaluator, he turned to Fidler because of his reputation for integrity and objectivity and for his research on college student outcomes. Fidler's UNIV 101 evaluation helped convince university administrators to provide ongoing support for the course and made its adoption at other colleges and universities possible. Fidler, along with Gardner, Witten, and Manning Hiers and John Zuidema from the Social Problems Research Institute, was a member of an unofficial UNIV 101 task force that made presentations and delivered trainings on the South Carolina model at national conferences and on in-dividual college campuses. Fidler published four articles on University 101, exploring the impact on retention and graduation rates, on African American students, and on faculty. He also worked with staff members of the National Resource Center for The First-Year Experience and Students in Transition to analyze and publish the results from the first three administrations of the triennial National Survey of First-Year Seminars.

### Keith Davis, Provost, 1974–1978

When Jones moved the leadership of University 101 to the Center for Cultural Development, Keith Davis, then associate provost, asked that a position de-scription for the course coordinator be developed. As provost, University 101 remained part of Davis's portfolio, and he was no doubt aware that President William H. Patterson was skeptical of his predecessor's educational experi-ment. Recognizing the potential value of the program and understanding that national recognition would increase credibility at home, Davis encour-aged John Gardner "to go out and sell this." Davis continued his early support of Gardner and University 101 as he moved from the provost's role to the dean of Arts & Sciences and then back to the faculty as chair of the psychology de-partment. When Gardner was looking to pilot University 401, Davis agreed to sponsor the course in the psychology department and even taught a section.

### Francis Borkowski, Provost, 1978–1988

Gardner met Borkowski at the 1978 annual meeting of the American Association of Higher Education when Borkowski was considering applying for the provost role at South Carolina. They developed a close relationship that ex-tended beyond Borkowski's tenure at South Carolina and translated into support for the course and for the larger first-year experience movement. It was during Borkowski's tenure that Gardner pursued a change in the course grading policy (from pass/fail to letter grade). Borkowski also pushed forward the proposal to establish a center at the university to study the first college year, which would support the popular conference series on the First-Year Ex-

Francis Borkowski

perience and the increasing number of inquiries from other colleges and uni-versities.

*Dennis A. Pruitt, Sr., Vice President for Student Affairs
and Vice Provost, 1983–2022*

Dennis A. Pruitt, Sr.

Pruitt has led student affairs at the University of South Carolina since 1983 and taught the University 101 course for more than 25 years. In 2007, then-provost Mark Becker realigned several student-facing academic support services to create synergy and boundary spanning to better serve students. As part of the realignment, University 101 Programs was moved under the Division of Student Affairs and Academic Support. While Pruitt is a proponent of hiring experts and getting out of their way, he encouraged a renewed emphasis on assessment for University 101 when the course was added to his portfolio. Despite a narrative of ongoing success, Pruitt wanted to ensure that the course had the current evidence to support that narrative and requests for institutional resources needed for program improvement and expansion. Pruitt is a staunch advocate for the course both within the division and outside it— notably, defending the course against proposed changes to its longstanding remuneration policy and encouraging student affairs leadership to provide release time for employees to teach UNIV 101. Similarly, he uses his role as the chief student affairs officer to sell the virtues of the course to parents and students through orientation, academic deans through his position on the Council of Deans, and the Board of Trustees by helping them see the course as a frame of reference for higher educators around the world. Finally, he supports the ongoing institutionalization of the course by ensuring the course has a central place in strategic planning initiatives, such as the 2021 Quality Enhancement Plan, Experience by Design, while simultaneously protecting it from mission creep.

# APPENDIX A

Case Studies of Programs Modeled on University 101

---

## BENEDICT COLLEGE

James Winfield, Director of Student Retention

### ■ The Institution

Founded in 1870 in Columbia, South Carolina, Benedict College (BC) is a small private historically black college. BC has been recognized as *HBCU Digest*'s HBCU (Historically Black Colleges and University) of the Year in 2019 and for excellence in STEM education. The undergraduate population is approximately 1,800 students.

### ■ Overview of the First-Year Seminar

In its previous iterations, the first-year seminar course resided in a now-defunct freshman program, then moved to the academic departments where faculty taught the courses. With the establishment of the Student Success Center (SSC) in 2019, the course quickly shifted in focus and philosophy and refined student learning outcomes. The courses, known as College Experience I and College Experience II, are each one academic credit and taken in sequence by students during their first year at Benedict.

The institution relies heavily on the College Experience courses as an extended orientation, educating students on the college's policies, processes, and expectations. The courses include uniform experiences that students participate in, such as an institution-wide career inventory and a financial literacy program. Otherwise, instructors have the flexibility and autonomy to tailor their in-class sessions.

Through reflective assignments and consistent engagement, the courses help students understand the history of BC and appreciate HBCUs in general, provide opportunities for engagement across campus, and focus on financial literacy and career exploration. The courses' curriculum emphasizes understanding the expectations of college life and using help-seeking skills to connect with on-campus resources. As many of BC's students are first-generation, building self-efficacy for completing college is an essential component, as is validating students as they persist.

The SSC houses the College Experience courses, and the program director is responsible for training instructors and curriculum development. Academic department chairs assist the SSC by identifying and supporting faculty to teach these courses.

The instructors for College Experience consist of a tight group of staff and faculty, who primarily include SSC staff members, other campus staff, and key faculty advocates. In 2020, staff in student activities and financial aid and scholarships became instructors to support course expansion.

Faculty training and development are done in conjunction with the institution's Center for Teaching and Learning (CTL). Sessions hosted by CTL and the SSC include orientation and refreshers on the learning management system and methods for unpacking and discussing content within the online learning modules. Ongoing faculty sessions also occur throughout the semester to discuss emergent themes, provide opportunities for engagement, and highlight changes in policies or campus navigation that would benefit the students enrolled in the course.

## ■ Benefits of the Course

With the evolution of the course, delivery models have adapted to meet the needs of students. In fall 2020, BC achieved its highest retention rate in years, increasing by 12%. The support and navigation provided in this course to students are pivotal factors in students' success.

An added benefit of the courses are the connections students develop with diverse staff and faculty. The instructional team's composition is intentional, since instructors possess the proper disposition to teach first-year students and work in areas that consistently interact with students. Having representation in the classroom provides a bonus to the accessibility and approachability of their services.

## ■ Variations on a Theme

The BC Student Success Center leadership has prior experience working with University 101 Programs at the University of South Carolina and has brought that knowledge to the College Experience courses. For example, vetted activities and lesson plans from the *University 101 Faculty Resource Manual* are shared among the instructors to use in their curricular planning.

In alignment with best practices in teaching and learning, appropriate scaffolding is prioritized to organize course content and assignments. This practice aligns with the UofSC philosophy of providing students with "what they need, when they need it, and when they are ready for it" (Friedman et al., 2019, p. 12). The course's underpinnings are grounded in practices and strategies that prioritize reflection and application versus information distribution. The SSC leadership consistently engages in professional development with the National Resource Center for The First-Year Experience and Students in Transition.

### Reference

Friedman, D., Winfield, J., & Hopkins, K. (2019). Faculty development for the University of South Carolina's first-year experience course. *Journal for Faculty Development, 33*(2), 11–18.

---

## COLLEGE OF CENTRAL FLORIDA

Julee W. McCammon, Lead Faculty, First Year Seminar
Karla B. Wilson, Director, QEP StartSmart@CF

### ■ The Institution

Founded as a two-year college in 1957, today the College of Central Florida (CF) has a population of approximately 10,000 students serving three mostly rural counties and offering certificates, associate degrees, and bachelor's degrees in business, education, and nursing.

### ■ Overview of the First-Year Seminar

In the fall of 2018, CF piloted SLS1122: The First-Year Seminar. The course is required for all first-time-in-college/AA-degree-seeking students and was developed around the foundations of the South Carolina model. The path to implementation was arduous. Fortunately, Dr. Dan Friedman, executive director of University 101 at the University of South Carolina, provided practical tips and thoughtful guidance.

In 2014, CF embarked on a year-long search to identify what was needed to improve the culture and learning environment for our students. Focus groups, surveys, and roundtables among staff, faculty, students, and community members resulted in a Quality Enhancement Plan (QEP) titled *StartSmart@CF: Enhancing the First-Year Experience*. The encompassing goal of the plan focused on improving the first-year experience for our students, which included the formation of a first-year seminar course.

Prior to the QEP, we offered a similar course, SLS1501: College and Career Success, which was mandatory for students in developmental education classes. The course had the stigma of being an "easy class with little academic rigor," and the general opinion of the course was lackluster. As such, we began to research best practices in first-year seminar organization and administration. We sent four faculty members from different departments to the National Resource Center's Institute on Developing and Sustaining First-Year Seminars in Savannah, Georgia, where we first learned about the South Carolina model.

Knowing after this meeting that we wanted to adapt the South Carolina model to CF, we invited Friedman to serve as a keynote for a campus-wide professional development day in the spring of 2018. His presentation struck a chord with those in attendance. We also asked Friedman to facilitate a training for potential first-year seminar instructors and prepared for up to 50 people to attend the session. We had to turn people away due to lack of space. The result was that more than 80 people applied to teach the seminar.

Through interdisciplinary efforts, we identified the institutional knowledge and academic skills our students needed to be successful. We had the framework of the seminar curriculum but needed to create actual assignments. In the summer of 2018, the lead instructor and director of the QEP attended the Teaching Experience Workshop (TEW) at UofSC. This three-day instructor training event armed us with an engaging curriculum and a pedagogical template to adapt lessons to our student population. We also gained insight into how to identify the individuals best suited to teach the course and how to cultivate instructional effectiveness. We developed a required training for potential first-year seminar instructors, using the TEW as a model.

## ■ Benefits of the Course

Central to University 101 is collaboration among students and fostering community. We strive for those same tenets in our first-year seminars. A comment from one student to her first-year seminar instructor suggests we are meeting this goal: If you never remember anything else, just know you inspired a change on my heart for helping people. Each day on campus I seek out students that are struggling and those who are too afraid to ask questions. I utilize my resources to ensure that students receive the help that they need. I remember when I was in their shoes. Students are not the only ones who benefit from the collaborative nature of the course. A biology professor adapted many of the teaching methods learned in first-year seminar to her discipline, finding they helped students meet the academic expectations in her courses. Many colleagues in her department have also adopted new approaches to teaching through her leadership. Several administrators and staff teach the course; one is a vice president at CF. Through this new role, he has become more in tune with the needs of students and has gained more credibility and respect from many faculty members. Perhaps most importantly, we have seen an institutional shift in thinking, which embraces the need for supporting and ensuring the success of our students during the critical point of entry to the campus and extends beyond the course.

Developing SLS1122, receiving approval from the curriculum committee, and training instructors are behemoth tasks. However, the work has just begun; maintenance, guidance of faculty, and constant review of the course's efficacy are ongoing. We have seen improvements in our retention, GPA, and sense of belonging at CF, and we anticipate with continued commitment to our students those trends will continue.

## KOÇ UNIVERSITY

Pınar Özbek, Instructor, Academic and Life Skills (ALIS) Program

### ■ The Institution

Koç University (KU) is a leading foundation (private) university located in Istanbul, Turkey. Founded in 1993, it is ranked among the top 500 universities in the QS World University Rankings in 2021. With seven colleges and four institutes, KU offers undergraduate and graduate degrees in medicine, nursing, engineering, basic sciences, social sciences, literature, administrative sciences, economics, and law. The medium of instruction is English. The undergraduate student population is approximately 5,700, of which half are residential and 5% are international. The university admits a first-year cohort of roughly 1,300 students each academic year, most of whom are recruited from the top 10th percentile of nationwide university candidates.

### ■ Overview of the First-Year Course

The Academic and Life Skills (ALIS) program was founded and is academically supervised by Zeynep Aycan, professor of industrial and organizational psychology in the Department of Psychology at KU. It is housed within the office of the Dean of Students, alongside other offices providing support and development services to students. These include counseling, the career development center, and newcomer advising offices. ALIS courses are offered by six full-time instructors with master's or doctoral degrees in psychological counseling, clinical psychology, industrial/organizational psychology, and positive psychology.

ALIS 100 is a one-credit required course for all first-year students at KU. It began with a pilot study in 2009 and became part of the curriculum for all departments in 2010. The course enables students to reflect on their personality, values, sources of motivation, areas of interest, and expectations about the future. It also aims to help students develop skills in communication, relationship management, teamwork, university citizenship, goal setting, time management, and stress management. These skills help students reconcile their aspirations with the demands of society. ALIS 100 is experiential: Learning is supported by simulations, team exercises, interviews, reflection logs, psychological inventories, polls, and group discussions. Sections are capped at 25 students, and classes meet once a week for a 75-minute session during one semester. The instructors work with students individually on skill development, if needed, and refer them to other university units such as psychological counseling, career counseling, and academic advising when necessary.

### ■ Benefits of the Course

In 2011, following the completion of the first academic year in which the course was offered, the effectiveness of ALIS 100 was assessed. A self-assessment questionnaire on self-awareness and life skills was administered to 347 students before and after the course. Significant progress was noted on students' knowledge of and attitude toward responsibilities as a university citizen, time management, communication styles, giving and receiving feedback, email communication, public speaking, psychologically risky behaviors, and stress management.

Following ALIS 100, new courses were offered for students who are in later stages of their academic career, namely ALIS 200 (Applied Life Skills), ALIS 350 (Transition to Professional Life), and ALIS 360 (New Generation Leadership and Transformation). In addition, ALIS grad workshops were offered to graduate students and ALIS staff training programs to administrative staff.

This program also proved to be a best practice in Turkey, which many universities aspire to adopt. Instructors published a book entitled *University and Beyond: Life Skills for Young Adults*, which serves as an instructor's manual for higher education professionals and a self-help book for students. The Turkish First-Year Experience Network was established in 2017 and now has 207 members from 80 Turkish institutions. The inaugural first-year experience symposium was organized in 2018 at KU, with 85 colleagues from 41 institutions around Turkey participating.

### ■ Impact of the South Carolina Model

Pınar Özbek, an ALIS Instructor, visited the National Resource Center for The First-Year Experience and Students in Transition and University 101 Programs at the University of South Carolina in 2016. She participated in the Teaching Experience Workshop to learn more about UNIV 101's history, philosophy, course-planning process, teaching strategies, and assessment methods. This exposure translated into a new approach for ALIS 100. A transitions perspective was integrated into the philosophy of the course. Initially conceived as simply a self-awareness and skill-building course, KU recognized its potential to help students adjust to the university. As such, more sections of the course were offered in the fall season (as opposed to the spring season) to expose students to the ALIS experience earlier in their college experience. Peer leaders were employed for many sections, and more rigorous assessment methods were implemented more frequently to measure and enhance course effectiveness.

## NOVA SOUTHEASTERN UNIVERSITY

Teri Williams, Assistant Professor
Kevin Dvorak, First-Year Experience Faculty Coordinator

### ■ The Institution

Founded in 1964 in Fort Lauderdale, Florida, Nova Southeastern University (NSU) is the largest private research university in the state. The US Department of Education classifies NSU as "high research activity" by the Carnegie Foundation for the Advancement of Teaching and as a Hispanic-serving Institution. The undergraduate population is approximately 5,000 students, and the average class size is 17.

### ■ Overview of the First-Year Seminar

The First-Year Experience Program at NSU began in 2015 and was designed to acclimate students to college life, engage them in experiential education opportunities, and teach them how to use many of the university's support services. The curriculum focuses heavily on experiential education to help students understand what it means to be a learner and to underscore the importance of active and beyond-the-classroom learning. Key components of NSU's FYE course include early immersion, which requires students to spend time working alongside a professional in their chosen field; an e-portfolio students use to showcase their accomplishments during the semester; and an upper-level peer embedded into each section. Sections are capped at 19 students.

The FYE program is housed in the Office of Experiential Education and Learning, which oversees hiring, training, and evaluating more than 80 FYE instructors and peer leaders each fall, manages the program's curriculum, and facilitates program assessment.

Instructors are intentionally comprised of faculty, administrators, and staff from across the university. In the fall of 2020, this included professional staff from student affairs and residential life, campus facilities, marketing and recruiting, and the library and faculty from the university's health professions division, college of education, and college of arts and sciences. This diverse group of educators participates in an ongoing professional development that begins with a spring orientation and continues with 10 summer workshops (all of which are complemented by an asynchronous platform within the university's learning management system). During the fall semester, instructors continue to participate in regular meetings and workshops designed to address immediate needs.

The peer leader (PL) program employs rigorous training that begins each spring semester and carries over to the summer. Through a combination of in-person and online activities, PLs are trained on classroom management and working with diverse student populations, public speaking, using various technologies, and employing mindfulness in their work. The PLs have strong working relationships with their instructors, who also provide them with ongoing mentorship. To provide leadership opportunities to senior PLs, cohorts are designated and guided by one senior PL.

### ■ Benefits of the Course

To date, the FYE program has proven to be a success. The retention rates for first-year students have risen in each of the past four years, and students have shown an appreciation for the course and the connections they have built with their FYE instructors and peer leaders. Upper-division students have also benefited from the professional development opportunities afforded by the PL program. The instructor training program has developed a strong community of professionals across campus among people who typically would have had fewer opportunities to work together. Bringing diverse professionals together to teach this course has been transformative for the NSU culture, creating a community with a common goal. We have all become better instructors, learned what it means to be truly student-centered, and renewed our passion for our institution.

## ■ Variations on a Theme

The FYE course draws heavily on the South Carolina model. In the first years under the Office of Experiential Education and Learning, the FYE team was fortunate to work with Dr. Dan Friedman from the University of South Carolina (UofSC). Friedman provided the knowledge, resources, encouragement, and support needed to grow the course successfully. Attending the First-Year Experience Conferences helped NSU's team continue to learn and strengthen the program. We have experienced the power of collaboration, the blessing of unwavering support, and the deepening of our mission through our work with John Gardner and Dan Friedman. The benefits of FYE and our partnership with UofSC have helped establish a strong foundation for all our undergraduate students.

# APPENDIX B

## Sample University 101 Assignments

### ■ Academic Success Strategies Assignment

One goal of this class is to help you be successful in your other academic courses. To help foster effective habits and behaviors that lead to academic success, you will be required to earn 50 points by choosing activities from the below list. You do not need to do all the activities on the list, but you do need to accumulate 50 points over the course of the semester (in any combination you choose). Evidence of completion of each activity is due one week after participation or task completion.

_____ Complete the Semester-at-a-Glance activity in *Transitions* (10 points).

_____ Attend a Supplemental Instruction session and bring signature from Supplemental Instruction leader (10 points each).

_____ Type your notes for one of your classes (10 points per week).

_____ Make a study guide for one of your exams (10 points).

_____ Make an outline for a chapter in one of your textbooks (10 points).

_____ Make flashcards to prepare for an exam (10 points).

_____ Take a draft of a paper for a class to the Writing Center or the Peer Writing and Communications Lab for review (10 points).

_____ Take a professor out to lunch and write a one-page reflection paper (20 points). For more information about how to get a free lunch ticket for your professor, as well as potential discussion questions to ask over lunch, visit the Student Success Center website: https://sc.edu /about/offices_and_divisions/student_success_center/academic -engagement/out_to_lunch.php

_____ Attend a Success Consultation session in the Student Success Center and bring a verification form (10 points).

## ■ Research Presentation

To further explore the course learning outcomes, you will develop a research presentation that will contribute to our learning in this course. This project will be your opportunity to enhance and practice your research, writing, group work, and presentation skills. These presentations will also contribute to the class's knowledge of issues related to academic or personal success.

Possible topics might include (but certainly are not limited to) those in this table:

| LARGER TOPIC | SPECIFIC RESEARCH QUESTION (THINK *MYTH BUSTERS*) |
| --- | --- |
| Time management | Can college students (or people in general) effectively multi-task? |
| Studying | Is group work more effective than studying alone? |
| Sleep | How much sleep do we really need? Or what is the impact of sleep on college student success? |
| Physical wellness | Is the "freshman 15" a real thing? |
| Drugs | What do we know about the effects (physical, ethical) of ADHD medication for those without ADHD? The presentation should provide relevant information about the larger topic and discuss the implications for college students. Strategies for success (regarding the larger topic) should be shared. In addition, the findings from the specific research question should be given. |

### *Requirements*

- Deliver a formal (in dress, speech, preparedness, and organization) 20-to-25-minute presentation.
- Involve all members of your team equally.
- Include some sort of activity, demonstration, or discussion to engage your classmates.
- Properly use and cite sources (minimum of six sources; at least three should be from scholarly sources (i.e., book or peer-reviewed journal article). If the topic is in *Transitions*, please use that as a source as well. Other sources could include books, newspaper or magazine articles, and white papers/reports from governmental or non-profit organizations.

- Submit an outline, works cited list, and copy of visuals (i.e., PowerPoint slides).
- Each individual will submit a summary of an article being considered as a source for the project (students will receive an individual grade for this component).

## Evaluation

Presentations will be graded on the following components:

- Presentation style and technique
- Demonstrated knowledge of material
- Relevance of information
- Quality of research
- Overall quality of presentation (i.e., organization, cohesiveness, thoroughness)

## Timeline

| STEP | ACTION | DUE DATE | NOTES |
|---|---|---|---|
| 1 | Form group and select general topic | 9/26 (in class) | See pages 143–146 in *Transitions* |
| 2 | Attend library workshop on finding sources | 10/8 (in class) | Read pages 141–154 in *Transitions* |
| 3 | Locate and evaluate possible sources. Each person should bring in a summary of one peer-reviewed journal article related to the topic. | 10/24 | |
| 4 | Submit outline. | 10/29 | |
| 5 | Presentations begin (submit detailed outline, PPT slides, and complete works cited list) | 11/12–11/19 | Works cited list due 11/12 (regardless of presentation date) |
| 6 | Complete evaluation of self and group members | 11/19 | |

■ Final Exam

The final exam in this course will consist of two parts: A letter to next year's first-year class and a 3-minute presentation.

*Part I*

Please write a letter to next year's first-year class that includes the following:

- *Introduction.* You should introduce yourself to next year's entering class, explaining briefly where you are from and why you chose UofSC. In addition, I want you to explain one or two new things you have discovered about yourself during this semester.
- *Transitions.* Next, I want you to explain the most difficult transitions in your move from high school to college. You might want to focus on life in the residence hall, meeting new people, roommates, adjusting to stress levels, or money management, among others. In the process, note ways in which the university, fellow students, UNIV 101, parents, or faculty or staff members have helped you make the transition.
- *Academic success strategies.* Discuss your level of academic readiness to succeed in college. To what extent are you prepared for success in college? What might you need to work on, or what skills might you need to develop?
- *Discovering South Carolina.* Another goal of our course has been to help you discover the full range of educational opportunities, university resources, support services, and institutional history. I would like for you to briefly explain to next year's first-year students the most important things you learned about UofSC in these categories.
- *Plan for next semester.* The first semester of college is a time of growth, exploration, trial and error, struggles, and joys. Now that you have a semester of college under your belt, what have you learned that you will need to do differently next semester? What changes do you want to make in your life as a college student, and how do you plan to make these changes? This can be in the form of advice about what new students need to understand to succeed in college.

Please write your letter in an easy, friendly style, paying attention to correct grammar, spelling, and so on. Illustrate your statements with examples, use logical transitions from one topic to another, keep the entire letter in essay form, and try to be as concise and clear in your comments as possible.

*Part II*

Design and deliver a creative presentation reflecting on and synthesizing your experiences during your first UofSC semester. The presentation will be given to the class on the day of the final exam and must be 3 to 5 minutes in length. The way you present is up to you: PowerPoint, video, poster board, interpretive dance, graphic novel, or some other creative form. However, the following messages must be conveyed during your time:

- *Introduction.* Who are you? Where did you come from? Why did you come to UofSC?
- *Transition.* Describe your first semester of college. What were your first thoughts moving onto campus? What are your favorite memories from your first semester? Where did you find challenges and struggles?
- *Academic strategies.* Transitioning from high school to college can be difficult. How did you make the academic transition? What UofSC resources did you use to help you become a successful college student?
- *Discovering South Carolina.* What is your favorite part of being a student at UofSC?
- *Plan for next semester.* What have you learned about yourself this semester? How will this new knowledge help you in the years to come? What is one suggestion you have for incoming students next year?

You will be graded on the overall quality of your presentation, evidence of self-reflection on the semester, and fulfillment of the questions asked above.

# APPENDIX C

Sample University 101 Course Syllabus

## UNIV 101: The Student in the University Sample Syllabus

| INSTRUCTOR | PEER/GRADUATE LEADER |
|---|---|
| NAME OF INSTRUCTOR | NAME OF PEER/GRAD LEADER |
| CELL AND/OR OFFICE PHONE NUMBER WITH AREA CODE | PHONE NUMBER WITH AREA CODE |
| EMAIL | EMAIL |
| CAMPUS ADDRESS | |

Office Hours: We are happy to meet with you anytime we are mutually available. Please call, text, or email to schedule a time.

Required Text(s): Sokol, K., & Friedman, D. (Eds.). (2022). *Transitions.* Columbia, SC: University of South Carolina.

First-Year Reading Experience book (provided at Orientation)

## COURSE DESCRIPTION

University 101 is designed to help first-year students adjust to the university, develop a better understanding of the learning process, and acquire essential academic success skills. The course provides a general orientation to the functions and resources of the university and also provides a support group for students transitioning to college by examining problems common to the first-year experience. Attaining an appropriate balance between personal freedom and social responsibility underlies all University 101 activities.

## COURSE GOALS AND LEARNING OUTCOMES

### I. Foster Academic Success

*As a result of this course, students will . . .*

a) Adapt and apply appropriate academic strategies to their courses and learning experiences.
b) Identify and apply strategies to effectively manage time and priorities.
c) Identify relevant academic policies, processes, and resources related to their academic success and timely attainment of degree requirements.

## II. Discover and Connect with the University of South Carolina
*As a result of this course, students will . . .*

a) Identify and use appropriate campus resources and engage in opportunities that contribute to their learning within and beyond the classroom.
b) Develop positive relationships with peers, staff, and faculty.
c) Describe the history, purpose, and traditions of the University of South Carolina.

## III. Promote personal development, wellbeing, and social responsibility
*As a result of this course, students will . . .*

a) Clarify their values and identity and articulate how these shape their perspectives and relationships with people who are similar to and different from themselves.
b) Explore the tenets of the Carolinian Creed.
c) Examine and develop strategies that promote wellbeing and explain how wellness impacts their academic and personal success.
d) Initiate a process toward the attainment of personal and professional goals and articulate potential pathways to employability.

## POINTS BREAKDOWN AND ASSIGNMENT EXPECTATIONS

| COMPONENT | WEIGHT |
|---|---|
| Participation | 15% |
| Resident Expert Presentation | 15% |
| Final Project | 15% |
| Midterm Reflection | 15% |
| Academic Success Strategies Assignment | 5% |
| True Colors Formal Paper | 15% |
| Informal Writing (Journals and Event Reflection paper) | 10% |
| Other Homework | 10% |

## GRADING SCALE

| | | | |
|---|---|---|---|
| 90–100 | A | 70–76 | C |
| 87–89 | B+ | 67–69 | D+ |
| 80–86 | B | 60–66 | D |
| 77–79 | C+ | 0–59 | F |

## DESCRIPTION OF ASSIGNMENTS, EXAMS, AND PROJECTS

1) Participation (15%)

   a. It is important that you not only come to class each day but that you participate fully. Participation is more than just contributing to whole-class discussion; it includes active engagement in activities and small-group discussions, listening respectfully, coming to class on time and prepared, and positive involvement in the classroom community. There will be opportunities throughout the semester to discuss your participation grade with us.

2) Resident Expert Presentation (15%)

   a. To further explore the course learning outcomes, you will develop a research presentation that contributes to our learning in this course. This project will be your opportunity to enhance and practice your research, writing, group work, and presentation skills. In small groups, you will develop a research question, collect information, and create an informative and engaging presentation for your classmates.

   b. Possible topics might include (but are certainly not limited to):
      i. Can college students (or people in general) effectively multitask?
      ii. How much sleep do we really need?
      iii. Is the freshman 15 a real thing?
      iv. What do we know about the effects (physical, ethical) of ADHD medication for those without ADHD?

   c. Timeline:
      i. Groups formed: Day 11
      ii. Topic selection due: Day 12
      iii. Information Literacy Workshop: Day 15
      iv. Article summaries/evaluations due: Day 19
      v. Presentation outline due: Day 21
      vi. Presentations begin: Day 23

3) Final Project (15%)

   a. You will be asked to write a letter to a 2022 freshman and create a 3-minute media presentation (movie, slide presentation, art collage, etc.) that synthesizes your first semester of college. More information will be provided later in the semester. We will hold a "film festival" during our final exam period at which each student will share their media presentation.

4) Midterm Reflection (15%)

    a. You will respond to questions (in video or written form) that are designed to encourage reflection on the first half of your first semester at UofSC. More information will be provided.

5) Academic Success Strategies Assignment (5%)

    a. One goal of this class is to help you be successful in your other academic courses. In order to help foster habits and behaviors that lead to academic success, you will be required to earn 50 points by choosing activities from the list below. You do not need to do all of the activities on the list, but you do need to accumulate 50 points over the course of the semester (due Day 23) in any combination you choose. Evidence (paper, confirmation slip, screenshot, etc.) is due no later than one week from when you complete the task or attend the event.

    b. REQUIRED: Complete the Semester at a Glance activity on pages 196–197 in *Transitions* (10 points)—Due Day 2

    c. Earn 40 more points from the list below:
        i. Attend an SI Session (10 points each)
        ii. Type your notes from one of your classes (10 points per week)
        iii. Make a study guide for one of your exams (10 points)
        iv. Make an outline of a chapter in one of your textbooks (10 points)
        v. Create flashcards to prepare for an exam (10 points)
        vi. Have the Writing Center review one of your papers for another class (10 points)
        vii. Attend a Success Consultation at the Student Success Center (10 points)

6) Informal Writing (10%)

    a. *Journals:* Each student will be asked to keep a journal and respond to journal prompts at specific points throughout the semester. More information will be provided in class.

    b. *Event Reflection Paper:* In order to foster your ability to integrate your learning (make connections between your coursework and what you are learning beyond the classroom), you will be asked to attend at least one beyond the classroom learning opportunity (cultural event such as a play, recital, dance performance, campus lecture, etc.) and write a 1–2-page reflection that addresses the following components:

    i. Describe something you learned from the experience (150–200 words)

    ii. Describe how the beyond the classroom experience connects to a larger concept, topic, issue, or UNIV 101 learning outcome (such as diversity, wellness, academic success, etc.) and/or to specific aspects of an area of study (history, math, science, etc.)? Be specific as to how your experience reinforced, contradicted, or provided a concrete example related to the larger concept you identified. (200 words or more).

We may choose to attend an event together as a class (such as the FYRE event) or you may choose an opportunity on your own.

7) True Colors Paper (15%):

    a. After completing the True Colors personality type assessment in class, you will write a formal paper synthesizing and analyzing your True Color type, explaining how your type may help and hinder your college success. More information will be provided.

8) Other Homework (10%):

    a. This will include your "All About Me" sheet, a one-on-one meeting with the Peer Leader or instructor to discuss your progress, your Lifeline, your Do You Know presentation, your Time Management Log, and other assignments throughout the semester.

## Course Policies

University 101 is a course in which regular attendance and active participation are critical to your learning and the experience of your classmates. Research has shown that regular attendance is a strong predictor of your academic success. Therefore, you are expected to be in class, on time, each day. Per university policy, for each unexcused absence after ONE, 3% will be deducted from your final course grade. Absences for a number of university-approved situations, including, but not limited to illness or injury, participation in university-sponsored events, required military duty, or observance of a religious practice or holy day will be excused with appropriate documentation as described in the Undergraduate Bulletin. If you will not be in class due to one of the university-approved excusable situations, you must contact us as early as possible to discuss a plan for obtaining and submitting documentation to excuse the absence. If you are absent, you are responsible for learning the material covered in class and for completing assignments that were due or assigned in your absence.

This course participates in the progress report initiative through the Student Success Center (SSC). At key points throughout the semester, we may alert the SSC of students who may not be meeting criteria that has been established for both attendance and/or course grade performance. Students who receive an alert will get an email, then be contacted via the SSC Call Center. The student will be encouraged to connect with additional academic support resources.

## Academic Integrity and Responsibility

Every student has a role in maintaining the academic reputation of the university. The university's guidelines for academic integrity are listed in our Honor Code (sc.edu/academicintegrity). Students are to refrain from plagiarism, cheating, falsifying work, and assisting other students in violating the Honor Code.

When a student is uncertain as to whether conduct would violate the Honor Code, it is the responsibility of the student to seek clarification from the instructor of record. To clarify your understanding of the Honor Code, refer to the Office of Student Conduct and Academic Integrity's website.

## Expectations for Classroom Behavior

To ensure an enjoyable, inclusive, and engaging learning environment, you are expected to openly share your ideas and express your opinions in class; respect the opinions, values, and identities of your classmates, instructors, and guests; and honor the open environment of the class by respecting confidentiality when appropriate. You are expected to do your best work, meet assignment deadlines, regularly engage in class discussion and activities, and treat other members of the class with courtesy and respect. Please be respectful of others by avoiding disruptive behaviors such as side conversations, cell phone or laptop use, arriving late, and/or leaving early, etc.

## Course Accomodations

The University of South Carolina provides high-quality services to students with disabilities, and we encourage you to take advantage of them. Students with disabilities needing academic accommodations should: (a) Register with and provide documentation to the Student Disability Resource Center in Close-Hipp 102, and (b) discuss with the instructor the type of academic or physical accommodations you need. Please do this as soon as possible. *All course materials are available in alternative format upon request.*

## Syllabus Clause and Contract

This syllabus may be revised and adapted throughout the semester to better serve the needs of the class. The instructor may assign additional reading and assignments and alter the course calendar (on the next page) as necessary. Students will be notified of any changes to the syllabus via email.

| DATE | CLASS TOPIC | ASSIGNMENTS DUE | NOTES |
|---|---|---|---|
| 1 | Introduction to University 101 | | |
| 2 | Building Our Community Semester at a Glance | DUE: All About Me, | *8/25 Last day to drop a course without a grade of a "W"* |
| 3 | Lifeline Presentations | DUE: Lifelines | |
| 4 | High School vs. College | DUE: Read *Transitions*, pp. 69–73 and 175–176 | |
| 5 | Campus Safety and Football 101 | DUE: Journal #1; Do You Know (DYK) presentation choices *(Note: you will be responsible for only one DYK presentation from the due dates on this calendar)* | *9/6 Labor Day* |
| 6 | Campus Involvement | DUE: DYK; Read *Transitions*, pp. 65–68 | |
| 7 | Time Management | DUE: DYK | |
| 8 | Alcohol Use In College | DUE: Read *Transitions*, pp. 19–24; Journal #2 | |
| 9 | Carolinian Creed/ Academic Integrity | DUE: DYK; Time Management Log | |
| 10 | TBD | | |
| 11 | Advising and Registration | DUE: DYK | |
| 12 | My 30 Values | DUE: Resident Expert presentation topics; DYK | |
| 13 | Off-Campus Living and Budgeting | DUE: DYK; Journal #3 | |

Syllabus Clause and Contract continued

| DATE | CLASS TOPIC | ASSIGNMENTS DUE | NOTES |
|---|---|---|---|
| 14 | True Colors | DUE: DYK | *10/5 FYRE Main Event* |
| 15 | Information Literacy | DUE: DYK; Midterm Reflection | *10/7–10/8 Fall Break* |
| 16 | Building Resilience | DUE: DYK; Read Transitions, p. 109 | |
| 17 | Healthy Relationships | DUE: DYK; Read *Transitions*, pp. 97–102; True Colors paper | |
| 18 | Carolina History/ Traditions | DUE: DYK; Journal #4 | |
| 19 | Managing Stress | DUE: DYK; Resident Expert article summaries | |
| 20 | Effective Presentations | DUE: DYK | |
| 21 | Diverse Identities and Values | DUE: DYK; Read *Transitions*, pp. 222–228; Resident Expert presentation outline | |
| 22 | Employability | DUE: Journal #5 | *11/3 Last day to drop a course without a grade of "WF"* |
| 23 | Study Abroad | DUE: Academic Success Strategies Assignment | |
| 24 | Resident Expert | DUE: Resident Expert Presentations | |
| 25 | Resident Expert | DUE: Resident Expert Presentations | |
| 26 | Resident Expert | DUE: Resident Expert Presentations | |
| 27 | TBD | DUE: Event Reflection Paper | |
| 28 | Closure. **NO CLASS— Thanksgiving Break** | | *11/24–11/28 Thanksgiving Recess* |
| 29 | Closure and Evaluations | | |
| 30 | FINAL: Due—Letter to next year's freshmen and Creative Presentation | | |

# NOTES

## Foreword

1. It is acknowledged that the integration of the University of South Carolina was more complex than what is described in the text and the use of the term *peaceful* is not meant to downplay the experiences of the individuals who would describe it as otherwise. For a full discussion, see *Invisible No More: The African American Experience at the University of South Carolina* (University of South Carolina Press, 2021).

## Chapter 2. The University 101 Model

1. National data on first-year seminars in this section are derived from the triennial survey on course goals, structure, and administration conducted by the National Resource Center for The First-Year Experience and Students in Transition. Documents consulted include Barefoot and Fidler (1992, 1996), National Resource Center (2002), Tobolowsky et al. (2005, 2008), Padgett and Keup (2011), Young and Hopp (2014), and Young (2019).

2. Betsy Barefoot was a graduate assistant at the National Resource Center in the early 1990s, later serving as co-director for Center. She analyzed course descriptions and materials, syllabi, and other documents from more than 500 first-year seminars to create the typology that would guide seminar research for the next three decades. In addition to extended orientation seminars, the original typology (see Barefoot, 1992; Barefoot & Fidler, 1992) included:

- *Academic seminars with generally uniform academic content across sections.* May be either elective or required courses for first-year students, sometimes interdisciplinary or theme-oriented, sometimes part of a general education core. Will often include academic skills components such as critical thinking and expository writing.
- *Academic seminars on various topics.* Specific topics are chosen by faculty who teach sections of these freshman seminars. Will generally be elective courses. Topics may evolve from any discipline or may include societal issues such as biological and chemical warfare, urban culture, animal research, tropical rain forests, and the AIDS epidemic.
- *Professional seminars.* Generally taught for first-year students within professional schools or specific disciplines such as engineering, health science, or education to prepare students for the demands of the major and the profession.
- *Basic study skills seminars.* Generally offered for freshmen who are academically underprepared. These seminars focus on such basic study skills as grammar, note-taking, and time management.

3. From 1991 to 2000, respondents to the National Survey of First-Year Seminars were asked to list the three primary objectives for the course, which were

coded. The themes meeting a certain threshold (e.g., 25 responses) were included in the final survey report. With the 2003 survey administration, participants were asked to select the most important objectives from a list of eight possibilities (plus *other*). That list has changed with subsequent administrations, growing to 26 options (plus *other*) on the 2017 administration of the National Survey of the First-Year Experience. Despite these changes, we do see some consistency in the primary goals being reported by respondents across administrations.

4. College adjustment was not among the choices offered to respondents beginning in 2003. A review of "other" responses to the course objective question in the 2009 and 2012 datasets did not find the words *transition* and *adjustment*. Thus, college adjustment may not figure as an important objective simply because it is assumed to be a core or essential purpose of the first-year seminar.

5. The choice "develop a connection with the institution" was added on the 2012 administration.

6. After noticing that respondents who identified their seminar type as "other" frequently described the course as "hybrid," researchers at the National Resource Center added this as a response option for the 2006 administration.

## Chapter 4. Key Ingredients to a Successful First-Year Seminar

1. Sense of Belonging was defined by three items: (a) ability to identify people with similar interests, (b) feeling accepted by other students at the institution, and (c) finding it easy to make new friends.

2. Course effectiveness is a factor comprised of the following questions: extent to which the students would recommend this course to other first-year students as well as extent to which the course included interesting subject matter, contributed to their ability to succeed academically, contributed to their ability to adjust to the college social environment, and covered topics important to them.

## Chapter 5. University 101's Impact on Students' Transition and Success

1. First-to-second-year retention data for the 2020 cohort and cohorts prior to 2008, first-year GPA data for the 2020 cohort, and 6-year graduation rate data for the 2015 cohort were provided by the University of South Carolina's Office of Institutional Research, Assessment, and Analytics. All other retention, first-year GPA, and 6-year graduation rate data were provided by the Enrollment Data Analytics division of the Office of Undergraduate Admissions.

## Chapter 8. Campus Partnerships

1. The Policy Center engaged an external panel of national experts in a blind review process to select institutions of excellence.

2. Palmetto College is part of the University of South Carolina system. Students can begin their studies at South Carolina on one of four two-year campuses.

## Chapter 10. Major Figures in University 101

1. Gardner, J. N. (2010). Foreword. In F. B. Newton & S. C. Ender (Eds.), *Students helping students: A guide for peer educators on college campuses* (pp. xi–xvii). Jossey-Bass.

# CONTRIBUTORS

*Dr. Christian K. Anderson* is associate professor of higher education at the University of South Carolina. His primary research focus is on the history of higher education and the organization and governance of higher education (particularly the role of faculty). He holds a PhD in Higher Education from Penn State University.

*John N. Gardner* is Chair and Chief Executive Officer of the John N. Gardner Institute. He is also the Founding Director and Senior Fellow of the National Resource Center for The First-Year Experience and Students in Transition, and Distinguished Professor Emeritus of Library and Information Science at the University of South Carolina. Gardner is the recipient of numerous local and national professional awards including USC's highest award for teaching excellence, the AMOCO Award for Outstanding Teaching. In 1986, John was selected by the American Association for Higher Education (AAHE) as one of 20 faculty in the United States who ". . . have made outstanding leadership contributions to their institutions and/or American higher education." Gardner is best known as the initiator (in 1982) of an international reform movement in higher education to call attention to and improve what he originally coined "The Freshman Year Experience" and then renamed "The First-Year Experience." Moreover, since 1990 he has developed a special focus on a second critical transition during the college years to improve and champion: "The Senior Year Experience." In 1995, he renamed the Center he directed at UofSC to The National Center for The First-Year Experience and Students in Transition, to signify a broader and more generic focus on the need for institutions to focus more intentionally on "students in transition." John and his colleagues at UofSC are currently driving a new national discussion about another critical transition in college and have authored a recent book, published by Jossey-Bass, on the sophomore year experience. Gardner has authored/coauthored numerous articles and books, including, *College is Only the Beginning* (1985 and 1989); *Step by Step to College Success* (1987); *Your College Experience* (1992–1993; 1995–2016 originally with A. Jerome Jewler and in subsequent editions also with Betsy O. Barefoot, Bedford/St.Martins; *The Freshman Year Experience* (1989) with M. Lee Upcraft, Jossey-Bass; *Ready for The Real World* (1994) with William Hartel and Associates, International Thompson Publishing; *The Senior Year Experience* (1998), with Gretchen Van der Veer, Jossey-Bass; *Challenging and Supporting the First-Year Student* (2005), with M. Lee Upcraft and Betsy O. Barefoot, Jossey-Bass; *Achieving and Sustaining Institutional Excellence for the First Year of College* (2005), with Betsy O. Barefoot and Associates, Jossey-Bass; *Helping Sophomores Succeed* (2010), with Mary Stuart Hunter and Barbara F. Tobolowsky and Associates, Jossey-Bass; *Developing and Sustaining Successful-First-Year Programs* (2013), with Gerald M. Greenfield and Jennifer R. Keup, Jossey-Bass; and *The Undergraduate Experience: Focusing Institutions on What Matters Most* (2016), with Peter Felten, Leo Lambert, Charles Schroder, and Betsy Barefoot.

*Catherine Flowers* coordinated departmental partnerships and presentations to develop high-quality educational experiences for first-year students. She provided support for Campus Partner Presentations, the First-Year Reading Experience, and the Outstanding Advocate for First-Year Students Award. Catherine supported the assessment of Campus Partner Presentations and provides feedback to campus departments. She also coordinated the development of Campus Partner Presentation support materials, including curricular materials for instructors. She holds an MA in Public History from the University of South Carolina.

*Dr. Daniel B. Friedman* is the executive director of University 101 Programs at the University of South Carolina (UofSC), where he provides leadership for six academic courses, including approximately 280 sections of the nationally renowned first-year seminar taught by over 240 instructors and 280 peer and graduate leaders. Dr. Friedman is also an affiliated faculty member in the Higher Education and Student Affairs program. His area of research centers on the first-year experience, first-year seminars, faculty development, and assessment. He holds a PhD in Higher Education from the University of Virginia.

*Catherine S. Greene* is responsible for University 101 Program's campus partnerships, including developing curriculum and training materials related to campus resources and managing the Outstanding Advocate for First-Year Students Award. Catherine also collaborates with the Office of the Provost in providing leadership for the First-Year Reading Experience. She holds an MA in Higher Education Administration from the University of Alabama Tuscaloosa.

*Mikaela Rea* assisted with the recruitment, selection, matching, and training of University 101 Peer Leaders and Graduate Leaders. In addition, she was responsible for creating and distributing the Peer Leader weekly newsletter.

She holds a MEd in Higher Education and Student Affairs from the University of South Carolina.

*Sandy Greene* oversees the communication and marketing efforts of University 101 Programs. Sandy also manages the University 101 Scholarship. She holds an MEd in Higher Education and Student Affairs from the University of South Carolina.

*Katie Hopkins* is responsible for the training and support of UNIV 101 instructors and serves as the primary point of contact for new instructors. Katie also oversees the Graduate Leader Program and the M. Stuart Hunter Award for Outstanding Teaching in University 101. She holds an MEd in Higher Education and Student Affairs from the University of South Carolina.

*Emma Reabold* is responsible for the recruitment, selection, matching, and training of University 101 Peer Leaders. She holds an MEd in Counselor Education and Student Affairs from Clemson University.

*Dr. Tracy L. Skipper* is senior thesis director and academic advisor for the University of South Carolina's Honors College. Previously, she served as the assistant director for publications of the National Resource Center for The First-Year Experience and Students in Transition at the University of South Carolina. She wrote *Student Development in the First College Year: A Primer for College Educators* (2005) and served as managing editor of the five-volume series, *The First-Year Seminar: Designing, Implementing, and Assessing Courses to Support Student Learning and Success* (2011–2012). She also coauthored the volume *Writing in the Senior Capstone: Theory and Practice* (2013) with Lea Masiello and edited *What Makes the First-Year Seminar High Impact? Exploring Effective Educational Practices* (2017) and *Aligning Institutional Support for Student Success: Case Studies of Sophomore-Year Initiatives* (2019). She holds degrees in psychology, higher education, American literature, and rhetoric and composition. In addition to her writing and editorial work, she has served as a student affairs administrator, taught writing at the college level, and presented on the application of student development theory to curricular and cocurricular contexts and the organization and administration of high-impact educational practices.

*Carrie Van Haren* is responsible for managing the end-of-course evaluation, survey, and performance analytics processes for all UNIV courses; the department's external assessment and compliance reporting; and the assessment of UNIV 101 course learning outcomes. She holds an MEd in Student Personnel Services from the University of South Carolina.

# PHOTO CREDITS

Page xv: Courtesy Dan Friedman

Page 8: WIS-TV News Story Number 70-93(A). Date filmed 1970-01-18. © University of South Carolina Moving Image Research Collections.

Pages 11–14: © The State Media Company. All rights reserved. For more information, contact the Walker Local and Family History Center at Richland Library, Columbia, SC 29201.

Pages 32, 50, 65, 69, 78, 82, 85, 125, 128, 131, 144, 145, 157, 203 (bottom): Courtesy University 101 Programs, University of South Carolina

Page 108: Courtesy Marvin Mitchell

Page 109: Courtesy Kate Snelson

Page 110: Courtesy of Issy Rushton

Page 111: Courtesy Tyler Heath

Page 161: Ryan Dawkins © University of South Carolina

Page 173: Leadership and Service Center, University of South Carolina

Page 202: Gardner Institute

Pages 203 (top), 207: University of South Carolina

Page 204: National Resource Center for the First-Year Experience and Students in Transition

Page 206: Appalachian State University

# INDEX